Reinhard Heydrich

Reinhard Heydrich

The Chilling Story of the Man Who
Masterminded the Nazi Death Camps

EDOUARD CALIC
TRANSLATED BY LOWELL BAIR

MILITARY HERITAGE PRESS
New York

This edition published by Military Heritage Press,
a division of Marboro Books Corporation,
by arrangement with
William Morrow and Company, Inc.

ISBN 0-88029-210-5
(formerly ISBN 0-688-00481-4)

Printed in the United States of America
M 9 8 7 6 5 4 3 2 1

Contents

Introduction

On the morning of May 27, 1942, as SS Obergruppenfuehrer Reinhard Heydrich, Acting Reich Protector of Bohemia and Moravia, was riding in his chauffeur-driven Mercedes convertible on the way to his office in Prague, he was attacked by two men. An official communiqué later gave this account:

> On May 27, at above 10:30 in the morning, an attempt was made on the life of Obergruppenfuehrer Heydrich. The Acting Reich Protector was in his car on Kirchmeyer Street in the Prag-Liběn district . . . when a man stepped in front of the car and tried to fire a submachine gun at its occupants. At the same time, another man threw a bomb which exploded when it struck the car.[1]

The two attackers then fled. Heydrich, wounded by the bomb blast, was taken to the Bulovka hospital.

Adolf Hitler had doctors sent to Prague from Berlin. While they tried to save Heydrich's life, more than sixty thousand policemen were searching for the assassins.

On June 4, 1942, the Prague radio station announced that Heydrich had died of his wounds.

Hitler ordered that the body be brought to the Reich Chancellery in Berlin. The funeral was attended by the Fuehrer, his ministers, and the General Staff. The leaders of the Nazi party mourned their "irreplaceable" policeman, the man who from 1931 until his death had been head of the SD (Sicherheitsdienst, the SS Security Service), and in 1936 had become the dreaded chief of the Security Police.

9

They had good reason to deplore the loss of their super-policeman. His contribution to the consolidation of the Nazi dictatorship in Germany had been unparalleled. When the Nazis set fire to the Reichstag on February 27, 1933, thus creating a pretext for seizing total power, it had been Heydrich who secretly had staged the operation. He had set up the first concentration camps and sent thousands upon thousands of his victims to them. The "Night of the Long Knives" on June 30, 1934, in the course of which at least two hundred of Hitler's adversaries within the party were massacred, also had been Heydrich's work. From 1933 to 1942, his imagination and executive ability had been the mainsprings of a whole series of clever provocations that had enabled Hitler to act implacably against his enemies.

Heydrich was thirty-eight when he died. His rank of SS Obergruppenfuehrer was equivalent to that of General in the army. He had never been a member of the government, but his command of the RSHA (Reichssicherheitshauptamt, Reich Central Security Office) gave him much more power than any minister. And he was the right-hand man of Heinrich Himmler, head of the SS, who had built a state within a state.

The funeral ceremony for that potentate of the Third Reich was held on June 9, 1942, in the Mosaic Room of the Reich Chancellery. After the funeral oration delivered by Himmler, Hitler stepped toward the coffin and spoke:

> I will devote only a few words to the dead. He was one of the best of all National Socialists, one of the staunchest defenders of the idea of the German Reich, one of the greatest adversaries of all enemies of that Reich. He has fallen as a martyr to the cause of the preservation and security of the Reich.
>
> As Fuehrer of the party and Fuehrer of the German Reich, I award you, my dear comrade Heydrich, after our comrade Todt [Fritz Todt, the engineer who built the Fuehrer's network of strategic roads and the fortifications known as the Siegfried Line; before Heydrich, Todt was the only man who had received the highest decoration of the German Order], the greatest distinction I can confer: the highest decoration of the German Order.[2]

Whenever Hitler had wanted to step up the persecution of Jews, Reinhard Heydrich, head of the Gestapo (Geheime

Staatspolizei, Secret State Police), had always gone into action. It was he who had organized the pogrom of November 9, 1938, that came to be known as *Kristallnacht,* or the "Night of Broken Glass." He had staged the sham attack on the German radio station at Gleiwitz, near the Polish border, that provided Hitler with a pretext for "counterattacking" Poland on September 1, 1939. On November 9, 1939, he had had two British intelligence officers, Captain S. Payne Best and Major R. H. Stevens, abducted in Dutch territory and brought into Germany. He had conducted the investigation into the alleged attempt to assassinate Hitler at the Buergerbräukeller in Munich on November 8, 1939, and had "discovered," as the interests of the Reich required, that it had been a plot hatched by the British Intelligence Service. On January 20, 1942, he had convened the meeting of high officials at Wannsee, a Berlin suburb, at which he had presented the plan for the "Final Solution of the Jewish problem," that is, the extermination of all European Jews.

In slaughtering members of "inferior races," Heydrich was acting in accordance with principles laid down many times by Hitler and Himmler. On one occasion, Hitler said simply,

Nature is cruel, so we must also be cruel. If I send the flower of the German people into the inferno of war without the slightest compassion for the precious blood that is shed, we certainly have the right to eliminate millions of human beings belonging to inferior races that multiply like vermin.

Himmler was more matter-of-fact:

I care nothing about what happens to Russians or Czechs. . . . Whether other peoples live in prosperity or die of starvation interests me only insofar as we need them as slaves. . . . If ten thousand Russian women die of exhaustion while digging an antitank ditch, it interests me only insofar as the antitank ditch is completed for Germany.

Heydrich's death was a heavy blow to the Nazi leaders, and they took savage revenge. Immediately after the assassination, seven hundred people were executed and thirteen thousand others were arrested. The Czech village of Lidice was annihilated as a reprisal. A Gestapo report described that crime: "The entire population of the village of Liditz [Lidice], numbering 483, was arrested on June 9 and dealt with as follows: the men were shot, the women were sent to concentration camps, and the children were taken away to be given a suitable education."

Reinhard Heydrich, one of the most monstrous criminals in history, has remained an even more enigmatic figure than the other important members of Hitler's entourage for two reasons. First, he always made careful efforts not to leave any documentary evidence of his crimes; and second, after the war, surviving members of the Gestapo gave all sorts of fictitious accounts designed to camouflage the real nature of Heydrich and his henchmen.

Contrary to what has been written by many historians, Hitler did not send Heydrich to Prague in the fall of 1941 to restore order in Bohemia and Moravia, and the Acting Protector had no intention of taking measures with a view toward an "honest" accord between the Germans and the Czechs. Immediately after his arrival in Prague, he had two hundred Czechs shot and several thousand imprisoned. He spoke quite openly of his intentions in his first speech to the political and military chiefs of the Protectorate on October 2, 1941:

This region must be colonized by Germans once and for all. I will not tell you vaguely that in order to make it permanently German we will try to Germanize this Czech rabble by using old methods; instead, I tell you that we are going to begin with things that can be undertaken today, but that we will disguise them. To examine what is Germanizable in this region, I must carry out a survey from the standpoint of peoples and races.[3]

For the moment, however, maintaining munitions production was the top priority. Heydrich's mission was to see to it that the Protectorate of Bohemia and Moravia, spared by British bombing raids, became the armory of the Third Reich. His closest collaborators already saw him as the Fuehrer's successor.

Today, forty years after his death, historians are still discussing Reinhard Heydrich's real character and his role in the Nazi regime. In trying to present an objective picture of him and his contribution to the rise and fall of Nazism, I will describe his youth, his training as a naval officer, his service in the SS before moving to the headquarters of the Nazi party in Munich, and his activities during the Third Reich.

Heydrich was a typical product of the German society of his time, that is, of the spirit that reigned in Germany during the first half of the twentieth century. In childhood he was marked by World War I, and in adolescence by the collapse of the German Empire and the founding of the Weimar Republic. As a young man, he was part of the Nazi movement. In 1933, he helped Hitler to take power. Within the Nazi regime he was able to begin making his dreams come true.

Examining this key figure of the Third Reich in the light of witnesses' testimony and documentary evidence will help us to understand how the Nazi state was able to function so efficiently, how propaganda and police terror contributed so greatly to its success, and how Germany came to be ruled by such men as Adolf Hitler, Joseph Goebbels, Hermann Goering, Heinrich Himmler, and Reinhard Heydrich.

Before his violent death, Heydrich was scarcely known outside of Germany, yet he was the architect of the death camps that annihilated six million human lives. People born after the war may wonder how that son of a great civilized nation could have become the most effective mass murderer of all time. After everything I personally experienced in the Third Reich, I consider it a duty to make my contribution toward a better understanding of that period. Knowing the truth about it may help to make future generations immune to the virus of Nazism.

But I realize that I will stir up protest from those who once identified themselves with Heydrich or one of his character traits. They will claim that the events I describe happened differently or not at all. When I published a book on Himmler, *Die Zeit*, a self-styled liberal weekly, upbraided me for presenting the Third Reich solely as a regime of provocations and machinations. According to the opinion that *Die Zeit* was still vigorously defending in 1979, Hitler and his associates did not act voluntarily, but only *re*acted to events imposed on them from outside the Reich. Likewise, Hitler committed his crimes only because external conditions happened to be favorable for him, or because unforeseeable mistakes by others gave him an opportunity, or because Goering's secret police enabled him to know his adversaries' diplomatic telephone conversations, or because strategic necessities forced him to act against his will.[4]

Endless theories and half-truths are propagated for the purpose of making official history accept the idea that the Third Reich was a chaos in which everyone ruled except those who were supposed to. But it is an undeniable fact that Hitler was not a weak, vacillating dictator. And the story of Heydrich's life shows that, *because of their efficient organization,* Hitler and his accomplices were able to bring about the conditions that triggered World War II. The presumption and arrogance of certain present-day German historians show that the malignant spirit of the Nazi dictatorship did not disappear with the military destruction of the Third Reich. It still manifests itself today, but in different forms.

1

The Child Prodigy
and the Lords of the Earth

The Absolute Wagnerian

Bruno Heydrich, Reinhard's father, was a music teacher and composer. During the years he lived in Halle, near Leipzig, he earned a certain reputation for himself, but the satisfaction it gave him was marred by the disdain inflicted on him because many of the people who knew him believed that he was at least partly Jewish. "Good society" placed a barrier between itself and anyone not thought to be of impeccably Aryan ancestry. Bruno Heydrich felt he could break through that barrier by establishing himself as an artist and being known as a fervent German nationalist. In accordance with his character and outlook on life, he became an enthusiastic partisan of the work of Richard Wagner, who, with his operas, had created the myth of Germanic culture.

As a young man, Bruno was determined to gain access to the upper strata of society through his art. He dreamed of becoming a composer, an orchestra conductor, and a tenor, and decided that he needed a diploma from the Dresden Royal Conservatory to make that dream come true. He entered the conservatory in 1879. When he left it three years later, with excellent grades, he was offered a contract as a double-bass player by Hans von Buelow, conductor of the Dresden Royal Orchestra, but he regarded that position as being only temporary. Since his ambition was still driving him on, he resumed his studies at the conservatory to become a composer and conductor. One of his professors, a Dr. Wuellner, decided that his voice was worth

15

cultivating and introduced him to Professor Georg Eugen Krantz, who was impressed by the passion and tireless zeal of his new disciple.

In 1887, on his professor's recommendation, the court theater of Sondershausen engaged him as an opera singer. He stayed there till 1889 and was highly successful with the local public, especially in the role of Lyonel in Flotow's opera *Martha*. But to him this period was only a brief phase in a career that would make him a celebrated Wagnerian singer. That had become his greatest desire, now that it was no longer possible to approach the master in person, Wagner having died in 1883, soon after Bruno Heydrich obtained his first diploma at the conservatory and before he had any serious intention of becoming a singer.

His professors' recommendations and his success in *Lohengrin* during a series of performances in Magdeburg enabled him to meet Cosima Wagner, his idol's widow, in Bayreuth, where he saw how she followed her husband's example in venerating great heroic figures. Filled with renewed enthusiasm, Heydrich left for Saxony. Engagements at theaters in Brunswick, Halle, Frankfurt am Main, Amsterdam, Ghent, Brussels, and Cologne gave him many opportunities to sing Wagnerian roles. While he was in Cologne, the press saluted him as the personification of Wagner's heroes.

This artistic success enabled him to demand as much as a thousand marks for a performance, and he was soon able to fulfill another dream. He intended to found a family someday and hoped to marry the daughter of Professor Krantz, with whom he had studied in Dresden. When he returned to Dresden as a well-known singer, Elisabeth Maria Anna Amalia Krantz proudly accepted his proposal of marriage.

Professor Krantz was known as an ardent Wagnerian, but Bruno Heydrich far surpassed him in fanaticism on the subject. He described himself as "an absolute Wagnerian."

During his stay in Cologne, he had used his free time between rehearsals and performances to write an opera of his own. Not being modest, he already saw himself triumphing as a composer, librettist, and singer at the Opera in Berlin, where he would be honored by the Emperor and the whole court.

Richard Wagner had found his patrons among the Wittelsbachs; Bruno Heydrich imagined that the Hohenzollerns would be his benefactors. Louis II, being simply the King of Bavaria, had been able to satisfy only part of his friend Wagner's demands; since Wilhelm II was Emperor of Germany, he would reward Heydrich in proportion to his genius. Heydrich had unreserved veneration for the nobility. Even in his boyhood, he had dedicated his first childish compositions to princes and princesses.

Whereas children of well-to-do families regarded studies at the conservatory as a kind of pastime, to Bruno Heydrich they had been a necessary condition for making a living. Afraid that the difference in background between himself and his fellow students might endanger his chances of success, he had been careful never to talk about his origins. But what did he have to be ashamed of? What was it that would destroy his social success if others knew about it?

Reinhard: A Symbolic Hero

Bruno's father, Karl Julius Reinhold Heydrich, born at Arnsdorf in 1837, had lived in the little town of Lommatzsch, near Meissen. Karl Heydrich was a carpenter, and since he usually worked only at irregular intervals, he was very poor. His wife, Ernestine Wilhelmine Linder, born at Lommatzsch in 1840, gave birth to their son Bruno on February 23, 1862. Soon afterward the family moved to Meissen, where Karl died a short time later. His widow then married a workman named Gustav Robert Suess and had five daughters with him.

Since the morbidly ambitious Bruno Heydrich's real family background could only hinder his social rise, he had transformed his father, a carpenter who was often out of work, into a talented and well-established piano maker who had taught him to love music. It was actually Bruno's schoolteachers at Meissen who had discovered and encouraged his musical ability; Karl Heydrich had died too soon to have any decisive influence on his son's development.

The genealogy that Bruno had invented for himself became more plausible when he married Professor Krantz's daughter: a carpenter's son would not have been granted that honor. Bruno was convinced that if he had honestly admitted his origin, his career would have been nipped in the bud.

His obsessive desire to gain a position in "good society" blinded him to the point where all progressive and democratic efforts, whose effects were slowly becoming felt all over Germany, aroused only contemptuous hatred in him. The ignorant rabble of the lower classes was incapable of appreciating his art. To him, art—in his case, music—belonged in a luxurious setting of castles and drawing rooms and ought to be appreciated by a rich, cultivated elite.

With his conviction that music was the prerogative of high society and that musicians, both performers and composers, were automatically members of that caste, he inevitably had reactionary and chauvinistic ideas. And he could not fail to see that all German aristocrats were faithful supporters of the great empire of the Hohenzollerns. It was in that circle that he expected to find his patron.

In Bayreuth, where Cosima Wagner had given him a final layer of authentically Wagnerian polish, the conversation had sometimes turned to national problems in addition to artistic endeavors. As was fashionable at the time, the assembled company ridiculed Jews who had made a name for themselves in finance and the world of German culture. To her friends and anyone else interested in such matters, Cosima Wagner handed out copies of the book that her English son-in-law, Houston Stewart Chamberlain, had written in German, *Die Grundlagen des Neunzehnten Jahrhunderts* ("The Foundations of the Nineteenth Century").

Chamberlain had been inoculated with the virus of Pan-Germanism by his German teacher in England, and he had then gone to Germany to devote his life to that country. He imagined that he recognized Aryan ancestry in all the great geniuses of the human race. Condemning the Jews, he maintained that Jesus Christ was the son of a Roman soldier. Following the example of Viennese anti-Semites, he hailed Dante Alighieri, author of *The Divine Comedy*, as a genius of German origin by the name of Aldiger.

Bruno Heydrich was stirred by the importance that Chamberlain attributed to ideas:

They [ideas] seize humanity with imperious power, they clutch thought like a bird of prey. No one can defend himself against them. As long as one particular concept is dominant, one can do nothing successful outside its sphere of influence. Anyone unable to feel in that way is condemned to sterility, no matter how gifted he may be.[1]

In writing his opera, entitled *Amen*, Bruno Heydrich made use of all the ideas that seemed momentous to him. The central figure of *Amen* is a rich and superior man named Reinhard who falls in love with Dora, a woman whose rank is equal to his. But the wedding plans of this noble couple are threatened by Thomas, a jealous peasant leader. One day when Reinhard and Dora are together, Thomas and a group of vengeful peasants try to kill Reinhard. At first, fate sides with good against evil: Reinhard repels the attack with superhuman strength and leaves Thomas lying wounded on the ground. But then the other peasants overwhelm the hero and, even though he wounded Thomas only in self-defense, he is unjustly thrown into prison.

Four years go by. Dora, of course, still loves Reinhard, but her father orders her to marry Konrad, a farmer. The wedding day arrives. The sorrowful Dora stands at the altar, but before the ceremony is completed Reinhard appears and sings, "In you, my love, is all my happiness." And the chorus concludes the act with a powerful "Amen, amen!"

But the melodrama is not yet over. In the next act the ignoble Thomas arrives, determined to prevent the two lovers from marrying. He takes out his dagger, stabs Reinhard in the heart, and sings, "Now my vengeance has struck you both!"

Refusing to go on living now that Reinhard is dead, Dora takes poison. The music expresses the tragedy of the situation, and the chorus again sings, "Amen, amen!"

Bruno Heydrich intended his opera to be a symbolic work. His message was that the Germans were threatened by a multitude of people inferior to them and that they had to oppose those inferior enemies in time to avoid being destroyed by them. Like Siegfried and Tristan, the heroic and tragic figure of Reinhard was a warning to future generations.

Amen had its first performance in Cologne in 1895. The bourgeois audience clearly recognized the Wagnerian elements in it and reacted so favorably to it that it was given several more per-

formances. But although Heydrich did everything in his power to
have his work presented at the Berlin Opera, the road to the
capital remained closed to him. He failed to communicate his
message to the whole nation, but at least he had created a new
hero: Reinhard.

The Composer's Nightmare:
The Jew Suess

Bruno Heydrich's marriage to Elisabeth Krantz in 1897 gave him
the social position he wanted. His wife had been educated in a
Catholic boarding school, and her parents would never have allowed her to marry outside their religion, so Bruno had converted
to Catholicism, disregarding the slogan that was common in nationalistic circles at that time: "Away from Rome." He was prepared to do anything necessary to consolidate his situation in
society because by now he had been forced to recognize that his
singing voice and his ability as a composer were only mediocre
and that he would always be a provincial in his artistic activities.
It was time to head in a new direction. His father-in-law got him
a post as a music teacher.

In 1899, Bruno Heydrich founded his own music school in
Halle, an administrative, industrial, and university city not far
from Leipzig, Dresden, and Berlin. Almost as soon as the school
was opened, twenty students enrolled in it to take singing
lessons. Two years later, Bruno changed its name: it became a
conservatory. The number of students eventually rose to about a
hundred and twenty. Elisabeth Heydrich was a member of the
faculty; she taught piano.

The students came mainly from the city's rich and influential
families. Heydrich kept making new contacts among those families and tried to join every organization that might be useful to
him. He attached great importance to impressing his listeners
with a witty remark or a wise saying whenever the opportunity
arose. He liked to stud his conversation with quotations from
Goethe's *Faust*. Cosima Wagner had told him that there were
"inexhaustible riches of the heart and strength of soul" in
Goethe. Anyone who quoted from Goethe, thought Heydrich, was
sure to be known as an ardent champion of the German spirit.

When he had been drinking abundantly, he sometimes forgot the serious purpose of a meeting and told jokes. But at regular gatherings of socially prominent ladies in his house, he was on his best behavior and gratified his guests with compliments that he had prepared in advance. With important businessmen, he used flattery and servility to win their favor.

The local patricians criticized his exaggerated joviality and enviously watched his conservatory becoming more and more profitable. They were intrigued by the fact that practically nothing was known about Heydrich's background. Finally, it was learned that he regularly sent money to a Frau Ernestine Suess, and then it did not take long to discover that she was his mother. A rumor soon began circulating that Bruno Heydrich was only his professional name and that he really bore the Jewish name of Isidor Suess. When this rumor reached him, Heydrich lodged a complaint against "a person or persons unknown" in an effort to find out who had started the slanderous story.

Bruno Heydrich was not the first to be threatened with ostracism for belonging to another racial or religious group, whether the "accusation" was true or not. For centuries, German guilds of merchants and craftsmen had tried to exclude competitors from the market by depicting them as foreign elements. Newcomers who spoke Yiddish were especially hated, even when they only set up a small family business that barely made enough profits to keep them alive. They were taunted, ridiculed, and caricatured, largely on the basis of alleged customs that were actually unknown to them. Even if a Jew was totally assimilated in his language, religion, and way of living, his enemies would still claim to see "typically Jewish traits" in him.

In Halle, there was soon widespread agreement that Bruno Heydrich really did seem Jewish.

Elisabeth Heydrich regarded this story about her husband's origin as a vicious insult that could cause the whole family great harm. She tried to combat it by repeating Bruno's claim that his father, Karl Heydrich, had been a talented piano maker in Meissen. She maintained that, at the time, piano makers had been as highly respected as violin makers, and that such piano manufacturers as Bechstein and Lambert had built their fortunes on the skill of craftsmen like Bruno's father.

The Heydrichs never succeeded in putting an end to rumors about Bruno's supposed Jewish extraction. He did not understand how such an affront could have been inflicted on him when he was second to none in zealously professing German nationalism. No one in Halle had the courage to mock him to his face, but people went on calling him Isidor Suess behind his back. He was consumed with resentment, and the rest of his life was embittered by the knowledge that he was powerless to stop that slander.

Birth of Reinhard Tristan Eugen Heydrich

On March 7, 1904, the Heydrichs had a second child, the son they had been hoping for after the birth of their daughter, Maria. Bruno Heydrich had already decided to give him the name of Reinhard, the main character in his opera *Amen*, who because of his love was killed by the vindictive peasant, Thomas. It was a name intended to symbolize courage, loyalty, honor, and undying love.

A son with dark hair and eyes would have been a disaster for Bruno Heydrich, that fanatical racist who was tortured by rumors that attributed Jewish ancestry to him. When he saw that his baby was blond and blue-eyed, he must have taken it as a sign that he was worthy of the three prenames he had chosen for him: Reinhard Tristan Eugen.

Four months after Reinhard's birth, the family moved into a new home. The number of students had increased to the point where a larger building was needed for the conservatory. The new building, at 21 Poststrasse, had many classrooms and a concert hall with a stage.

In 1905, another son, Heinz Siegfried, was born.

Elisabeth Heydrich gave her three children a rigorously Catholic upbringing. Bruno taught them that they must respect soldiers and that the army was the concentrated embodiment of the people. Hoping to counter the effects of the Isidor Suess rumors, he saw to it that everyone noticed his family's militaristic Prussian spirit, which he confirmed by maintaining close relations with his friend Major Ernst von Eberstein and the latter's entourage of career officers. He often told anecdotes beginning with such phrases as "When my opera *Amen* was performed in Cologne . . ." or "When I was with Cosima in Bayreuth. . . ." The implication was that his close friendship with Cosima Wagner entitled him to refer to her by her first name only.

With Major von Eberstein, his conversations were almost exclusively political. He railed against the Social Democrats, accusing them of trying to weaken the Reich with their campaigns against military spending. He never forgot to make some laudatory mention of "the Iron Chancellor" (Bismarck) and present himself as a stalwart supporter of the glory of Prussia.

But his efforts to show his devotion to Prussianism brought him only short-lived successes. When he asked the authorities to grant him the rank of Professor, since many students had graduated from his conservatory and some had become well-known musicians, his request was denied. His conservatory, he was told, was not an official institution. He felt that this was only a pretext and that the real reason for his rejection was the cloud that hung over his origin.

Meanwhile, however, he was prospering financially. In 1906, when Reinhard was two, the family moved into a building at 20 Gütchenstrasse, in a well-to-do residential neighborhood.

As Reinhard and his brother, Heinz, grew older, fighting with wooden swords became their favorite game. They were later to become enthusiastic athletes. Their father encouraged their growing inclination toward developing physical strength and skills. In Reinhard, it was an inclination that lasted all his life and made him tend to judge men by their athletic ability.

The two boys soon became interested in everything military, and when Major von Eberstein came for a visit, they looked him over admiringly, from the tips of his boots to his epaulets. They also admired their father because he was an accomplished fencer and belonged to the Fencing School of the German Reich.

Reinhard, of course, had to study music. But it soon became apparent that he would never be an opera singer: the poor boy had a falsetto voice. So Bruno Heydrich's favorite son studied piano and violin in the family conservatory.

Reinhard was only ten when World War I began. From then on, every phase of the war was discussed at length in the Heydrich household. "Uncle Ernst" von Eberstein's son Karl had

just turned twenty and therefore had the good luck of being able
to fight for the Kaiser and the Fatherland. The assassination of
Ferdinand, Archduke of Austria, cried out for vengeance. Karl's
and Reinhard's mothers began collecting gifts that the Red Cross
distributed to soldiers at the front. Bruno Heydrich supported
their efforts by organizing patriotic meetings at which music was
provided by the Patriotic Singing Association.

Reinhard cared very little about those activities: it was weapons that aroused his passionate interest, and especially the warships he had seen with his own eyes during vacations on the
Baltic shore at Warnemünde. His childish view of the war was
centered on those formidable ships that could take their gigantic
cannons all over the world.

"Heil, Emperor of Germany, Heil!"

When it was time for Reinhard to enroll in a *Gymnasium* ("high
school"), his parents chose a "reformed" *Gymnasium* in which
the curriculum stressed technical subjects and modern languages, rather than the humanities. Emperor Wilhelm II, who
was regarded almost as a god by German nationalists, had urged
educators to give priority to technology, for understandable reasons. He was not satisfied with having the largest army on the
European continent: he needed a transatlantic fleet strong enough
to compete with those of other countries and bring from the colonies the raw materials necessary for the further development of
German industry.

When Reinhard looked in his atlas and was surprised by the
great number of British colonies throughout the world, he asked
his father how the English had acquired them.

"It's simple," he was told. "The English have more than
enough warships."

"Could we build even more warships than the English?" asked
the boy.

"Of course. Uncle Ernst says it's only a question of money."

Reinhard's interest in seafaring, and particularly the navy, did
not diminish. He dreamed of someday being a shipbuilder, or a
ship's captain, or even an Admiral. He decorated the walls of his
room with colored pictures of warships.

His teachers at the reformed *Gymnasium* were pleased by the interest he showed in mathematics and chemistry, as well as German and history. He was a boy who would amount to something when he grew up, especially since his parents had taught him to respect the authorities in general and the Emperor in particular. The people of Halle still remembered that for the twenty-fifth anniversary of Wilhelm II's accession to power Bruno Heydrich had organized a celebration at which his conservatory students performed an "authentically German program" of works by German composers from George Frederick Handel to Richard Wagner. He had also composed a march for the occasion, and written the words himself. Reinhard, nine years old at the time, had learned those words by heart:

> Lord God, give they blessing . . .
> Lead us on all paths
> And protect the Emperor as always.
> May unity and peace
> Always uplift us in this world.
> Look upon us in thy grace.
> Without thee, nothing is done.
> Heil, land of Germany!
> Heil, Emperor of Germany, heil!

Reinhard keenly felt the tragedy of the loss inflicted on the Austrians by the assassination of Archduke Francis Ferdinand at Sarajevo, in Bosnia, which was part of the vast Austro-Hungarian empire. "There's nothing surprising about it," his father told him. "Those Serbs even killed their own King Alexander Obrenovich and replaced him with a puppet who made it possible for them to have good relations with France. Then there was that anarchist Luchieni, who killed Empress Elisabeth, Franz Josef's wife, at Geneva in 1898." And Bruno Heydrich explained to his two sons that such outrages could only come from the pernicious ideas that had become widespread, especially in France.

Bruno Heydrich, the "absolute Wagnerian," naturally knew every sentence that Wagner had written against the Jews. Wagner was of the opinion that the Jews really belonged in Palestine, and since he hated "Judeo-French democracy," he had recommended destroying Paris during the Franco-Prussian War of 1870–71. The Heydrichs were sure that this time Wilhelm II would accomplish what his grandfather had not been able to do in 1870.

As the World War continued, Reinhard's developing mind became better able to understand what was happening. His father explained events to him, as he saw them. He also imbued Reinhard with contempt for the Jews, considering it his duty to bring up his children to be zealous anti-Semites, and hoping that this would help to protect them against the effects of the Isidor Suess rumors. Things had reached the point where the two Heydrich boys were sometimes taunted in the street with shouts of "Isi! Isi!" (Isi was the diminutive of Isidor.) Their father urged them to silence their tormentors with their fists, and Heinz once went so far as to threaten one of them with a knife.

Because of his family's special situation and the intense interest with which the course of the war was followed in his home, Reinhard acquired a certain political awareness at an earlier age than his classmates. As he grew older, he often displayed an arrogant attitude, and he was generally criticized for his aggressiveness. This tendency toward physical violence was fully manifested whenever one of the other boys dared to call him a goat, a teasing he received because of the bleating quality of his high-pitched voice. His brutality was nourished by discussions with his parents concerning the war and the best ways of annihilating the hated enemy.

In 1916, the Heydrich family's hopes, for a German victory in the near future began to fade: the French were defending Verdun with unexpected tenacity, and it became clear that the German Navy had no chance of wiping out the British fleet. But Bruno could still look forward to a personal victory: a new edition of Hugo Riemann's *Musiklexikon* ("Dictionary of Music") was about to be published, and he hoped that it would recognize his worth as an artist.

He was outraged when the dictionary appeared and he saw that the entry concerning him began as follows: HEYDRICH, BRUNO (REAL NAME SUESS). . . ."

Elisabeth Heydrich had great difficulty calming her husband. By threats of legal action he was finally able to obtain the assurance that the words REAL NAME SUESS would be omitted from the next edition of the dictionary. But the experience left its mark on him; from then on he was more and more determined to be recognized by everyone as a pure Aryan.

While the German people became increasingly tired of the war, Bruno Heydrich maintained his unshakable belief in victory; he wrote articles describing how the enemy could be overcome. But suddenly the workers began demanding an end to the war, and there was a sailors' mutiny in the seaport of Kiel. The German Army was headed for collapse, but the bourgeois citizens of Halle continued to believe that it would finally triumph. After all, German soldiers were still in enemy territory. All they had to do was hold their positions and eventually they would be victorious. Reinhard acquired this conviction from his parents, and it influenced his military thinking the rest of his life.

Reinhard Joins the Free Corps

As a fourteen-year-old *Gymnasium* student, Reinhard already showed his aptitude for science and technology. No experiment in chemistry or electrical engineering seemed too complicated to him, but he was especially interested in radio communications between ships and their home bases. He read all the books he could get on great naval battles and famous seafarers. On a shelf in his room was a photograph of Hans Kinau, a sailor who wrote *Seefahrt ist Not* ("Seafaring Is a Necessity") under the pseudonymn of Gorch Fock. Reinhard almost knew that book by heart. Fock was one of his idols, partly because he had died for the Emperor and the Fatherland in the naval Battle of Jutland. Years later, when the Nazis had taken power, a German training ship was named the *Gorch Fock*.

Reinhard often told his parents that he wanted to be a naval officer, already seeing himself commanding a whole fleet. He knew the chemical composition of the explosives used in torpedoes and bombs, and often took cartridges apart and burned their powder in the garden. His experiments had also made him familiar with the use of phosphorus. His parents were afraid he might someday blow up the whole building.

He felt different from other boys his age, and superior to all of them. In his view of science and art, all important advances were

made by men of genius. He believed that since Germany had
given the world a great number of geniuses, it would be unjust if
such a superior country lost the war.

At fifteen, he attended mass meetings of workers and heard
them demand a return to peace. But his own attitudes were reflected in the nationalistic speeches of his teachers and other
patriots, who angrily said that the soldiers fighting in France and
Russia were being stabbed in the back by those treacherous
workers at home. He decided to oppose their criminal activities
by supporting an antirevolutionary movement.

When, in 1918, the city of Halle learned that Wilhelm II had
abdicated and that the Imperial Chancellor, Prince Max of
Baden, had resigned and turned over power to the Social Democrat Friedrich Ebert, Reinhard heard the same accusation repeated again and again: "Treason!"

The German defeat, the proclamation of the Republic, and the
appearance of the Spartacists, a radical group of German Socialists, led Reinhard, whose father still regarded him as a child
prodigy, to join the rightist bands of volunteers known as the
Free Corps (Freikorps). He gathered parts of cast-off uniforms for
himself, including a steel helmet, and began training with his
companions to prepare for fighting against the armed workers.

At the end of February 1919, a Free Corps commanded by
General Maercker marched into Halle to crush the rebels in the
city. Reinhard applauded enthusiastically, and he had already
drawn up a list of the most dangerous leaders of the workers,
those whom, he felt, should be arrested or shot as agitators. From
the first to the third of March, the Maercker Free Corps conducted a ruthless mopping-up operation. Reinhard and his companions, who could not participate in it because of their youth,
supported it with their denunciations. This was what Heydrich
was later to call his "service as a liaison agent for the Maercker
Free Corps."

Meanwhile, the bourgeoisie of the city, with General
Maercker's help, organized the Halle Free Corps. Reinhard
Heydrich joined and remained a member until the middle of
1920.[2]

Heydrich's family, and especially his widow, Lina Heydrich,
naturally disagree when his early antidemocratic activities are

denounced. According to her, he only did his military duty all through his adult life, and in his youth he did not voluntarily join the Free Corps, but was drafted.

"The family now [after World War II] denies that much importance should be attributed to his belonging to the Free Corps," writes Shlomo Aronson, "especially since all his classmates automatically had to join it."[3]

Lina Heydrich did not meet her future husband until ten years after his service in the Free Corps. Karl von Eberstein, who also served in the Free Corps, was better able to depict his friend Reinhard's frame of mind at that time:

> It has been said that during the war [World War I] Reinhard was already a "nationalistic extremist," that he was greatly interested in nationalistic historical ideas, that he developed into a "racial purity fanatic," and that he joined many nationalistic organizations. Considering his nationalistic upbringing, impregnated with the Wagnerian cult, this seems plausible.[4]

Karl von Eberstein reported that Reinhard acted as one of the nationalist movement's "bodyguards" at meetings and in street fighting, and that this took up so much of his time that he neglected his schoolwork.[5] In 1937, when Heydrich filled out a questionnaire for Heinrich Himmler, head of the SS, he stated that from 1920 to 1922 he had belonged to the Offensive and Defensive League of the German People. In the statutes of the league there is the following paragraph:

> The league strives to bring about the moral rebirth of the German people by awakening and fostering their healthy nature. . . . The league undertakes to explain the nature and extent of the Jewish danger and threats from other non-German races, and to combat them with all legal means at its disposal.[6]

Versailles and the Red Peril

According to Heydrich's own declarations, he also belonged to the Escherich Organization, a right-wing extremist group led by

Georg Escherich, whose name had become known in Halle at the time of the Kapp putsch. (In 1920, Wolfgang Kapp had organized a revolt against the Republic that failed when President Ebert mobilized workers all over the country for a general strike.)

The sailors' mutiny in 1917 had given Heydrich food for thought. He regarded it as a case of high treason. Two years later, he heartily approved when he learned that Karl Liebknecht and Rosa Luxemburg, the leaders of the Spartacists, had been murdered.

He tried to find out everything he could about the sailors' mutiny and the revolt of the Reds in Berlin. Those revolutionary events interested him so much that he decided to learn Russian and began studying it in a textbook for beginners.

Karl von Eberstein told the Heydrich family about Lenin's successes in Russia. The Reds had captured railway junctions, stations, military depots, and munitions factories. The White Guards, though outnumbered, had fought valiantly, said Eberstein, but the Reds had been able to take advantage of their superiority in men and equipment. The populace, gathered in large groups under the control of "Jewish ringleaders," did not realize that they were being deceived in accordance with the principles set forth in the *Protocols of the Elders of Zion*, a supposed report of secret sessions of the Elders of Zion in Basel, Switzerland, about a vast Jewish plot but actually written in France by anti-Semites working for the Czar.

Reinhard's history teacher told him that all this was perfectly true. The Czar had been weak in dealing with the Jewish revolutionary leaders, he said, and as a result the Jews were now creating a state based on the *Protocols*, with the aim of dominating all of Europe. Marx and Engels were only bait used for misleading the German workers.

The basis of the concept of "Judeo-bolshevism," which the Nazis were later to develop more fully, had been implanted in Heydrich's mind.

When he was seventeen, he had long discussions about the Russian Revolution with Günther Gereke, a friend of his father's, each time he went to the Gerekes' estate to admire their horses. Gereke held a high political post in the Weimar Republic and was later a member of Hitler's first government. After World War

II he recalled that in 1921 young Reinhard Heydrich had told him how important it had become for him to learn Russian: one could not fight effectively against an enemy country without knowing its language. Reinhard, still in high school, had seen the nationalist movement, the *Voelkische Bewegung*, as an opportunity to awaken Germany. The emblem of the movement bore a swastika and the motto. "We are the lords of the earth." Reinhard had that emblem in his room.[7]

According to Gereke, after graduating from high school, Reinhard became even more fanatical in his nationalism: "Where politics was concerned, he acted like a hunting dog coming into a forest."[8]

During the time he spent in the Free Corps, he always found new reasons to hate the Versailles Treaty, and he learned to describe the "Red peril" in a particularly alarming way. To him, politicians who advocated abiding by the terms of the Versailles Treaty were, like the Jews, traitors to Germany. Thinking only of their careers and personal well-being, they paid tribute to foreigners with the German taxpayers' money. The French were the hereditary enemy; they could be expected to ally themselves with the Bolsheviks against Germany. The "Jewish danger" was a justification for imperialistic dreams of a greatly expanded German territory.

In 1920, when he was sixteen, Reinhard had admired Kapp's attempt to overthrow the Weimar government with the help of officers who had remained faithful to the Emperor, and he even expected a return of the Emperor. When the attempt was defeated by a general strike, he had one more reason for hating the German workers. Far from discouraging him, this episode strengthened his convictions still more.

Years later, he proudly told how in May 1921, with the Escherich Organization, he had taken part in crushing the third Polish insurrection in Upper Silesia.[9] The experience convinced him that the Polish people were contemptible. From then on he hated not only the Jews and the French, but also the Slavs.

He fully agreed with his father's view that nothing good could be expected of France. At Versailles, Germany had been forced to accept a treaty that robbed her of Alsace-Lorraine and gave large portions of her territory to Poland. To give Poland access to the sea, East Prussia had been separated from the rest of Germany by a corridor that extended to the Baltic. A group of artificial states had been built on the ruins of the Hapsburg monarchy: Czechoslovakia, Hungary, Austria, and Yugoslavia. To young Heydrich, this new order meant that more than ten million Germans had to live outside the borders of the Reich. Furthermore, Germany had lost her whole naval fleet and all her colonies, and the Versailles Treaty had forbidden her to have more than a hundred thousand soldiers and fifteen hundred naval officers.

Like many German conservatives, Heydrich felt that acceptance of all this constituted treason by the members of the Reichstag (the lower house of the German parliament), who had proclaimed the Republic.

Long before he graduated from high school, Heydrich's mentality had already been deeply imprinted by the upbringing his father had given him, the influence of his teachers, the devastation of the German defeat of 1918, his activities in the Free Corps, and his participation in the nationalistic and racist movement.

The Navy, a Focus of National Awakening

When he graduated from high school at eighteen, Heydrich's early decision to become a naval officer remained unchanged. Not only would he have a respected profession, but he would be working with men whose political views were in harmony with his: the German Navy was noted for the conservatism of its officers, and this was not likely to change, since the Social Democrats had no thought of encouraging their sons to become part of that military elite.

His father approved of his choice, knowing that the postwar difficulties, which had not spared his conservatory, ruled out a musical career for his son. Bruno Heydrich had joined the *voelkisch* (racist-nationalist) party of the German Nationalists and, like everyone of that political persuasion, he believed that the Versailles Treaty would be only temporary. The German Nationalists had become an important political factor: in 1920–22 they obtained 4.25 million votes out of a total of 28 million.

In Reinhard's opinion, however, it was the strength of the Nationalists' convictions, not the number of votes they could obtain, that would tip the balance in their favor.

The Emperor was living in exile in the Netherlands, but the politicians, generals, industrialists, and university professors who hoped for his return had kept their positions, and many veteran officers had entered the Reichswehr, the postwar German Army. A considerable number of former soldiers who had fought in the Free Corps—including Karl von Eberstein—had formed a nationalist movement centered in Munich and chosen as their leader an Austrian named Adolf Hitler, who had joined the German Army in 1914 and remained in it all through the war without rising above the grade of Corporal. After proving himself to be a brilliant orator at far-right anti-Semitic political meetings, he was elected *Fuehrer* ("leader") of the National Socialist German Workers' party.

Karl von Eberstein soon established personal relations with Hitler and began working in Munich, Dresden, Leipzig, and Halle to recruit former soldiers into the movement. He naturally described the new *voelkisch* party to young Reinhard Heydrich, and to give him a better understanding of it, he had its newspaper, the *Voelkischer Beobachter*, sent to him regularly from Munich.

The party newspaper explained that Hitler wanted to organize the movement on a military basis to achieve power, and that if necessary he would lead an uprising to renounce the Versailles Treaty. To assure the success of such an uprising, the Marxist workers would have to be enrolled in the National Socialist party. Hitler expected the Reichswehr to join in with the people once the rebellion was under way. Since the country's borders had to be defended, the Regular Army would not oppose the formation of a national militia.

To Reinhard Heydrich, a fanatical nationalist and racist and a veteran of the Free Corps, these were exciting prospects. He believed that the new German Navy could be a powerful force in awakening the nation and counteracting the effects of the betrayal of 1918. Count Felix von Luckner, the legendary captain of the *Seeadler*, was traveling all over Germany and captivating lecture audiences with stories of the feats of German warships in the Atlantic and Pacific. His *Seeteufel* ("Sea Devil"), describing his adventurous life, was one of Reinhard Heydrich's favorite books, and the author never failed to visit the Heydrich family when he was in Halle.

Bruno Heydrich had enough connections to get his son accepted as a naval cadet. When it was time for Reinhard to leave, his father went with him to the station and, at the last moment, handed him his violin. During his last visit to the Heydrichs, Count von Luckner had told them that music was highly appreciated in the navy.

2

The Would-be Admiral

On March 30, 1922, at the age of eighteen, Reinhard Heydrich was admitted into the German Navy at Kiel.

He differed from his fellow cadets in many ways. Very sure of himself and sustained by the certainty that he had many friends in the *voelkisch* movement, he could behave, even toward his superiors, with a casual ease that was unusual in an officer candidate.

His first period of instruction took place between October 1922 and March 1923 aboard the warship *Braunschweig*. According to some witnesses, he was unhappy at first and often went off by himself for hours at a time. Whenever he began feeling sad, he "took refuge in an isolated part of the ship's bow, with his violin."[1]

We also have a description of his appearance: "Heydrich was tall and slender. His neck was a little too long; above it was a long, horsy head, with a receding chin and forehead, a large nose, and light blond, wavy hair."[2]

With his entrance into the navy, the second stage of his development began. Since he was at first either unwilling or unable to become involved in political activities, he attached even greater importance to his technical studies. He was soon called "the blond Siegfried," not only because of his appearance but also because of his undisguised aversion to everything "non-Aryan." He continued to develop his athletic abilities; his favorite sports were swimming, running, and fencing.

Heinrich Beuchke, one of his companions at the time, later

said of him. "In theoretical and practical subjects at the naval school, he never showed any unusual intelligence or knowledge. His general culture was average, at most."[3] Beuchke did see "a certain peasant shrewdness" in him, however.

When Heydrich had become an Ensign, he produced this impression:

> The most noticeable aspects of his character were vanity, self-satisfaction, a desire to please, indolence, and hypersensitivity. On the whole, he seemed to be full of contradictions. He quickly became the favorite butt of jokes among nearly all his companions. . . . He was the only one in his class who had no friends; he became completely solitary.[4]

If we are to believe these descriptions, Heydrich's father was deluded in regarding him as a prodigy. His strong points were evidently limited to making the most of his "peasant shrewdness" and his physical appearance, and an ability to "spot opportunities, guess his superiors' wishes and [use] his faculty of adaptation."[5]

In the navy, Heydrich made no secret of his anti-Semitism. To him, the Jews were a people who ought to be sent to hell; they had imposed the Versailles Treaty on the Germans, fomented uprisings among the workers, and broken the backbone of the Reich. This was what Heydrich had learned in the Offensive and Defensive League of the German People, and his conversations with Karl von Eberstein had confirmed his belief in it. The Russian Revolution was the work of the Jews. The Romanovs had brought on their own downfall by not forcefully opposing Jewish revolutionary activity. The *Protocols of the Elders of Zion* were often quoted in the Offensive and Defensive League; in *Mein Kampf*, Hitler had regarded that forgery as a genuine document proving the existence of a worldwide Jewish conspiracy.

Heydrich's second training period took place aboard a sailing ship, the *Niobe*. In the course of it, he acquired a passion for sailing as a sport. He began reading every book on the subject he could get, and he was fascinated by the exploits of the Spanish conquistadors and such great sailors as Columbus and Magellan.

In July 1923, he began the final phase of his training as a naval cadet, aboard the cruiser *Berlin*, and it ended in March 1924. One of his instructors was Lieutenant Commander Wilhelm Canaris, the future head of the Abwehr (the German military intelligence service). A feeling of friendship soon grew up between Canaris and his student. In their long conversations, Canaris sometimes told of his experiences in the World War. He had served in Latin America, Spain, and the Mediterranean sector; finally, with the Austrians, he had tried to resist the far superior fleets of the British, French, and Italians.

When he learned that Heydrich was particularly interested in radio, Canaris told him that a large number of warships could be built as soon as the Reich had enough money, but that the shortage of qualified technicians would be a problem. In addition, the German Navy would have great need of radio experts who were not only technically proficient but also completely trustworthy. Hearing this, Heydrich decided to become a specialist in radio communications.

Wilfried von Loewenfeld, the captain of the *Berlin*, was quite different from Canaris, the executive officer of the ship. Canaris sometimes disapproved of Loewenfeld's harsh training methods, but Heydrich appreciated them and quickly adapted to them; he had already experienced "Prussian-style training" in the Free Corps.

The friendship between Heydrich and Canaris was based on certain affinities: they both had a strong hatred of the victorious Allied powers and a keen interest in politics. They often discussed Adolf Hitler's unsuccessful putsch in Munich on November 8, 1923. Canaris felt that it should not be regarded merely as an act of protest; in any case, General Erich Ludendorff, the brilliant strategist of the World War, had supported Hitler. If the putsch had succeeded, Hitler would have made Ludendorff Commander in Chief of the German armed forces, and in Canaris's view that would have been a great change for the better, because the tough old soldier would have stood up to the French, rather than giving in to them as Chancellor Gustav Stresemann had done.

Years later, when Canaris was head of the Abwehr and Heydrich was in command of the SD and the Gestapo, their friendship, born on board the cruiser *Berlin*, was to be of great importance to both of them. Unfortunately, historians have persistently underestimated it and propagated the legend that when Canaris became head of the Abwehr in 1935, he immediately began working against Heydrich. In his biography of Canaris, Heinz Höhne has proved that this was not the case. "The good and loyal patriot Canaris, the friend of his country, constantly fighting against Heydrich, the satanic chief of the SD—this picture may meet the profoundly apologetic needs of Canaris's biographers, but it is not the truth."[6]

It was precisely because Canaris was a staunch supporter of Hitler, and because Heydrich shared his political views from the start, that ten years later Canaris fell under the influence of his former subordinate, so that Heydrich, as head of the SD, the Gestapo, and then the RSHA, was able to act on the powerful Abwehr through Canaris.

Heydrich's meeting Canaris in 1923 was undoubtedly a factor in determining his political viewpoint, as was his meeting Himmler eight years later. His widow has acknowledged this:

> Heinrich Himmler played a decisive part in Reinhard's life. Only Wilhelm Canaris, head of German military intelligence, had an equally fateful influence on him. They met for the first time on the warship *Braunschweig*, where Canaris was a Captain.[7]

The two men first met on the *Berlin*, not the *Braunschweig*, and Canaris was a Lieutenant Commander at the time, not a Captain, but those details do not alter the essential accuracy of Lina Heydrich's statements. She does not mention, however, that the shaping of her husband's political mentality began in childhood, first with his father, then with his teachers, the officers of the Free Corps, the agitators of the *voelkisch* movement, and finally Karl von Eberstein, who became a Nazi soon after the party was founded in Munich.

From his conversations with Canaris, young Heydrich learned that a naval intelligence officer could, by means of his reports, influence not only his country's armed forces but also its government. Because of this, Heydrich decided to specialize in intelligence work as well as telecommunications.

He left the *Berlin* in March 1924. On April 1, he was promoted to Midshipman. That same month, he entered the naval officers' school at Mürwik, in Schleswig-Holstein, where he was to stay until March 1925. Canaris had already sent the commandant of the school a letter of recommendation for his young friend. Hans Rehm, one of his classmates, said after the war, "At the naval school, Heydrich was average in practical training and scientific and technical subjects."[8]

He, however, again showed a special interest in sports: swimming, sailing, fencing, running. He also took up horseback riding, which was new to him, and became an excellent rider. After the war, his widow claimed that he had broken his nose in a riding accident and that the break had left his nose with an accentuated curve. But people who knew him very well did not notice such a change at the time, and failed to recognize it in photographs taken later. It is possible that Lina Heydrich's statement was prompted by the family obsession: on one must be able to say that her husband had a non-Aryan physical characteristic from birth.

At Mürwik, Heydrich resumed his study of Russian. He worked hard for six months, but without achieving any significant results. Most of his free time was taken up with sports.

Many writers have maintained that Heydrich had no interest in politics while he was in the navy. It is not surprising that this view has been adopted by his widow and the surviving officers who knew him during that time. But we can safely rule out the possibility that any naval officer could have remained indifferent to the tumultuous events that were shaking Germany. Objective contemporaries have reported that Heydrich was overjoyed when he learned that the *voelkisch* political groups, including Hitler's, had won 1.9 million votes in the elections of May 1924. He showed the same enthusiasm a year later when Field Marshal Paul von Hindenburg was elected President of the Reich. Heydrich considered it a good omen that the nation had chosen a famous soldier as its leader.

The Intelligence Officer:
Opportunist or Idealist?

From April to December 1925, Heydrich took numerous courses in weaponry. From January to September 1926, he was aboard the *Braunschweig*. Next he was sent to the flagship *Schleswig-Holstein* and, at his request, given training as a technical intelligence officer. He zealously studied all aspects of radio communications and equipment, and served as second radio officer on the *Schleswig-Holstein* until the fall of 1928. On July 1 of that year, he was promoted to Lieutenant, Junior Grade.

A year later he was stationed at the Kiel naval base as an intelligence officer.

He had, of course, fulfilled every requirement for his new post. He was familiar with all sorts of weapons and had been given "special military training" in these fields: infantry, artillery, torpedoes, signals, navigation, and intelligence. He spoke several foreign languages: English (in which he had passed the preliminary but not the final examination for qualification as a military interpreter), Spanish, Russian, and French. In Russian and French he considered himself only a beginner, but he could make himself understood with the help of a dictionary. His health was excellent and his political views left nothing to be desired: he was known as a steadfast nationalist.

He firmly believed that national socialism would soon triumph, and his conviction was strengthened by each of Hitler's successes. His friend Karl von Eberstein kept him posted on the progress of the movement.

In the course of his duties, Heydrich had occasion to visit many German coastal towns. At Wilhelmshaven he met Hermann Behrend, an innkeeper's son. The two young men became friends, partly becuse they shared the same political views. After the Nazis' spectacular gains in the 1930 elections, Heydrich said to Behrend, "Now there's nothing for Hindenburg to do but appoint Hitler as Reich Chancellor, and then our time will have come!"[9]

In the light of everything we have so far learned about Heydrich, Hermann Behrend's testimony seems quite plausible, and it gives the lie to stories circulated after the war in which

Heydrich is presented as an apolitical naval officer who read only sports newspapers and detective novels.

Lieutenant Reinhard Heydrich was proud of himself for having succeeded in becoming an intelligence officer at Kiel, where the naval High Command had its headquarters. He regarded his new post as an important step toward much greater advances.

Kiel, the capital of Schleswig-Holstein, was a city of two hundred thousand people. Heydrich's companions noticed an abrupt change in him as soon as he arrived there. He attended all sorts of social events and played his violin at musical gatherings. But he now tried to keep his former comrades at a distance. He suddenly became very mistrustful and even broke off with one of his oldest shipboard friends, Baron Hubert von Wangenheim, who later said that Heydrich "did not trust others and was afraid they would hate him and draw him into a trap."[10]

What was he afraid of? Did he want to avoid all political conversation? Or did he think he was being watched because he held a position that demanded secrecy? Important information passed through his hands. He did not deal only with requests for promotion or leave, or communications between naval commanders and ships at sea: the papers that came to his desk also concerned personal intrigues within the officer corps and political reports for the intelligence service, and he usually had to transmit this information in code. He felt the need for secrecy more than any of his companions. But it may also be that he broke off with them because he felt that he now belonged to another, more important world: the world of the secret service.

His former friends came to regard him almost as a stranger; very few of them dared to strike up a conversation with him when they happened to meet him. He had given up his habit of talking about his successes: he was afraid of arousing jealousy in others. But his free time was as important to him as his work; he frequented "good society," went sailing, and took an interest in women. In Kiel he soon acquired the reputation of a Casanova.

He was a good talker, especially on subjects that he knew well: music, sports, seafaring adventures, politics. But he also knew how to listen, occasionally making a pertinent remark at the right moment. He had a carefully collected stock of jokes that he had heard either in the navy or in his parents' home, and they were appreciated in the more lighthearted circles of Kiel society. Conservatives admired him because he could boast of having fought against the Communists, rifle in hand, at the age of fifteen. Another point in his favor was that he came from an esteemed family: his father was a composer and the director of a conservatory.

He had all the characteristics he needed for making a good impression, those that corresponded to the Nazi ideal. First, his physical appearance: if Nazism had looked at itself in a mirror, it would have been the image of Reinhard Heydrich. The vision of a racial elite that would dominate the future Nazi utopia was centered around a type of man precisely described by Hans Günther, the racial theorist of the Third Reich: this type was tall, with a long skull; a narrow face; prominent cheekbones; a high, thin nose; soft blond hair; light blue, deep-set eyes; and pink and white skin. [11]

According to Heydrich's companions, "in relations with his subordinates he was cold, disdainful, arrogant, and often insulting in words as well as in his way of treating them." And "on two occasions acute conflicts with the crew of the *Schleswig-Holstein,* provoked by his behavior, nearly led to a mutiny directed against him." [12] He had probably felt that his brutal attitude toward his subordinates would help him to win promotion.

But now that his apprenticeship was over and he had become an intelligence officer at Kiel, such conduct was no longer called for. His colleagues were officers, like himself, and they appreciated only his professional competence and political reliability.

Fascinated by Technology and Politics

We can now ask why, after seven years of effort to become a radio officer at sea, Heydrich suddenly requested a post as an intelligence officer onshore. Did he intend to make a career for himself as a bureaucrat? Did he want to become more highly specialized from a technical viewpoint? Did he have political motives? Did he feel that as a staff officer he would be better able to serve his country and further his own well-being at the same time? One thing is certain: with his ruthless determination to get ahead, he had already aroused the antipathy of nearly all his associates.

Shlomo Aronson, an Israeli historian, has concluded that Heydrich was apolitical, but that conclusion is based only on what Heydrich's family and friends have said since the end of the war. To counter the view of him as one of the worst Nazi criminals, a demon in human form, they have tried to humanize him and take away his satanic character by presenting him as an ordinary man with no interest in politics, a man whose only ideal in life had been to have a successful career as a naval officer.

This version of Heydrich's nature raises a question. Here we have a man who at the age of fifteen had fought in the ranks of the *voelkisch* movement; who had been photographed as a member of the Free Corps, proudly wearing a steel helmet; and who from childhood had been taught by his father that the Jews were a diabolical race—is it reasonable to assume that when he entered the navy he completely reversed himself and became apolitical? The instruction given in the German Navy at that time was known for its particularly violent indoctrination against the *"Diktat* of Versailles."* Political and strategic aspects of the world situation that were ignored in civilian schools were taught in great detail to officer candidates.

Heydrich received that political education. He was also instructed in the Prussian military tradition and the glories of the German Navy. Every year the nation commemorated the anniversary of what was regarded as the greatest naval battle in history: the Battle of Jutland. On May 31 and June 1, 1916, the German high seas fleet, commanded by Admiral Reinhard Scheer, had defeated a numerically superior British fleet. The British lost 6,700 men, the Germans only 2,400; British losses in ships totaled 115,000 tons, German losses only 60,000. To every German sailor, the Battle of Jutland was a stirring example of his leaders' skill and daring. Such leaders, with brave men serving under them, could also be victorious in the future, even if their forces were greatly outnumbered.

Students in military academies were indignant at the provisions of the Versailles Treaty that limited the German Navy to six

light cruisers armed with 150-millimeter guns. Was it for this
that thirty-five thousnad German sailors had given their lives in
the World War?

The annual commemoration of the Battle of Jutland was regarded by German military men as a protest against the Versailles Treaty. The political education that Heydrich received in
the navy could have only reinforced his personal hatred of what
to him was the betrayal represented by that treaty.

Many of his companions were already dreaming of establishing
a new order in Europe: Germany, with its advantageous geo-
graphical situation, its formidable industrial potential, and a pro-
portionate number of invincible soldiers, should be able to break
the chains of Versailles and create a new Europe.

Heydrich thus broadened his political horizon as he increased
his technical knowledge. He soon realized that the progress of
science could serve the greatness of the Reich and the strategic
plans that it required.

In 1924, when the period of great aerial exploits began, his
ideas on the relation between technology and politics became
clearer and more concrete. He shared the national pride that all
Germans felt when Hugo Eckener flew across the Atlantic in his
zeppelin. In 1926, he was fascinated by the American Richard
Byrd's flight from Spitsbergen, Norway, to the North Pole and
back. In that same year, Umberto Nobile and Roald Amundsen
flew from Europe to North America across the North Pole in the
dirigible *Norge*. In 1927, an American pilot, Charles Lindbergh,
flew his airplane from New York to Paris. In 1928, Nobile set off
for the North Pole in the dirigible *Italia*, but crashed, and
Amundsen was killed in an attempt to rescue him and his crew.
As a radio officer aboard the *Schleswig-Holstein*, Heydrich followed these events closely. Because he deeply hated the Russians, he was disappointed when a Soviet rescue team reached
the Italians on an ice floe near Spitsbergen. "I would have applauded any other team," he said, "but not the Russians!"

When Eckener experimentally carried passengers in a dirigible
in 1928, German naval officers discussed the possibilities of air
travel with keen interest. Did the future belong to the sea or to
the air? Heydrich, the sailor, was enthusiastic when the newspapers announced that Germany was building a ten-engined sea-
plane that would be the largest in the world.

By radio, Heydrich was also able to follow the flight of the Germans Günther von Hünefeld and Hermann Köhl, and the Irishman James Fitzmaurice, who in April 1928 were the first to cross the Atlantic from east to west in an airplane. Novelist Thomas Mann witnessed the two German heroes' triumphal return to their homeland. In a personal letter to the writer Arthur Hübscher he described their reception as "nationalistic acrobatics" and said that the two pilots themselves were only "witless aviators." When Hübscher revealed the contents of this letter, it immediately set off a controversy in the press. Heydrich, who was strongly interested in aviation and regarded Hünefeld and Köhl's feat as a German victory, felt that Mann's statements were an insult to Germany and never forgot them.

It was at this time that Heydrich began toying with the idea of getting a pilot's license. Meanwhile, however, he was a radio officer, and that specialty was as important in aviation as it was in the navy. All the routine activities of a naval officer were a waste of time as far as he was concerned. Feeling that he was destined for high positions, he intended to study only what would be really useful to him later. He wanted to concentrate on the techniques of diving, laying cables, transmitting information, and intercepting enemy radio communications. Canaris had stressed to him the importance of gaining knowledge of the enemy and using it to defeat him. To Heydrich, this principle had political as well as military applications.

Germany would not regain her proper place in Europe unless she had a new government capable of using the latest scientific advances to serve the nation. "If only we had the right kind of government, we could do wonders!" Canaris had said to Heydrich. And after his disappointment at the failure of the Kapp putsch, Canaris had placed all his hopes in the movement led by Adolf Hitler.

Secret Warfare and Armed Revolt

Heydrich and Canaris continued the friendship that had begun aboard the *Berlin*. Canaris and his wife, Erika, treated Heydrich as a member of the family during his frequent visits to their home. Erika loved music. She and Heydrich played duets—their

favorite composers were Wolfgang Amadeus Mozart and Joseph
Haydn—while Canaris sat reading with his two basset hounds at
his feet. This love of dogs was another bond between Canaris and
Heydrich. Each time Heydrich came to the house, he brought not
only a bouquet for Erika but also some sort of treat for the dogs.

When the musical interlude was over, the two men would begin discussing politics and military strategy. They agreed that
strategists of the future would emphasize naval, air, and tank
warfare; the time of fortifications was past. Canaris often spoke of
his experiences as a submarine officer in the Atlantic and the
Mediterranean, and Heydrich listened attentively.

The transmission and interception of information was still one
of their favorite topics. They discussed all aspects of secret warfare, such as espionage, counterespionage, and sabotage. They
both regarded the politicians of the Reich as traitors and were
convinced that American, French, British, Polish, and soviet secret agents had woven a web of espionage all over the country;
everything that happened in Germany was immediately transmitted by radio to Washington, Paris, London, Warsaw, and Moscow. If there was a national uprising, the enemy networks and
their numerous agents would have to be wiped out as quickly as
possible.

The failures of the Kapp putsch and Hitler's "beer hall" putsch
in Munich, and the street fighting that was constantly forced on
the Nazis, showed that the Social Democrats and the Communists
were bent on fomenting not only strikes but also civil war. Canaris and Heydrich were confident that in the event of civil war
following a takeover of power, the Reichswehr and the police
would side with the nationalists against the Catholics, Social
Democrats, and Communists, who would oppose a Hitler government.

In such a confrontation, technology and military training would
be crucial factors in determining which side won. Canaris and
Heydrich believed that a secret struggle for power was already
under way. Heydrich decided to make a thorough study of all
available material on civil war. A counterespionage officer
brought him a copy of Der bewaffnete Aufstand ("Armed Revolt")
by A. Neuberg, published in 1928, which maintained that at the
decisive moment the class struggle could take on a revolutionary

form: "Armed revolt is the supreme form of the political struggle of the proletariat."[13]

Heydrich resolved that from then on he would prepare himself for armed conflict. With his technical knowledge and proven courage, he was well qualified to play an important part in the struggle. Karl von Eberstein had told him that with Hitler it would be all or nothing.

Hitler's *Mein Kampf* had strengthened Heydrich's conviction that a well-equipped army could easily conquer, in the East, the "living space" (*Lebensraum*) that the German people needed. He knew that Italy, Hungary, Austria, and Bulgaria did not accept the terms imposed by the victors in the World War; the multinational states of Czechoslovakia and Yugoslavia would therefore have to disappear.

Heydrich was sure that once Hitler came to power he would renounce the terms of the Versailles Treaty concerning limitations on Germany's army and navy, and that he would place special emphasis on building a modern air force. Heydrich suspected that Hitler would favor the air force at the expense of the navy; he had read in *Mein Kampf* that England was Germany's natural ally, in view of the world situation.

In 1930, Heydrich maintained close relations with his friend Karl von Eberstein, who now belonged to the staff of Heinrich Himmler, head of the SS, and he shared Eberstein's enthusiasm when, on September 14, Hitler's National Socialist party won 6.4 million votes, a spectacular increase over the 800,000 votes of 1928. As a result of the election, 107 brown-shirted Nazi deputies took their places in the Reichstag.

Eberstein assured Heydrich, who was now more interested in politics than ever, that Hitler's conquest of power was only a question of time and that the economic depression was driving the lower middle class into the party. President von Hindenburg and the German Nationalists now had to be persuaded to take measures against the Communists, who had polled 4.6 million votes.

Heydrich was among those who, for propaganda purposes, had been repeating Hitler's assertion that the German nation had to make a choice: "National socialism or communism, Berlin or Moscow." This choice was supposed to decide the presidential election to be held in 1932.

Remaining in Kiel all through 1930, Heydrich hoped that he would soon be promoted to a staff position in Berlin. Berlin was his prime objective: that was where he could do good work. He knew that Hitler had sent one of his party leaders there, Dr. Joseph Goebbels, a man of exceptional intelligence who, with the SS and the SA, would combat the Red hordes as the Free Corps and the militia had done in Halle. The party's decisive victory would take place in Berlin, and Heydrich wanted to be there.

One evening, after a musical interlude with Erika Canaris, Heydrich received a gift from her husband: a copy of Machiavelli's *The Prince*. Canaris agreed with Machiavelli in believing that a statesman had as much to learn from the fox as from the lion. Man was both a human being and a beast of prey; a real statesman must never lose sight of that truth. "Man is and always will be a beast of prey," Heydrich would later say to his collaborators.

His zeal was increased still more by the example of Colonel Ludwig Beck, commander of a regiment stationed at Ulm. In 1930, there were charges of a Nazi conspiracy in the regiment and three officers—Lieutenants Wendt, Ludin, and Scheringer—were arrested by the police for activities hostile to the state. The whole officer corps condemned this civilian intervention in the armed forces as a violation of the army's prerogatives and an affront to the patriotic young lieutenants. But the government insisted that they be punished for having tried to impair the country's defenses. Colonel Beck, who had strong political opinions, opposed the government's action with a firmness that made him the idol of Heydrich and all other German officers.

Heydrich was also deeply affected by an affair that involved his friend and mentor Wilhelm Canaris in 1927–28. Canaris had been transferred to the Reichswehr Ministry in Berlin, where he dealt with important matters concerning the secret services. He was attacked by a left-wing newspaper, *Die Weltbühne*, which claimed that he had played a double role, like so many other officers, at the time of the Kapp putsch. Then he was accused of having been partially responsible for the execution of several rebellious sailors in 1917–18. His chief accuser was Philipp Scheidemann, a Social Democrat who in 1918 had proclaimed the Republic to the people gathered in front of the Reichstag building. Heydrich followed the whole affair in the press, including *Die Weltbühne* itself.*

On January 23, 1926, when Canaris appeared as an expert witness before a parliamentary commission investigating the disturbances that had taken place in the fleet in 1917–18, he had reproached the Social Democrats with having incited the sailors to revolt. The deputies had silenced him with boos and shouts of "Provocation!" From then on, he had been discredited from a political viewpoint, but the Reichswehr Ministry, that state within a state, had stood by him.

Die Weltbühne further accused Canaris of having supported the Wikingbund, a right-wing extremist league, when he was in Kiel. This league, wrote the newspaper, was a reconstitution of Erhardt's terrorist organization, which had inspired several political murders, and Canaris had given it money taken from government funds.

The Reichswehr Ministry now felt that Canaris could no longer be kept in Berlin. On June 22, 1928, he was transferred to the *Schlesien,* an old warship serving in the North Sea. For a year, nothing more was heard of him. It was during this period that Lieutenant Reinhard Heydrich was stationed in Kiel as an intelligence officer. There is no documentary evidence that the two men were still in contact with each other, but one thing is certain: those who knew Heydrich at the time reported later that he had cut out and collected all newspaper articles about Canaris.[14]

On September 29, 1930, Commander Wilhelm Canaris was promoted to Chief of Staff of the North Sea Command, which was far from satisfying his political ambitions.[15]

Departure from the Navy

While he was still in the navy, Heydrich swore to take revenge on the journalists Carl von Ossietzky, editor of *Die Weltbühne,* and Berthold Jacob. The latter had "specialized in revelations

*Heydrich hated Carl von Ossietzky, editor of *Die Weltbühne*. After the Reichstag fire in 1933, he had Ossietzky arrested and sent to the Sachsenhausen concentration camp. Under pressure from public opinion, he had to release him. Ossietzky, already gravely ill, died soon afterward.

concerning the Reichswehr and radical rightist organizations."[16] Heydrich never lost sight of him, and eight years later he tried to even his score with him.

But Ossietzky and Jacob were not the only objects of Heydrich's hatred. Dr. Ernst Oberfohren, leader of the German Nationalists in Kiel, was, like Heydrich, an adversary of the Versailles Treaty, but he could not overcome his aversion to "the Bohemian Corporal," to use Hindenburg's description of Hitler. He had a more personal reason for being displeased by the growing success of the Nazis: the number of his own party's seats in the Reichstag had fallen from 71 in 1928 to 43 in 1930, while the Nazis had increased theirs from 12 to 107. Because Oberfohren opposed the policy of "all or nothing" that Hitler advocated in his speeches, the SA and the SS disrupted all his meetings. In Kiel, the SS regarded Oberfohren as the foremost enemy of their movement, and Heydrich was well aware of his hostility to the Nazis.

Heydrich's rise to great power in the Third Reich cannot be understood without taking account of his previous development and activities in Kiel, because it was there that his political views and social attitudes took on their final form.

On December 6, 1930, he met Lina von Osten, a nineteen-year-old student whose father was a teacher on the Baltic island of Fehmarn. Conversation between the two young people naturally turned to politics because, like her brother, a student at Oldenburg, Lina von Osten was already a fanatical Nazi. She enthusiastically praised Adolf Hitler and his talent as an orator. The SS, with their "absolutely military" appearance, pleased her greatly, especially since they maintained order with an iron hand at meetings where the Fuehrer spoke.

After knowing each other only two days, Heydrich and Lina von Osten became engaged and announced the happy news to their friends and relatives. Heydrich had no objection to the fact that, because of their rigorous Nazi convictions, his fiancée and her family were not held in high esteem in Fehmarn.

Three weeks after the couple agreed to marry, their official engagement was celebrated in the house of Lina's parents. But Heydrich must have been somewhat distracted from full enjoyment of the festivities: the father of a woman he had abandoned after having an affair with her had just demanded that he marry her. Heydrich told Lina that the woman herself had made her father take this action because she wanted revenge.

Soon afterward, Heydrich was dismissed from the navy. A number of historians have accepted the idea that his dismissal resulted entirely from his refusal to marry the woman he had abandoned.

Lina Heydrich said the following after the war:

> Politically, he had no opinions. . . . He looked down on all parties, especially the Nazi party, and to him politics was something crass. In that respect, he gave the impression of being rather snobbish. He considered his naval career the most important thing in his life. Nothing else mattered.[17]

She also said that he made fun of the Nazi party because it was headed by a "Bohemian Corporal" (Hitler) and a "crippled orator" (Goebbels).[18] According to her own statements, she was an enthusiastic supporter of the party and its leaders; if Heydrich really spoke about them so disrespectfully in front of her, we must conclude that, politically, the two of them were at opposite poles.

Four months after Heydrich's dismissal from the navy, a miracle occurred: that supposed adversary of Hitler became head of the Nazi party's secret service, with an office in the Brown House, the Fuehrer's headquarters in Munich.

A year after they became engaged, Lina von Osten and Reinhard Heydrich were married in Fehmarn. He was now an SS Obersturmbannfuehrer, which meant that his rank was higher than the one he had held when he was thrown out of the navy.

Were the Nazi leaders really so blind or foolish as to place their secret documents in the hands of an apolitical man who had only scorn for their party?

Be that as it may, the SA and SS men in Fehmarn took part in Heydrich's wedding. They were all there, standing at attention in two rows when the couple entered the church. The pastor quoted Luther: "Even if the world be full of demons, we must succeed," and gave a patriotic speech. The organist played a composition by Bruno Heydrich, Reinhard's father, that he had written for this solemn occasion. The wedding procession left the church to the strains of the Horst Wessel song. The SA and SS men waiting outside beneath their swastika flags greeted the newlyweds with the stiff-armed Nazi salute.

Circumstances or Innate Evil?

Before taking up Heydrich's career in the SS, we will consider some of the efforts that have been made to explain why he committed his monstrous acts.

Charles Wighton, Heydrich's first biographer, describes him as a highly gifted man whose depraved character drove him to become "Hitler's most evil henchman." But what we have learned of Heydrich's youth and the time he spent in the navy does not support that view. After the war, Felix Kersten, Himmler's masseur, tried to exonerate the SS by claiming that one man, Reinhard Heydrich, was responsible for the murder of millions of Jews, and that he had a satanic character resulting from an inferiority complex produced by his awareness of his "impure blood," that is, his partially Jewish ancestry. Wighton was influenced by this fabrication and therefore failed to present an accurate picture of Heydrich.

Another interpretation depicts Heydrich as a thoroughly ordinary man who was never capable of having political ideas, though he did have a craving for authority. After long conversations with Heydrich's widow, Lina, the Israeli historian Shlomo Aronson reached the conclusion that Heydrich was apolitical and that he entered the SS only by chance. Aronson made that mistake because he neglected to consider Heydrich in the context of the Weimar period and the antidemocratic, nationalistic, and racist doctrines to which he and millions of other young Germans were exposed. Having been indoctrinated and contaminated from early childhood, they remained faithful to the *voelkisch* convictions that had been instilled in them.

Part of their indoctrination was the idea that the enemy had to be not only defeated but destroyed. The consequences of that idea were expressed after the war by Karl Wolff, a former SS officer who was tried for war crimes by a West German tribunal.

When the judge reproached him for having written to the director of the German railways to congratulate him on the speed and efficiency with which Jews were transported to Auschwitz and other death camps, Wolff replied, "We were systematically brought up to be like that."

Those who have studied Heydrich's life have seldom carried skepticism far enough to see through the tendentious accounts given by his friends and relatives, who depict him as having no political ambitions. Associates from his days as a naval cadet usually describe him as a rather eccentric young man who had great difficulty in adapting to ordinary social usages.

But from what we now know about him, he had all the qualities required for a normal career in the navy. He was self-disciplined, eager to learn, and full of ambition, and he liked his profession. If he had remained in the navy, he would have had a good chance of making his boyhood dream come true: he might have become an admiral. But he had grown up in a world of political fantasy. "Patriots" ranted about the fateful, decisive role of the German nation and its position as a predominant power. By technology and armed conflict, Germany was to conquer the rights that inherently belonged to her. Since the fate of the nation would be decided not on the high seas but in Berlin and Munich, Heydrich gave up his naval ambitions and turned to politics.

It was neither chance nor the accusation of having "impure blood" that made him a fanatic. What determined his decision was the same vision that had prompted him to become a naval officer so that he could contribute to Germany's struggle for world domination. He came to believe that because of his superior qualities he could go farther outside of the navy than within it. From his experience in the Free Corps he had learned that a command center could function well only if it had an efficient system of gathering information. That was the reason for his departure from the navy and the cordial welcome he was given in the Brown House.

No, Heydrich was not a born monster. Like many of his contemporaries, he took the path laid out for him by circumstances. A barbaric ideology created the murderous dynamics of Nazism. It was not chance that made Heydrich first an intelligence officer and then the head of the SD. This key man of the Third Reich cannot be understood without knowing about his youth and his professional training. He and the other overlords of the Third Reich epitomized a whole period of their country's history: *they reflected the German society of the first half of the twentieth century*.

Günther Deschner, another of Heydrich's biographers, also fails to present an accurate picture of him because he accepts the theory of chance: if Heydrich had not been dismissed from the navy, he would not have "happened" to enter the SS. Deschner does not consider the question of how a man who was supposedly interested only in sports and military technology could have built up a gigantic police organization. He oversimplifies when he says that Heydrich was only swept along in the wake of fascism and that, following the example of left-wing revolutionary movements, he merely placed advanced technology in the service of the Nazi dictatorship. According to Deschner, although the SS acted harshly, basically all it did was to add "one layer to the veneer of National Socialist ideology."[19] But in that case, how are we to explain all the murders that the SS committed for the Fuehrer and the state? Could those bestial crimes have been committed on such an incredible scale by men who had no deep ideological convictions?

Heydrich eventually took command of the war of racial extermination that the Nazis waged in Europe, and he was already a "political soldier" in that future war when he came to the Brown House in Munich, just as he had already been a right-wing extremist before he entered the navy.

He fervently believed in the historic role of the Nazi party and its militias, the SA and the SS. Convinced that Hitler was on the verge of taking power, he wanted to devote all his knowledge and energy to the coming Nazi victory.

3

Hitler's Fouché

The view that Heydrich was forced to leave the navy because of "trouble with a woman" has been accepted by most writers who have described his past. Some add that a second reason was misconduct toward his superiors.

If he was really dismissed because of his refusal to marry a young woman after having an affair with her, there ought to be some written trace of it, because most of the German Navy's records from that time have remained intact, but we have no documents concerning the cause of his dismissal. It also seems strange that no one, not even Heydrich's widow, has been able to remember the name of the woman in question. His associates who said after the war that he had been dismissed by a naval court of honor not only because he had wronged a woman but also for insubordination were unable to give any precise information about the woman he had wronged.

But even if there actually was such a woman, and even if Heydrich's refusal to marry her actually was the basis of charges brought against him, we cannot exclude the possibility that his dismissal was politically motivated. The great confidence shown in him by Hitler and Himmler as soon as he arrived at the Brown House, his rapid advancement in the SS, the respectful way he was treated in the headquarters of the Nazi party—all this suggests that the Nazi leadership wanted to reward him for services rendered to the party.

If someday it is established by unquestionable documentary evidence that Heydrich appeared before a naval court of honor because of his misconduct toward a woman, that will not disprove the statement he often repeated during his years in the Third Reich: that he was dismissed from the navy for political reasons.

In any case, the Nazis did not hold his dismissal against him. It took effect on May 31, 1931; the next day, June 1, he was enrolled in the Hamburg section of the Nazi party with the number 544916. And no one protested when he became a member of the SS with the number 10120.

According to those who present Heydrich as having been completely apolitical, his fiancée, Lina von Osten, persuaded him to accept the post in the SS for which his friend Karl von Eberstein had recommended him. Eberstein now had the rank of SS Oberfuehrer, equivalent to Brigadier General in the army. He made an appointment for Heydrich with Heinrich Himmler, who had just been ordered by Hitler to create an SS intelligence service at Nazi party headquarters in Munich.

When Heydrich came for his interview, Himmler said to him, "I need an Ic [an officer in charge of an intelligence service]. I'll give you twenty minutes to write a summary of how you would handle the job."[1] "Heydrich wrote something, using his professional military vocabulary . . . and was given the post."[2]

Supporters of the Third Reich who survived its collapse later realized that if they described the Nazi leaders as rather foolish they would find listeners inclined to believe their version of the facts. Karl von Eberstein was among those who went to great lengths to establish the idea that Himmler was so dim-witted that he did not understand Heydrich's naval background. Eberstein told his story to anyone willing to hear it, including Shlomo Aronson. In accordance with Eberstein's fanciful account, Aronson wrote, "Himmler showed interest in the former intelligence officer, unaware that he was not an expert on intelligence in the sense of espionage and counterespionage, but was trained only in radio and had actually been an intelligence communications officer."[3]

While it is true that Himmler was one of the Nazis' foremost racial ideologists, it is impossible to take seriously the story that he was decisively influenced by Heydrich's blond hair and blue eyes when he was looking for the right man to head the party's intelligence service. Himmler's alleged mistake about Heydrich's naval background can only be an invention by Eberstein. When Himmler said, "I need an Ic," he and Heydrich both knew exactly what that meant. The term *Ic* had been in common use as far back as the Imperial Army to designate the commander of an intelligence service. If Heydrich had not had experience in naval intelligence, he would have pointed out Himmler's mistaken assumption.

According to Eberstein, Himmler showed no particular interest in Heydrich's training and experience, hired him mainly on the basis of his military bearing and Nordic appearance, and then immediately turned over all his secret files and documents to him. Otto von Heydebreck, Hans von Kessel, and Udo von Mohrenschildt, three German journalists whose families suffered from Heydrich's brutality (each of them lost a brother in the Blood Purge of June 30, 1934, which Heydrich organized as head of the Security Police), reported after the war that in the summer of 1931 Himmler chose Heydrich because of his professional ambition, his military training, his ideological fanaticism, and his excellent knowledge of intelligence operations.

Heydrich was instructed to create an organization on the model of the British Intelligence Service and the French Deuxième Bureau, as well as a "secret league" of Nazi party members who could carry out murder and terror missions. By the end of October 1931, according to Udo von Mohrenschildt, there was a secret troop of assassins that owed its existence to Heydrich. Its purpose was to terrorize political parties and individual politicians opposed to Hitler.

Mohrenschildt, who was a supporter of Nazism at the time, met Heydrich at the Brown House in the fall of 1931. Heydrich, wearing the impressive black uniform of the SS, acted with great self-importance and tried to persuade young Mohrenschildt to join the secret staff of his branch office in Berlin.

Otto von Heydebreck has reported that in 1931 Hitler was concerned with putting pressure on the upper middle class to make large financial contributions to the party. At the time when Heydrich assumed his post in the Brown House, the Fuehrer had entrusted the secret party funds to Martin Bormann. Otto von Heydebreck's brother, Hans-Peter, then an SA Gruppenfuehrer in Mecklenburg, was on friendly terms with Bormann, who had

boasted of the great amounts of money he had brought into the
coffers of the SS. Bormann admiringly told Hans-Peter von
Heydebreck that Hitler had a group of blackmail specialists
gathering information on a number of rich people and using it to
extract money from them. To increase the number of geese that
laid golden eggs, the Fuehrer needed detailed information on
prominent people in all walks of life.

The Fuehrer's Mythology

Before Himmler placed his secret files in Heydrich's hands, he
called his attention to the basic elements of Nazi ideology. Although the official slogan was "National socialism or communism,
Hitler or Lenin, Berlin or Moscow," he said, the real enemy of
the party was, and always had been, the Jews. For tactical reasons, Hitler had decided to move toward power in successive
stages. "We must present an alarming picture of the Bolshevik
peril, whether it exists or not," said Himmler, "and that won't be
hard to do, because of the present activities of the Comintern and
the German Communists. But for the moment it's even more
urgent to build up detailed files on everything concerning the
Jewish problem."

He handed Heydrich a copy of *Literarisches Lexikon*, by the
anti-Semite Philipp Stauff, published in 1913, and said that
Hitler had found it extremely useful when he decided to devote
himself entirely to politics.

That book became one of Heydrich's favorite reference works.
He recommended it to all his associates. And in December 1931,
he showed it to a visitor from Pomerania whom he esteemed
highy: SA Gruppenfuehrer Hans-Peter von Heydebreck, a World
War veteran who had lost his left arm in the Argonne Forest and
was a friend of Ernst Roehm, head of the SA. In 1931, the SS
was only a section of the SA. Roehm had faithfully served Hitler
since the early days of the movement, and Hans-Peter von
Heydebreck, founder of a Free Corps, had fought the Poles from
1918 to 1923 in Silesia and Upper Silesia. Heydrich and
Heydebreck could therefore regard themselves as comrades who
had served on the same front. They were to have intense political
discussions until Heydebreck's death in 1934.

When the *Muenchener Post* published information on the new man in the Brown House, Heydrich must have been afraid that the Isidor Suess story might resurface and, in the face of such danger, he must have cultivated the acquaintance of people who could be useful in counterbalancing any painful discoveries that might be made. Hans-Peter von Heydebreck was one of those people, if only because his brother, Otto, worked for an important newspaper, the *Neuesten Muenchener Nachrichten*. Though the two brothers had fundamentally different views of the world, they were still bound together by strong family feelings. Otto was regarded as a friend and supporter of Heinrich Bruening, Reich Chancellor and leader of the Center party, who was greatly respected by President von Hindenburg. In the struggle for power, Bruening, the head of a party that then commanded more than four million votes, could play an important part.

Heydrich therefore had a strong interest in maintaining cordial relations with Hans-Peter von Heydebreck. He carefully chose the information he passed on to him, convinced that the two brothers would discuss it together. "You may have heard," he once told him, "that some people claim I have Jewish ancestry. If that were true, there would be some mention of it in Stauff's book."[4] He opened the book to the chapter on composers, singers, and instrumentalists, and showed Heydebreck that his father did not appear in it as either Heydrich or Suess.

While he was in Kiel, Heydrich had already realized that workers were not an important part of the Nazi party. Now, in Munich, he soon discovered that secret funds from the army, the police, and industry formed the party's economic base, and that without the support of those "national forces" Hitler could never have developed the party as he had done. But Heydrich knew it was effective propaganda to present Hitler as having been chosen only by "fate" to be the savior of the German nation.

Like Roehm, head of the SA, and Alfred Rosenberg, the party's philospher, Himmler was one of those who had developed and propagated the Hitlerian mythology. Adolf Hitler, born at Braunau am Inn, Austria, in 1889, described himself as a painter and a writer and attached special importance to the fact that as a young man in Vienna he had earned his living as a construction worker. He had enlisted in the German Army as

soon as war broke out in 1914, and was eventually awarded the
Iron Cross, First Class. In 1917–18, he had agitated against leftist ideas. Immediately after the war, when he had been given
a brief indoctrination in the nationalistic view of Germany's
defeat—treason, the *Diktat* of Versailles, the stab in the back,
the worldwide Jewish conspiracy, the *Protocols of the Elders
of Zion*—he had begun going to leftist political meetings to
spy on the people who attended them and argue against the
speakers.

Nationalistic agitators of Hitler's type had their bourgeois
counterparts in the Thule Society, which met regularly in the
luxurious Hotel Vier Jahreszeiten in Munich. Members of the
Thule Society denounced the clergy, socialism, and, of course,
the Jews. Their program was simple: Germanic tradition, mili-
tarism, and the swastika.

Alfred Rosenberg was considered a specialist on the Jewish
question. It was he who had the idea of a "workers' party" that
would voice anticapitalist slogans but fanaticize its members
against the Jews. His proposal fell on fertile ground: the Thule
Society founded and financed the German Workers' party,
headed by a machinist and right-wing agitator named Anton
Drexler. When Drexler heard Hitler speak at a meeting, he said
to one if his companions, "We could use him."[5]

Drexler's favorable impression of Hitler is understandable.
Hitler had the courage to attend opposition meetings, take the
floor, and call the previous speakers traitors or mercenaries in
the pay of foreign powers. On October 16, 1919, shortly after
joining the German Workers' party, he spoke at one of its meetings and produced such a strong effect on its members that Dietrich Eckart, its ideological chief, soon had to yield his position
to him.

Sometime earlier, Ernst Roehm had contacted Drexler. As an
intelligence officer, Roehm belonged to the upper stratum of the
army which, prompted by monarchist and anti-Semitic convictions, planted spies in all leftist movements and gave moral and
financial support to rightist extremists. It had been Roehm who
persuaded the leaders of the small German Workers' party to
place Adolf Hitler at its head.[6]

Heydrich knew that although the Nazi party had grown out of

the German workers' party, it was not in fact a workers' party. It owed its existence to the Thule Society, the Offensive and Defensive League, and the most reactionary segments of German society. Beginning in 1919, there must have been an agreement between Roehm and Hitler according to which Hitler would direct the party's political activities while Roehm would be in command of its military forces, even after it had come to power.[7]

In the early stage of the movement, an Adolf Hitler was more acceptable to prospective financial backers than an Ernst Roehm or an Alfred Rosenberg. Hitler was an excellent fund raiser. Rather than feeling humiliated, Roehm and Rosenberg proposed a propaganda campaign to make Hitler the messianic leader (Fuehrer) of the German people. In 1931, Heydrich accepted him without reserve as the great man of the party.

During his first weeks at the Brown House, Heydrich also read Rosenberg's *The Myth of the Twentieth Century*. From it he learned that Christ was to disappear as an object of worship and be replaced by Hitler. Heydrich had long since rejected the religious upbringing given to him by his mother, becoming instead a fanatical opponent of Catholicism. He was convinced that German Catholics, if only because of the existence of the Pope, would never recognize Hitler as a divine figure, and he was therefore determined to deal as harshly with the Catholics as with the Marxists and the Jews. Being a realist, he knew that the Fuehrer would never achieve his goals by parliamentary means. The Nazi party would have to take total control of the state, then eliminate other parties as well as labor unions, religions, and adversaries of racism.

Heydrich also knew he would have to do many things that would bring him no immediate advantage but would benefit him later. Once the Nazis had come to power, he would use his police organization to dethrone Christ and consolidate the position of Adolf Hitler, the new messiah. Since the tactic of forming a sham "workers' party" had been successful, he would continue in that direction. The upper middle class, the army, and President von Hindenburg had to be deceived into regarding Hitler's party as a mass movement. Those who would put Hitler in the saddle must be convinced that the Social Democrats, who had dominated German politics since 1918, had to be replaced with the National

Socialist German Workers' party, as the Nazi party was officially
called.

In 1931, Heydrich was still only an obscure member of that
German Fascist movement, but his political background already
enabled him to distinguish between German and Italian fascism.
In Italy there was still a hereditary monarchy, and Benito Mussolini had no thought of deposing the King. Nor could the Italian
government simply ignore the interests of the Vatican and the
Church, which had considerable influence on public life. Mussolini was not the prophet of an implacable racist religion. Unlike
the Nazis, the Italian Fascists had not made racism an integral
part of their ideology. The only elements that the two parties
shared were the concept of an authoritarian state, the suppression
of workers' movements and unions, and the demand for a revision
of the peace treaties.

Heydrich had learned that Hitler's "workers' party," with its
voelkisch Germanism, was a hoax, but he was ready to do everything he could to support that deception of a whole nation. He
believed that Hitler's racial policies could not be carried out in a
climate of political morality and religion. In the silent struggle
taking place behind the scenes, brutal power was the only argument that counted. Heydrich had read in *Mein Kampf* that in
1918 it was fighting in the streets that had forced the imperial
government to surrender, and he wholeheartedly supported
Hitler's principle that terror had to be broken by terror.

Having seen that the Munich bourgeoisie had helped to launch
the Nazi party, he hoped that powerful groups in all other German cities would help conservative forces to make their breakthrough. For the moment, however, he felt that the main task was
to drive the enemy from the streets. Experience had shown that
in a conflict between the Reds and the Brownshirts, the police
could be counted on to side with the Brownshirts.

According to Himmler's directives, the SS was not only to gain
mastery in the streets but also infiltrate enemy fortresses. Once
the fortress of Berlin had been taken, it would no longer be difficult to attract even the workers to Nazism. There had to be a
march on the capital, and careful preparations had to be made for
it. To make it succeed, the party would require an organization
capable of spying on the enemy and procuring all the means of

crushing government terror. Hitler, Goebbels, and Himmler were satisfied that Heydrich was the man who could do what was needed.

The Strike Force 𝒱
of a Terrorist Organization

According to Otto von Heydebreck, Heydrich drew up a detailed plan specifying how each man regarded as an adversary was to be slandered and implicated in a real or invented case of corruption that would finally lead to a trial. But complications arose in the SA secret service: its agents proved to be so incompetent that they ran afoul of the Munich police, and Moulin-Eckart, its leader, was arrested for illegal activities. His network had become filled with police spies. Heydrich was given the task of reorganizing it and turning it into an effective instrument.

What Otto von Heydebreck reported after the war, in the course of many conversations with me, is only partly confirmed by documents. Moulin-Eckart had counted on subsidies from the Reichswehr, while Hitler, Bormann, and Himmler wanted to extract money from the great magnates of finance. To do this, they needed a team of young men united by two basic ideas: anti-bolshevism and anti-Semitism. Moulin-Eckart had been told to give his men training that would enable them to escape police surveillance, but he had failed to do so.

On the pretext of coming to the aid of the Reichswehr in case of war, a number of adventurers had formed "defense groups" to draw money from the secret funds of the Ministry of the Interior and the Reichswehr. They were thus in competition with the Nazis, and Heydrich, as the new head of the SS Security Service, set about getting rid of them, using force when necessary.

Heydrich soon made enemies within the party and in the SA. He was not greatly disturbed by this. What mattered to him was that his acts were approved by Hitler, Bormann, and Himmler. The journalist Hans von Kessel later reported that Moulin-Eckart, wanting to discredit his rival, began collecting information on Heydrich's father, his youth, his service in the navy, his dismissal from it, and the "work of corruption" that he was carrying on in Munich. In doing this, Moulin-Eckart condemned himself to death.

What he learned about Heydrich's origins was unimportant compared with the evidence he gathered concerning relations between Heydrich and Karl von Eberstein. That was forbidden territory because Hitler had publicly declared that he would use only legal means to achieve power. Spying on officers of the armed forces was severely punished by the law and regarded as an act incompatible with the principles of patriotism. Moulin-Eckart, and others who wanted Heydrich out of the way, would not have missed a chance to use that argument in their struggle against him within the party. According to Hans von Kessel, Heydrich's adversaries underestimated the danger of what they planned to do. Revealing the true reason for Heydrich's dismissal from the navy might set off a scandal that would jeopardize Hitler's efforts to increase his support in the Reichswehr. Worried about the effects of such a revelation, the party leadership finally began circulating a story to counteract it: Heydrich had been dismissed from the navy because he refused to marry a woman after having an affair with her. That is Kessel's thesis. Is there documentary proof of it? No. But logic and common sense speak in its favor.

In any case, Heydrich's position was soon firmly established, and his rise in the Nazi hierarchy seemed assured. He was already working in an area where he was beyond the control of everyone except Hitler and Himmler. His activities were vitally important to a party that had half a million members, could count on the support of wealthy backers, and was preparing to take supreme power.

At the end of 1931, Heydrich married his fiancée, Lina von Osten, and was promoted to SS Obersturmbannfuehrer, which corresponded to Lieutenant Colonel in the army. In the Brown House he was already called "Hitler's Fouché," an allusion to Stefan Zweig's book on Joseph Fouché, sometimes considered the father of the modern police state, which was widely read at the time.

As Minister of Police, Fouché had served the successive French regimes of the late eighteenth and early nineteenth centuries. Heydrich saw him as a virtuoso of opportunism, but not as an example he could follow: now that he had committed himself to the policies of the Nazi party and all their consequences, there was no turning back. He was determined that after the party came to power he would create an organization far superior to the British Intelligence Service, the French Deuxième Bureau, and the Soviet GPU. Meanwhile, the party needed a powerful terrorist organization to undermine the Weimar Republic and, if necessary, wage civil war, provided the Reichswehr and the police fought on the side of the party.

The first necessity was to neutralize the informers who had infiltrated the party. But since Heydrich could not rapidly organize a system of espionage to cover the Reichswehr, the police, and the other parties, on September 4, 1931, an SS directive stated that the SD (Security Service) would first have to "limit its action to nongovernmental organizations."

Everyone in the Brown House was impressed by the self-assurance of the new head of the SD. Great things were expected of him. The party was preparing for the elections of the following year (1932), and there was a good chance that it would elect more deputies than any other party, in which case the President of the Reichstag would be chosen from its ranks. Hitler already had a candidate in mind: the former World War I pilot Hermann Goering. He regarded Goering not as a true revolutionary but as a man who saw great possibilities for himself in the coming Nazi victory. If Goering, a personification of the Prussian military tradition, became President of the Reichstag, he would be better able than anyone else to persuade Reich President von Hindenburg that control of the state should be turned over to Hitler.

But for the moment Hitler, born in Austria, was not even a German citizen, and he was therefore not a danger to the political establishment in Berlin. It was Heydrich's responsibility to use his secret connections and launch a campaign in favor of granting Hitler German nationality. At the end of November, he announced that he had succeeded: Hitler could choose the date when he would become a naturalized German citizen.

Hitler's Palace

No official written description of the Brown House, the Nazi party headquarters on Briennenstrasse in Munich, is in existence. The building was the former Barlow Palace, which had housed the Italian embassy in the nineteenth century. It stood on one of the most distinguished streets in the Bavarian metropolis. Bormann and the party treasurer paid half a million marks for it, and its renovation cost about the same amount.

Ordinarily, it was Rudolf Hess, the Fuehrer's deputy, who took important visitors on a tour of the palace, but on the day when Heydrich came to take possession of his post, Himmler himself showed him around the building. "The Fuehrer is a brilliant architect," Heydrich later said to him.

The architect Paul Troost had carried out the renovation of the Brown House on the basis of Hitler's plans. The result was a palace that made a powerful impression on all visitors, whether they were Nazi sympathizers or not. When the Fuehrer was present, silence had to reign. Visiting from one office to another was forbidden. Everyone had to concentrate on making his own personal contribution to the overthrow of the Weimar Republic.

Four months earlier, Richard Breiting, editor of the *Leipziger Neuesten Nachrichten*, had been given one of Hess's guided tours. Breiting took extensive notes, which have come down to us. Here are portions of them:

Hess leads us through the marble entrance hall of the palace. On a plaque are the names of the thirteen National Socialists who fell at the Feldherrnhalle. One of the walls is covered with banners, and Hess tells us that the others have been left bare because they are reserved for an honor roll containing the names of the three hundred murdered National Socialists, that is, those who have died for the party. This large room gives an impression of stern dignity. Swastikas have been placed all over it. . . .

There are countless offices on the ground floor and in the basement. Everything is brand new and shows clever organization. We are taken to the records department, which has steel walls to resist fire and forced entry. This is where personal information is kept on each of the five hundred thousand members of the National Socialist German Workers' party. There is enough space for files on a million members. Hess tells us that when the party reaches that number, it will accept no more members. "Either we succeed with a million, or not at all." Anyone who asks to join the party is not accepted as a member until a year later; during that time he must prove himself. Members who do not pay their dues are immediately thrown out.

Hitler and his closest collaborators have their offices on the second floor. These offices show really exquisite artistic taste. They are made of high-quality wood, decorated with valuable old paintings, and lighted by antique Venetian chandeliers converted into lamps.

Hess next takes us to the Senate Hall, an immense room that is prodigiously impressive from an artistic viewpoint. In it are sixty-one armchairs in bright red leather. The marble ceiling has a mosaic representing the emblem of the National Socialist party, and countless swastikas are woven into the large, luxurious carpets. Hanging on the wall facing the door are four paintings, surmounted by a gigantic swastika, depicting the four stages in the development of the National Socialist German Workers' party: foundation, program, first decline, "renewal" on September 14, 1930. According to Hess, this Senate Hall will later be a meeting place for the worthiest National Socialists, those who are qualified to rule Germany.

The courtroom on the upper floor is also interesting. This is where the supreme arbitration tribunal of the National Socialist party holds its sessions. It is a room of imposing dignity. In front of a crescent-shaped table is the armchair of the President of the tribunal. Facing it is a gold swastika, and above it a large portrait of Christ. ?

A tour of the huge building brings one surprise after another. This palace, decorated with precious objects and showing exquisite artistic taste, forms a striking contrast with the headquarters of a "workers' party." It gives the impression that Hitler resides in it as a King, and he probably feels that as the future ruler of Germany he must live in a setting like the one he has created for himself. . . .

Hess says that Hitler works incredibly hard from early morning till nightfall. Most of the visitors he receives are German and foreign politicians. Rumors that he avoids visitors out of shyness are false. He receives no journalists because of the bad experiences he has had with them. We are a praiseworthy exception.

Hitler sits behind a gigantic desk in an office next to the Senate Hall. On the desk is a photograph of Mussolini, and on the wall is an enormous oil painting of Frederick the Great.

This description clearly shows that no one could maintain that the Brown House was the headquarters of a workers' party. We can deduce from it that the Nazi party received large sums from the magnates of German finance, though since the end of World War II there has been a tendency to pass over that fact in silence.

The authenticity of Breiting's notes has been called into question by people who claim that Hitler never had a fixed plan. Even the journalist Alfred Detig, who was present during a conversation between Hitler and Breiting, has said in an unpublished letter to a magazine that the description of the Brown House is too grandiloquent to have been written by Breiting. But Detig reached that conclusion only after having been subjected to great pressure from former Nazi propagandists, such as Helmut Sünderman, for example. Earlier, Detig had confirmed the authenticity of the notes in front of witnesses, and stated that during the conversation between Hitler and Breiting, Hitler had forced Breiting to "donate" a sizable sum to the party. According to Breiting's widow and daughter, Heydrich also forced him to make payments, particularly in 1932. Breiting, who was on the Gestapo's blacklist in 1934, escaped death in the purge of that year only through the intervention of an influential friend. But he died mysteriously in 1937, after being interrogated by the Gestapo.

Before Breiting was "invited" to the Brown House, he had been the target of political attacks by the *Freiheitskampf,* the Nazi newspaper in Saxony, which called him a "flunky of the Jews." Nevertheless, Otto Dietrich, the liaison man between the Nazi party and the *Leipziger Neuesten Nachrichten,* arranged for Breiting's visit to the Brown House, where he was told that his newspaper would have to pay the enormous sum of ten million marks to make all official attacks cease.

This was a common procedure with the Nazis. It enabled them to curb the political activities of prominent figures in the Weimar Republic and also make them pay tribute if they wanted to keep their respectability. In the summer of 1931, Otto Dietrich had already arranged for several other such meetings between the Fuehrer and his victims. In his book *Mit Hitler in die Macht,* published in Munich in 1934, he wrote, "Anyone who had seen the powerful, convincing influence that Adolf Hitler exerted in personal conversation, even with his most determined adversaries, knew that this plan for destroying the system would achieve valuable victories."

Two months after coming to the Brown House, Heydrich took charge of "preparing" the people chosen for this kind of extortion. Breiting was one of the journalists he called from time to time. And Karl von Eberstein, whose task was to organize the SS in Saxony and Thuringia, seldom came to Leipzig without visiting Breiting to bring him "greetings" from the Brown House. Breiting, a resolute opponent of Nazism, always interpreted those visits as a bad omen. "When men like Heydrich, Eberstein, and Dietrich come to power," he once said to his wife, Emmy, "we'll soon be in hell!"[8]

The "Brown Olympus" and Its Gods

In his early days at the Brown House, Heydrich applied a basic military rule: first reconnoiter, then attack. So that he could form a clear idea of the political and personal attitudes of the men at the top, he tried to attract as little attention as possible. The adaptability that he had shown as a schoolboy, a naval cadet, and an officer was manifested once again at the beginning of his new career. He made a good first impression on the racists of the Brown House because of his strikingly "Nordic" appearance.

Very few people were allowed to see the party's membership files, but the man who had been placed in charge of reorganizing the secret service was naturally entitled to look up any information he wanted on any member. When Heydrich came into the file room, the clerks working there looked at him respectfully; if he stopped in front of a desk, the man or woman sitting at it quickly stood up and asked him what he wished.

It was the Fuehrer himself who had decided where the file room would be located and how work in it would be organized. A member's file card contained only "official" information: date of birth, address, occupation, marital status, references in the party, etc.

Besides the membership files, party headquarters also housed various departments: press, legal affairs, organization, propaganda, SS, SA, finance. Each department head had his own staff.

To further his chances of rapid advancement, Heydrich studied the high priests in that temple of racist religion. He learned that they wasted a great deal of time on speechmaking even among themselves, and that each tried to outdo the others in praising Adolf Hitler. He observed that the party was still too loosely organized.

Himmler had told him that the Fuehrer needed a "brain trust" that would be created within the SS and function as the General Staff of all Nazi activity. Hitler already had the men he needed in order to take power and rule the country, Himmler acknowledged, but measures had to be taken to guard against conflicting ambitions and overlapping jurisdictions.

One of the first Nazi leaders to whom Himmler introduced Heydrich was Alfred Rosenberg, editor of the party newspaper, the *Voelkischer Beobachter*. Born in 1893 at Revel (now Tallinn), in what were then the Russian Baltic Provinces, Rosenberg had fled to Germany at the time of the Russian Revolution. Since 1919, he had been living in Munich, where he had become associated with Hitler in political action. At his first meeting with Heydrich, Rosenberg explained to him that history was basically nothing but the eternal struggle among races. "The French and Russian revolutions must also be understood as struggles for power between the blond elite and an inferior racial stratum with dark hair and eyes."[9] This interpretation of history was to the liking of our "Nordic giant" from Halle. Rosenberg promised to lend him all his works, even those in manuscript form.

He began by lending him his most important work, *The Myth of the Twentieth Century*, and Houston Stewart Chamberlain's treatises on foreign policy. He asked Heydrich if he would write something for his monthly magazine, *Nationalsozialistische Monatshefte*, and suggested an article on Communist terrorist organizations in Germany.[10]

Within a short time, Heydrich became acquainted with all of the most powerful party leaders.

Hermann Goering was responsible for military planning and future rearmament. As a fighter pilot in the World War, he was already a squadron commander in 1915, and in 1918, he commanded the famed Richthofen squadron. His exploits had won him the highest military decorations. He now spent most of his time in Berlin, where he acted as Hitler's political observer and maintained the party's relations with the Reichswehr, Hindenburg's entourage, and important industrialists.

Joseph Goebbels, Hitler's propaganda chief, was to be one of Heydrich's models and teachers. He had been given a pious Catholic upbringing, but he was a born agitator and he now had a fierce hatred of Catholics as well as Communists and Jews. Publisher of the Nazi newspaper *Der Angriff* ("The Assault") in Berlin, he was respected in the party as the author of numerous propaganda works and he immediately gave Heydrich one of them, a printed speech entitled "Lenin or Hitler." Heydrich soon realized that Goebbels's influence on Hitler was much greater than one might think, and he held that "propaganda genius" in high esteem the rest of his life.

At first he regarded Goebbels, Goering, and Rosenberg as the only men in the party, aside from Hitler and Himmler, who were capable of giving the Reich the new form it needed. He later revised his opinion of Goering and Rosenberg, but at the time when he was organizing the SD, those three men were among his idols.

He placed Rudolf Hess in the first rank of the "secondary deities." Hess governed party affairs in the Brown House, and soon became friendly with Heydrich, working closely with him. Born of German parents in Alexandria, Egypt, in 1894, he had been a front-line soldier and a pilot in the World War. He appreciated the fact that Heydrich did not listen to his war stories only out of politeness. His participation in the 1923 putsch attempt and his eighteen-month imprisonment, half of it spent with Hitler, had made him one of the most fervent Nazis. He knew *Mein Kampf* almost by heart and was a fanatical believer in Hitler's racial mystique. Since 1925 he had belonged to the "general staff" of the party as Hitler's private secretary and he was said to be his right-hand man. He recognized that Heydrich was capable of organizing the party's secret service on the model of the British Intelligence Service. Relations between the two men were always marked by mutual respect.

Heydrich also found support in Martin Bormann, who handled Hitler's personal finances as well as the party treasury. Before going to Munich, Bormann had been a Nazi leader in Mecklenburg. Violent and brutal, he had been sentenced to a year in prison in 1924. Not long after his release, he was given a high rank in the SA and, after 1930, had administered the party's funds. It was he who had procured the money necessary for the

Brown House and made possible the financing of Hitler's feudal residence at Berchtesgaden. He and Heydrich had two things in common: their passion for iron discipline and their absolute devotion to their leaders. Bormann was as faithful to Hitler as Heydrich was to Himmler. Himmler had seen to it that Bormann could also regard himself as one of the heads of the Fuehrer's Praetorian Guards by giving him exhaustive information on all the secret affairs of the party; Heydrich could thus be sure that his reports would reach the Fuehrer directly. For tactical reasons, Himmler and Heydrich explained to Bormann that good intelligence work was essential to keeping the party's coffers well filled.

However great Heydrich's influence may now have been, he went on playing the part of an insignificant underling in Hitler's court, to ward off malevolent jealousy. He was an accomplished tactician in the internal warfare of the party. Outwardly, it seemed that Himmler had total control of the intelligence service. No one suspected that the future head of the Third Reich's secret police was already in the Brown House.

Postwar Epilogue

Since World War II, some of the people who worked with Heydrich during this period have described their experiences, but in a way that makes their activities in the Brown House seem trivial. They tend to present themselves as rather naive and not very bright. According to some of them, the employees of the secret service were all squeezed into one small room where they did nothing but fill out file cards on enemies of the party, and the party was so poor at this time that they had to keep the cards in old cigar boxes.[11] If we are to believe these postwar stories, we must also believe that the Nazi party carried on no conspiratorial activities and underpaid its top leaders, who were motivated only by idealism, a spirit of self-sacrifice, and a concern for the welfare of the German nation. Correspondingly, like all idealists, Heydrich and his collaborators had no precise political ideas; they did only the routine work of looking through the newspapers to learn who the enemies of the nation were, then taking notes on them that went into the card files kept in cigar boxes.

Heydrich's widow has played an important part in propagating this innocuous version of his work. She has said, for example, that soon after their marriage she and her husband rented a two-room apartment at 23 Türkenstrasse which, besides being their home, also housed the party's secret service, and that at this time he had only three employees who spent most of their time keeping files on friends and enemies.

And it has been claimed that at the beginning of 1932, when Hitler was transforming Germany into a political battlefield, the head of his secret service did not even have a typewriter:

> Even after the SD had moved into new quarters, the wretched state of its equipment did not change. Heydrich had the same old furniture as before, and still no typewriter. When there was an urgent need for one, Hildebrandt, the Chief of Staff, had to borrow it, bring it to the office by streetcar, and then take it back after it had been used.[12]

The purpose of such stories is to minimize the importance of Heydrich's work and disguise its nature. At first, it is said, his post was inconsequential and would not even have been created if it had not been for the chaos that reigned around Himmler. In short, Heydrich's secret organization dealt only with petty details and played no part in the Nazis' conquest of power. This is the version given by his widow and Karl von Eberstein, who have succeeded in getting it accepted, at least provisionally, by some German historians.

But no defender of this version has ever raised the question of why such a supposedly insignificant functionary was placed in charge of setting up a gigantic police organization immediately after the Nazis came to power. Werner Best, a former high official in the SS, has a different view of Heydrich, who was his immediate superior for five years: he has described him as "the most satanic of all the top Nazi leaders."[13]

From Bodyguard to Guard of the Nation

The truth is, of course, that Heydrich's activities at the Brown House in 1931 and 1932 were not as innocuous as his family, his

friends, and some historians have claimed. He and his SD were
concerned with infiltrating agents into important business and industrial groups, the universities, the Reichswehr, and the police;
recruiting new helpers (those whom Heydrich would later call
"honorary collaborators"); and undermining the structure of the
state so that eventually the Reich President, in accordance with
Article 48 of the Weimar constitution, would have no choice but
to turn over the government to Hitler.

For the moment, this strategy prevented the Nazi party from
designating the Jews as the main enemy of the nation. Anti-Semitism could be used in elections and propaganda slogans, but to
attract the upper class, on whom the success of the Nazis' attempt to take power would depend, the German Communist party
and its leader, Ernst Thaelmann, had to be presented as the most
pressing danger. The German nation was faced with a choice:
national socialism or communism, Berlin or Moscow, Adolf
Hitler or Ernst Thaelmann. This was the party line that became
increasingly prominent from the summer of 1931 onward. The
Nazi leaders believed that as long as they made anticommunism
their primary doctrine neither the German nor the foreign Jews
would take a position directly opposed to Hitler.

After the Communists, the next target would be the Social Democrats, and then the Christians, especially the Catholics, who,
with their claim that only they could assure salvation and their
principle of human equality, might hinder the "consolidation of
the state" and the establishment of a dictatorship. Furthermore,
they seemed to owe too much allegiance to the Vatican.

Neutralizing the Social Democrats would be easy: it could be
done simply by jailing their leaders. With the Christians, it
would be more difficult. The method of "the carrot and the stick"
would have to be applied to them. It was in these terms that
Heydrich explained the party's strategy to Hans-Peter von
Heydebreck in December 1931.

"To Heydrich, an indoctrinated racist, crushing 'the Jewish
influence' was as necessary as eliminating capitalism was to the
Marxists," remarked Hans von Kessel, whose brother, Eugen,
frequented Heydrich's confidential agents in Berlin and reported
their plans and objectives to his Jewish friends.

In June 1931, at a convention of SS leaders in Berlin, Himmler made a speech in which he said, "The SS must be trans-

formed from a bodyguard into the guard of the nation, the guard
of the Nordic race, which will lead a master race of two hundred
million Germans into battle against bolshevism all over the
world."[14]

Heydrich also had such ideas, as is known from several witnesses as well as an article that appeared in the *Muenchener
Post*, a Social Democrat newspaper, on November 25, 1931. In
that article, Heydrich was presented as an eccentric, and its author remarked, "This is the man who writes down these great
thoughts in the course of his tedious work."

This description of Heydrich's activities as "tedious work"
suited the purposes of the Nazis, who did not want anyone to
suspect that they were plotting to overthrow the Weimar Republic. Legends in the style of the "cigar-box story" were already
current in 1931. In Munich there was a great deal of joking about
the amateurish Nazis trying to set up a secret service. They were
considered ridiculous, and Hitler and Goering were often the
subject of satirical songs in cabarets. While six million fanati-
cized men and women stood ready to obey Hitler's orders, the
government authorities went on closing their eyes to the increasingly grave danger.

Heydrich's "tedious work" was actually part of a far-reaching
conspiracy that threatened the world's peace and, ultimately, a
large segment of its population. To the Nazis, seizing power in
Germany and indoctrinating the German people in a racist religion were steps on the road to a war whose goal would be world
conquest, and once that war was under way the extermination of
non-Aryan peoples would begin.

Heydrich's Plans

On the basis of the overall strategy conceived by Hitler, Rosenberg, Goebbels, Roehm, and Himmler, Heydrich was to draw up
two plans for maximum mobilization of forces.

The first plan would be used in case of a Communist insurrection. If open warfare against the Reds became necessary, the SS
and the SA would go into action immediately, and soon afterward
they would have the support of the right-wing Stahlhelm ("Steel
Helmet") and other paramilitary organizations. This combined

force would occupy army weapons and depots and make the Reichswehr and the police fight on their side.

Heydrich was ordered to obtain all the Communist literature on armed revolt, though he had already become familiar with much of it during his time in the navy. The fight against the Communists would be led by Free Corps veterans, most of whom had become Nazis. Heydrich drew up a list of adversaries, with the treatment to be given each of them: some would be arrested, others killed on the spot.[15]

Many politicians would also be arrested. This would frighten them so much, it was believed, that they would then be glad to collaborate. Not all of them would get off so lightly, however: a special organization was created for political assassinations.[16] Offices of the Communist and Social Democrat parties all over the country would be burned. The Nazis would seize all radio stations and begin broadcasting the news that Adolf Hitler's revolution had triumphed. (There were three million radio receivers in Germany at that time.) Forty thousand cars would take SS and SA men to strategic points, such as industrial centers. Soldiers of the Regular Army would be transported in requisitioned trucks. Their task would be to support the SS and SA in taking important objectives. In the large cities, police headquarters would immediately be taken by force, with the help of Nazi agents and sympathizers within them.

This plan would not be put into effect unless it seemed to the Nazis that they had no other choice. Only thirty-five leaders would be acquainted with the whole plan; they were to be notified at the first sign that action might be necessary. A list of those leaders is still in existence. Fifteen of the names are underlined, and Heydrich's is among them.

The second plan was for taking power by legal means, which was what the Nazis preferred because it would spare them the need to use violence against the state and the working class. Goebbels had given a simplified version of it: "We will strike down democracy with its own weapons." In preparation for that possibility, Heydrich had set up a powerful SS organization in Berlin. Posts in the police and various ministries were occupied by his agents. After being trained at the secret SD school in Braunschweig and becoming experts on sabotage, SS men were sent to Berlin to "fight the Communists," if Hitler were to become Chancellor. In that case, the police would be brought under total Nazi control and a dictatorship would be legally established. Each of Heydrich's agents in Berlin was instructed in the general line to be followed: "It prevented a confrontation with twelve million Marxists and seven million Christian members of the Center and Bavarian People's parties."[17]

Preparations for the coup were enveloped in rigorous secrecy. Not even the German Communist party's experts on defense and civil war, whose first duty was vigilance at all times, had any idea of what was being planned. The success of such a vast enterprise naturally depended on an efficient system of gathering and transmitting information. For that aspect of the operation, Heydrich drew on his training and practical experience, and if necessary he could use his knowledge of explosives and incendiary substances for the destruction of carefully selected strategic points.

No member of Heydrich's team who survived the war could be induced to say a word about what took place in the Brown House during that period: they were all afraid of revealing their own individual crimes or their share of responsibility for the crimes committed by their organization against their own people. They took refuge behind caricatures; according to them, Heydrich was only an eccentric dreamer and his fellow conspirators were a collection of naive visionaries who belonged in an insane asylum. And after everything that happened later, after all the atrocities, there are still people who take such stories seriously.

In 1932, as Goebbels had predicted, democracy was defeated with its own weapons. Hitler used the presidential election to create an atmosphere of panic and chaos in the country. As he had often said, the period before an election was to his party what spring was to the peasants: a time for preparing the soil. In the first eleven days of March, he made eleven speeches in major cities. In a conversation with the American journalist H. R. Knickerbocker on March 11, he predicted that he would obtain at least twelve million votes.

When the election was held on March 13, he came close to that figure, with 11,340,000 votes, but Hindenburg had

18,650,000. The remaining votes were divided between Thaelmann for the Communists (4,980,000) and Theodor Duesterberg for the German Nationalists (2,560,000). Since Hindenburg had not won an absolute majority, a second election would have to be held.

The results of the first election showed that Hitler could have won it even with the votes of the German Nationalists. But the Nazis hoped to make a better showing in the second election. This time the German Nationalist party withdrew its candidate and urged its members to vote for Hitler. With their two and a half million votes, he could win by drawing another two and a half million away from Hindenburg. He launched into his second campaign, stressing the idea that Germany was about to choose between the forces of nationalism and those of chaos. He was supported by a large part of the lower middle class and nearly all of the German Nationalists. Even the former Crown Prince, Friedrich Wilhelm, made a statement in favor of Hitler.

But the Nazis were disappointed again: in the second election, on April 10, the results were 19,360,000 votes for Hindenburg, 13,420,000 for Hitler, and 3,710,000 for Thaelmann.

During the election campaign, some of Heydrich's men came into serious conflict with the government and the Reichswehr Ministry. At Wilhelmshaven, an SS man named Franz Nawroth, who worked in the transport branch of the Kommandantur of the Reichswehr, was suspended for having transmitted secret information to Herbert Weichardt in Oldenburg. Hans von Kobelinski, one of Heydrich's collaborators, was also implicated in the Nawroth affair. He had already been given several important missions by the SD, in Braunschweig and Berlin.

These illegal activities against the Reichswehr prompted General Kurt von Schleicher, a close adviser to President von Hindenburg, to send a letter of protest to Ernst Roehm, head of the SA, in the name of the Reichswehr Ministry. During this same period Karl Severing, the Minister of the Interior, discovered a number of Nazi activities against the state, all directed by the SD.

Because of the protests from Severing and Schleicher, Heydrich judged it necessary to organize his SD even more rigorously. In 1932, the SA was temporarily banned because it had been constantly provoking bloody incidents. Newspapers opposed to Hitler wrote that he was instigating acts of terrorism by armed groups on the pretext that his adversaries were preparing to set off a Communist insurrection.

Hitler had noted that the national electorate was increasingly impressed by his men's spectacular fights against "the Red populace." When Chancellor Franz von Papen's government decided that the Reichstag elections would be held on July 31, 1932, Heydrich was told to organize even more of those fights, at opposition political meetings and in the streets.

Hitler wanted to intimidate his adversaries by a gigantic demonstration in Altona, a working-class suburb of Hamburg. Masses of Nazi supporters poured in by train and bus from all over nothern Germany, particularly Schleswig-Holstein. Preparations for that march on Hamburg, a prelude to the march on Berlin that was to take place in the near future, posed many problems for Heydrich. Hitler had given him full power to organize it behind the scenes, specifying only that it was to be an impressive demonstration of Nazi strength, no matter what the cost. Heydrich succeeded so well that the march and the clashes it provoked entered history as "the Bloody Sunday of Altona" and took a toll of eighteen dead and sixty wounded.

Here is what Lina Heydrich wrote in her memoirs about the events of that summer:

> Hitler's struggle for power became more violent. In Schleswig-Holstein the *Landvolk* movement set off bombs. Peasants carrying black flags paraded to draw attention to their problems. A terrible massacre began. There was trouble everywhere.

On July 20, 1932, the Army General Staff, supported by Chancellor von Papen, overthrew the Social Democrat government of Prussia by force. The fact that Army officers were able to carry out what amounted to a coup d'état showed that the Weimar regime was not going to last much longer. This episode brought on an increase in the street fighting that Hitler had been fomenting.

The police were given broader powers to combat the Marxists. Rudolf Diels, who was to become the first head of the Gestapo

after the Nazis' victory, later wrote that after July 20, 1932, as an
official of the political police, he had devoted himself "to preparations for crushing communism in Germany, in close collaboration with the men who directed the National Socialist party." The
police laid great stress on the "Communist peril" to influence the
middle class in its choice between Hitler, who would restore
order, and the Weimar politicians. Heydrich and his accomplices
all over the country made a large contribution to poisoning the
atmosphere during the election campaign.

In the parliamentary elections of July 31, 1932, the Nazis won
13.8 million votes and 230 seats in the Reichstag, more than
double the number they obtained in the 1930 elections.

Chancellor Hitler

The Nazis now had more seats than any other party and were able
to elect Hermann Goering as President of the Reichstag. Because
of his bourgeois background and his military exploits in the
World War, Goering was well suited to the task of inducing Hindenburg to accept Hitler as Chancellor.

After this success in the elections, Hitler continued his propaganda on the struggle that had to be waged against the "Red
Cheka." He proclaimed that his party would no longer tolerate
the Reds' campaign of terrorism which had resulted in six thousand wounded the year before and already eighty-two hundred in
the first seven and a half months of 1932.

In view of the "all or nothing" policy that Hitler was pursuing,
many Germans began wondering uneasily what would happen if
he organized a march on Berlin, a larger version of the Altona
bloodbath. Hitler tried to allay that uneasiness; in August 1932
the *Voelkischer Beobachter* reported what he had said to the
American journalist Louis Lochner: "Why should I march on
Berlin? I'm already there. The question is not who will march on
Berlin, but rather who will come out of Berlin? The SA will not
undertake an illegal march."

In 1940 I had several conversations with Lochner about the
Nazis' struggle for power and the way they had reached their
goal. He confirmed to me that in August 1932 Hitler was convinced that within six months Hindenburg would make him Reich
Chancellor to save Germany from anarchy.

In 1932, the Nazis' adversaries suddenly realized that the street fighting was part of a precise plan, and that if Nazi terrorism continued it would inevitably lead to civil war. Since the Nazis were abusing the right to hold public demonstrations, there was an increasingly strong demand for limitations on that right. On August 23 Hitler protested: the accusations against the Nazis, he said, were only a pretext for persecuting them.[18]

But his adversaries' firmness made him lose more than two million votes in the elections of November 6, 1932. He was now forced to abandon his hard line, and Heydrich had to apply methods other than those of the Altona bloodbath.

The Nazis began concentrating all their propaganda efforts on influencing Hindenburg to make Hitler Reich Chancellor. Hitler promised Hindenburg and the upper middle class that he would restore order in the state. He would be satisfied with having Nazis in only two other positions: Reich Minister of the Interior and Prussian Minister of the Interior. Hindenburg could not simply appoint a Prussian Minister of the Interior; the constitution did not give him that power. But Hitler knew that he could install a Nazi in the post as soon as he became Chancellor. The decomposition of the Weimar Republic was accelerating. Hindenburg's entourage, the Reichswehr, and the magnates of industry and finance believed that the social and political crisis could be resolved by applying Article 48 of the constitution, which authorized rule by decree during a state of emergency.

Under pressure from the industrialists and the Reichswehr, and with the consent of Franz von Papen, leader of the Center party, and Alfred Hugenberg, leader of the German Nationalists, Hindenburg finally made Hitler Reich Chancellor on January 30, 1933. As agreed, Hitler settled for two ministers: Wilhelm Frick was Minister of the Interior and Hermann Goering, already President of the Reichstag, became a Minister without Portfolio, but he exercised the functions of the Minister of the Interior of Prussia, the largest of the German states.

Although the forces led by Hitler, Papen, and Hugenberg were in perfect agreement on the suppression of democracy, they immediately began competing with each other for key positions in the state. We now know that Hitler had already decided on his future course of action before that coalition was formed: as head of the government, with the police controlled by his collaborators

Goering and Frick, he would be able to carry out a rapid coup d'état. But first, to create the right conditions for success, the Nazis would again have to place the country in a state of tension by playing up the "Red menace" and the idea that only Hitler could destroy it.

Only a few of the Nazi leaders knew about this secret plan, which had one extremely important provision: when Hitler became Chancellor, he and the other members of the coalition would dissolve the Reichstag and call for new elections. During the campaign period, more fighting would be provoked in the streets and at political meetings to convince the bourgeoisie that the Chancellor had to be given emergency powers so that he could crush Red terrorism. A week before the date of the elections, a shocking example of the Communists' determination to create turmoil, the "signal for an insurrection," would prompt Hindenburg to grant Hitler the full powers that would enable him to restore order.

A Secret Mission for the Head of the SD

On January 27, 1933, three days before Hitler became Chancellor, Himmler sent Heydrich to Berlin on a secret mission. No one else in the Brown House knew why Heydrich was needed in Berlin, but those who had closely followed his activities suspected that his mission was connected with Hitler's intention to take drastic measures that would dismantle the parliamentary system soon after he was made Chancellor. Though they naturally did not know the details, many of them thought that the pretext might be a simulated attempt to kill Hitler, which would enable the Nazis to set the police in motion and establish a dictatorship "legally."

On January 30, there was a torchlight procession in Berlin to celebrate Hitler's appointment as Chancellor. Heydrich took part in it, along with the top Nazi leaders. As already mentioned, no one knew exactly why Heydrich had come to Berlin, but his arrival made an unpleasant impression on Goering's associates. Rudolf Diels, Goering's political adviser, began to worry. He had played an important part in the military coup in Prussia the year before and therefore expected, not without reason, to become head of the Prussian secret service, but he now guessed Himmler's and Heydrich's ambitions with almost perfect accuracy. He quickly informed Goering of Heydrich's presence and, according to trustworthy witnesses, he even notified the entourages of Hindenburg, Hugenberg, and Papen, who immediately feared that the Nazi secret service was going to become involved in government affairs. According to the same sources, Hitler solemnly assured Goering that he did not want to interfere in matters already controlled by the SS in Prussia. One source was Dr. Ernst Hanfstaengl, Hitler's foreign press adviser, and other well-informed people have confirmed and completed his account.

Many of them have told me that Heydrich mysteriously disappeared soon after his arrival in Berlin and that later he went out only at night, "disguised" as a civilian. But it was known that he had come from Munich with a group of men who called themselves the "pirates of the state" and that he was in close contact with the high officials of his service in the capital.

What was the mission that the head of the SD was to carry out in Berlin once Hitler had become Reich Chancellor?

4

A New Era

Berlin, February 27, 1933. Hitler had been Chancellor for less than a month, and in six days a new Reichstag was going to be elected. That evening, Hitler was the guest of Goebbels, his propaganda chief; Goering, President of the Reichstag and now a minister as well, was conferring with his closest collaborators in the Prussian Ministry of the Interior. And that evening, at 9:14, an alarm was sounded at Firehouse No. 6 on Linienstrasse: the Reichstag building was on fire.

It was one of the monumental buildings of the German capital. In the time of the Empire it had been called the House of the Reich.

While the fire was still blazing, Hitler stated that it had been set by the Communists and was the signal for an insurrection. But it is hard to imagine how that fire could have been useful to the Communists. With the Nazis it was a different matter. The burning of the Reichstag gave them a chance not only to influence the coming elections in their favor by stirring up fear of civil war, but also to pressure Hindenburg into granting dictatorial powers to Chancellor Hitler before the elections.

Political logic suggests that the Nazis had a great deal to gain from the Reichstag fire. Examination of what happened after January 30, when Hitler became Chancellor, confirms it.

Although the Nazis had received only a quarter of the votes cast in the last elections, Hitler had felt strong enough to make his partners in the coalition accept new elections. His party had 196 seats in the Reichstag and the German Nationalists had 52;

85

together they were far from constituting a majority, since there were 584 deputies in all. Yet in spite of his partners' unfavorable predictions, Hitler succeeded in having new parliamentary elections scheduled for March 5.

The Weimar constitution guaranteed basic civil rights; a division of power among the legislative, executive, and judicial branches; and an important degree of sovereignty for the individual German states. The program of the Nazi party included the slogan "One people, one Reich, one Fuehrer"; it demanded that the parliamentary system be abolished and that all power be placed in a central government headed by a Fuehrer with unlimited authority. Achieving this would involve revoking all the rights guaranteed by the Weimar constitution: freedom of speech, the right of association, freedom of the press, the right of political parties and labor unions to function without governmental control, freedom of religion. The state had to be totally transformed in order to reach the goal that Hitler had set forth in *Mein Kampf:* the Great German Reich was to become the dominant power on the European continent and procure the *Lebensraum* that the German people needed.

To institute that program legally, the Nazi party and its allies would have to obtain enough votes in the March 5 elections to gain the two-thirds parliamentary majority required for altering the constitution. The Nazis tried to convince the German people that they had to make a vitally important choice, expressed in such terms as "Lenin or Hitler," "Moscow or Berlin," "bolshevism or national socialism," "chaos or order," "Jewish world conspiracy or community of the German nation." To make these slogans credible, the Nazis created conditions that seemed to support their accusation that their adversaries were planning a violent overthrow of the government. The SA and the SS provoked bloody clashes that gave Hitler and his two ministers, Goering and Frick, a pretext for taking "countermeasures." The new election campaign provided an excellent opportunity for intensifying that atmosphere of dangerous conflict.

Finally, the Reichstag building was burned. The news that this symbol of the parliamentary system had been destroyed was meant to make most of the German people believe that the revolutionaries had launched an all-out attack. Within a few hours after the fire broke out, some twenty thousand opposition politicians had been arrested all over Germany, by means of lists prepared in advance, and interned in concentration camps that also had been prepared in advance. The Communist and Social Democrat newspapers were banned. At one stroke, the Nazis' most determined adversaries had been silenced and made unable to act.

Hitler now appeared as the man who had saved the nation from a bloody civil war. The Reichstag fire, presented as the signal for a Communist insurrection, became the pretext for harshly repressive measures whose purpose, according to the Nazis, was to make sure there would be no further attempts to overthrow the government.

"After the burning of the Reichstag," Hitler said at a cabinet meeting on February 28, "the government of the Reich will undoubtedly win the elections with fifty-one percent of the vote." And in a speech on March 3, Goering gave an idea of the atmosphere in which the elections were to be won: "My measures will not be hindered by any judicial considerations, and no bureaucracy will interfere with their application. I am not concerned with justice. My only task is to destroy and exterminate, nothing more."

Hitler was right: on March 5, 1933, the Nazis won 43.9 percent of the vote and the German Nationalists 8.0 percent, making a total of 51.9 percent between them.

But Hitler had already scored a victory before the elections: on the day after the Reichstag fire, he had induced Hindenburg to sign an emergency decree suspending the sections of the Weimar constitution that guaranteed civil rights. This decree remained in effect until the end of the Third Reich, providing the legal basis of Hitler's totalitarian regime.

The Nazis' story that the Communists had burned the Reichstag was by no means universally accepted, however. A report that the arsonists had entered the Reichstag from Goering's palace immediately became current. On the night of the fire, Willi Frischauer, Berlin correspondent of the *Wiener Allgemeine Zeitung*, cabled to his newspaper in Vienna:

> There can scarcely be any doubt that the fire which is now destroying the Reichstag was set by henchmen of the Hitler government. By all appearances, the arsonists used an underground

passage connecting the Reichstag to the palace of its President, Hermann Goering.

That same night, Goering ordered an investigation by a special commission composed entirely of members of the political police, who had already exchanged information with the SS and its Security Service before the fire. The criminal police were thus prevented from carrying out an investigation of their own. The next day, Goering officially announced that the fire had been set by the Communists, acting on orders from Moscow. Hitler had already said this as soon as he saw the flames—as if he were clairvoyant.

The first individuals to be accused of the crime were Marinus van der Lubbe, a Dutch mason who was arrested at the scene, and Ernst Torgler, the Communists' parliamentary leader. Torgler was said to have hurriedly left the building twenty minutes before the fire broke out. Karwahne and Frey, two Nazi deputies, and Koryer, an Austrian Nazi, stated that on the afternoon of the fire they had seen Torgler with Van der Lubbe and an unknown man in a hall of the Reichstag.

On March 9, three Bulgarian Communists, Blagoi Popov, Vassili Tanev, and Georgi Dimitroff, who was had of the Comintern bureau for Eastern Europe, were arrested and taken before the commission investigating the fire. Dimitroff had been living in Germany under an assumed name; on March 10, he admitted his real identity.

The Nazis claimed that Dimitroff had planned the destruction of the Reichstag, that Torgler had made preparations for it, and that Van der Lubbe had set the fire. Goebbels began a propaganda campaign to show that international communism was directly responsible for the crime. Two weeks later, he was appointed Reich Minister for People's Enlightenment and Propaganda.

The alleged conspirators were accused of having burned the Reichstag to give the signal for an uprising that would lead to civil war and thus deprive the Nazis of an election victory. The absurdity of this accusation, the dissolution of all political parties except that of the Nazis, the systematic use of terrorism, the creation of concentration camps—all this strengthened the opinion, widely held in Germany and abroad, that the Nazis them-

selves had burned the Reichstag, for the purpose of putting their
program into action as quickly as possible.

At the trial, held before the Supreme Court in Leipzig, Van
der Lubbe proved to be incapable of repeating the confession he
had supposedly made in fluent German before Goering's commission. Observers in the courtroom had the impression, and said so
at the time, that Van der Lubbe was drugged. During a recon-
struction of the crime, he was unable to follow the path he was
said to have taken when he set fire to the building in several
places; a policeman had to be substituted for him.

Van der Lubbe was sentenced to death and executed, but
Torgler and the three Bulgarians were acquitted. The trial was a
political defeat for the Nazis.

The most common opinion was that the SA had burned the
Reichstag, but those with inside knowledge of the Nazi party
believed that Hitler would never have given such an assignment
to that gang of street brawlers. The SA leaders defended themselves by saying that Himmler and Heydrich had carried out the
operation from beginning to end. Heydrich had set up a special
team for the purpose, and Himmler had sent him to Berlin three
days before Hitler became Chancellor, with instructions to create
an opportunity to put the plan into action. According to that plan,
a week before the elections the burning of the Reichstag, presented as the beginning of a Communist uprising, would enable
Hitler, with Hindenburg's consent, to proclaim a state of emergency, as authorized by Article 48 of the Weimar constitution.
Then, on the pretext of maintaining the date of the elections and
suppressing the Communist uprising, Hitler could bring off his
coup d'état.

But in 1933, only a relatively small number of people maintained that Hitler had entrusted the operation to the SS and its
Security Service; this view was not accepted by the general public because the SS was still overshadowed by the SA at that time.

The arson specialists of the fire department and the administrative and technical personnel of the Reichstag were all convinced that the arsonists had come into the building through the
underground passage connecting it to Goering's palace, that Van
der Lubbe was only a puppet, and that the fire had been started by
well-trained Nazi agents using incendiary substances. This was also
the conviction of many German politicians, including the Social

Democrat Paul Loebe, Goering's predecessor as President of the Reichstag. But it was not possible to explain all the details of the fire, for the good reason that the Nazis now held supreme power and had no intention of allowing an objective inquiry.

The Solution of a Crime

In 1964, the German historian Hans Mommsen published a study in which he tried to prove that the Nazis had no responsibility for the Reichstag fire because their main concern at that time was to have calm elections. This thesis still has supporters in West Germany, especially among those unwilling to acknowledge that they themselves contributed to the seizure of power by men who, among other crimes, burned the Reichstag and then lied to the German people about it.

Here is how Mommsen demonstrates the Nazis' innocence:

1. He arbitrarily declares that Van der Lubbe took no more than two minutes to transform the gigantic plenary meeting hall of the Reichstag, with a volume of eleven thousand cubic meters, into a sea of flame.

2. Without having examined the scene or consulted plans of the Reichstag and the palace of the President of the Reichstag, he says that the arsonists could not have come from that palace because the underground passage ended beside a room occupied night and day by a doorman.

3. He maintains that the Nazis would never have burned the Reichstag because they regarded it as being almost sacred. (A reading of *Mein Kampf* would have shown him that Hitler, a would-be architect, despised that building because of its stucco walls.)

4. He rejects out of hand all testimony by experts and takes as his main witnesses the officials of the criminal police who testified at the trial in 1933 and later became collaborators of Heydrich; he fails to cite any documentary evidence and postwar statements by those same officials that contradict their testimony at the trial.

In 1969, an international committee headed by the Swiss historian Walther Hofer was convened in Luxembourg to study the Reichstag fire. Its findings were published in three volumes—the first in 1972, the second and third in 1978. These three books reveal the inadequacy of the inquiry made by the Institute of Contemporary History in Munich, which supports Mommsen's view that the Nazis were innocent and only Van der Lubbe was guilty. In 1978, Hofer stated that "the mystery of the Reichstag fire has now been definitively cleared up." In Germany and abroad, newspapers that must be taken seriously declared that the committee's long-awaited scientific investigation was an outstanding success.[1] Besides solving the crime, it showed that some West German historians writing on the subject had merely repeated assertions made after the war by former members of the Gestapo.

Heydrich had his propaganda agents spread the rumor that international Jewry was behind the accusation that the Reichstag had been burned by the Nazis. This was the beginning of the anti-Semitic campaign directed by Goebbels and Heydrich. To Heydrich, it was the beginning of a racist revolution: the Jews, those "kings of our time," had to be overthrown.[2]

After the Reichstag fire, Reinhard Heydrich's brother, Heinz, was given a position in the Berlin office of the *Muenchener Neuesten Nachrichten*, against the will of the newspaper's director, Otto von Heydebreck.[3]

In the paper Heinz wrote: "The First and Second Reichs failed because they refused to take account of biological and racial principles resulting from the laws of nature. But the Third Reich, which will be built by the German messiah, is founded for all eternity. This Reich will be cleansed of its Jews." On April 1, 1933, Heinz Heydrich figured prominently in the first organized boycott against the Jews. Through his brother, he became an "honorary member" of the SD, which meant that under cover of ordinary journalistic activity he could take every opportunity to spy on his colleagues.

Reinhard Heydrich was also in Berlin on April 1, when the first official anti-Jewish violence took place. Jews were harassed and attacked in the streets, cafés, and restaurants, and Jewish shops were destroyed. This aroused a storm of protest all over the world. Hitler had to recognize that the time for acting openly against the Jews had not yet come. He therefore sent Heydrich back to Munich, where he stayed for a year before the Fuehrer placed him in charge of the Gestapo at its headquarters on Prinz-Albrechtstrasse in Berlin.

Was Heydrich really the man who planned the Reichstag fire? The international committee headed by Walther Hofer concluded that Hitler assigned the operation not to the SA, as was commonly believed for many years, but to the SS, and that Heydrich played a great part in its planning and execution. The committee's findings are summarized below.

The arsonists were led by SA Standartenfuehrer Erwin Villain, who was killed in the Blood Purge of 1934. His name was cited by several witnesses, along with those of Willi Schmidt and the SS men Rudolf Steinle and Kurt Eggert, among others. Steinle and Eggert later murdered the famous seer and astrologer Eric Jan Hanussen. At a social gathering, Hanussen had predicted the Reichstag fire the day before it happened. This knowledge was considered dangerous, and it cost him his life.

Goering's SS bodyguard, Walter Weber, and the SS men Woite, Gepke, Sander, and Toifl appear several times in the declarations of trustworthy witnesses, and those declarations are supported by the fact that Toifl and Sander were also eliminated in the 1934 Blood Purge.

The team of arsonists, composed of eight to ten men, went to Goering's palace at least forty-eight hours before the fire and took up quarters in the great hall, with cots to sleep on and newspapers and decks of cards to help them pass the time. This room, ordinarily used only for formal occasions, was heated during those cold February days, which meant that their presence had to be known to three workers in the heating plant, Heinrich Grunewald, Johann Wittkowski, and Erhard Cyron, who were told by their supervisor, Alexander Scranowitz, that the men were special guards assigned to the building because there was fear of a Communist attack in that time of political turmoil.

To everyone's surprise, Goering had left the palace three weeks earlier, just when he had finished having it completely renovated, but he had left the second floor at the disposal of his friends and the Fuehrer's foreign press adviser, Dr. Ernst Hanfstaengl. Goering had also left behind a small SS troop commanded by Weber.

The three heating-plant workers—Grunewald, Wittkowski, and Cyron—felt that there was something a little strange about those "guards" because Paul Adermann, the night doorman, had told them six times in the previous four weeks, on six different occasions, that someone had gone into the underground passage between the palace and the Reichstag. Wittkowski, goaded by curiosity, went up to the great hall to have a look at the "guards" on the pretext of asking them if the room was heated to their liking. He saw them sitting or lying on their cots, playing cards, reading newspapers, and drinking beer.

Adermann tried an experiment on the evening of February 27: he sprinkled ashes on the bottom steps of the staircase leading down to the heating plant. The next day, after the Reichstag fire, he saw that several men had left footprints on those steps. The evening before, he had been ordered to stay in his room till the last of Goering's guests had come back into the palace.

The three heating-plant workers were questioned by the Gestapo after the fire. Their questioning was obviously a warning: they were told to say nothing about anything they might have seen or heard. They did not appear as witnesses at the trial.

Adermann, however, had to be summoned to testify; he had spoken too openly and too often about his nocturnal experiments in the underground passage and the palace. He declared under oath that, by means of pieces of thread and strips of paper attached to doors, he had been able to ascertain six times in four weeks that someone had used the underground passage. But the identity of the mysterious visitor or visitors was not established.

Two of the heating-plant workers, Grunewald and Cyron, survived the war and told what they had seen. They declared that the "guards" in the palace were actually the arsonists.

In 1975, Dr. Heinz Leferenz, director of the Criminology Institute of Heidelberg University, personally examined the underground passage and determined that the statements made by Grunewald and Cyron were strictly accurate, and he confirmed that defenders of the Nazis had published falsified plans to support their version of the facts.

Shortly after the Reichstag fire, two experts, Dr. Wagner and Professor Josse, stated that if the moderate fire burning in the meeting hall was transformed into a sea of flame between 9:21 and 9:26, it could only have been done by means of incendiary substances. It is important to remember that the head of the Berlin fire department was courageous enough to declare, even at the trial held in Leipzig, that he had found traces of incendiary substances in the meeting hall after the fire.

Policemen reported that immediately after they arrived at the scene they found a drunken man on the lower floor of the burning Reichstag, and that he was taken to the police station. After that, no trace of him was ever found. One of the arsonists had obviously drunk so much that he was unable to find his way out of the building.

Dr. Wilhelm Schatz, a chemist who appeared as an expert witness at the trial, was also courageous: he testified that Van der Lubbe could not have set the fire by himself, that the arsonists were skilled professionals, and that he had discovered traces of phosphorus, sulfur, and gasoline in seven different places.

After officials of the Nazi police had succeeded in making the German public believe that the arsonists could not have come into the Reichstag through the underground passage, they claimed that the experts were unreliable and incompetent, and they even went so far as to say that Dr. Schatz, the chemist, was a "charlatan." The historian Hans Mommsen, who, as we have seen, later supported the police officials' thesis, also seconded their efforts to discredit the experts.

In 1971, Dr. Karl Stephan, director of the Institute of Thermodynamics of the Berlin Technical University, verified the experts' testimony given in 1933. He too is of the opinion that Van der Lubbe, acting alone, could not have set the whole meeting hall ablaze in six minutes.

The part that Van der Lubbe played in the operation has now been completely clarified. The Nazis chose him because he was already wanted by the police, and that "political child," as Dimitroff called him, fell into the trap. His "friends" kept close watch on everything he did. Shortly before the Reichstag fire, they incited him to "act like a conspirator"; he made speeches, handed out leaflets, and set less important fires, after which he was able to escape without any risk of being arrested. He was thus gradually prepared not only to take part in burning the Reichstag but also to serve as the scapegoat that the Nazis needed. Since the fire was to be presented as the outcome of a Communist plot aimed at triggering an insurrection, the Nazis even arranged to have "witnesses" who would testify that they had seen Van der Lubbe with Dimitroff and Torgler.

But this plan misfired at the trial. Van der Lubbe was so dazed from the drugs administered to him that he was unable to follow the proceedings. He could not explain how he had come to Berlin, how he had found his way in the city, or how he had gone about setting the fire. Each time he did not know what to say, the prosecution answered for him, trying to depict him as a tool of the Communists.

The German historian Friedrich Zipfel later proved that the Nazis had infiltrated some of their agents into the Dutch Spartakus group to which Van der Lubbe belonged. These agents finally lured their victim to Berlin. The Nazis also tried to draw three German anti-Fascists into the same trap, but they pulled back in time, and the Nazis were left with only one puppet, Van der Lubbe, to bring before the court in that farcical trial. To have him sentenced to death, the Nazis had to promulgate a retroactive law and produce 180 carefully selected "witnesses."

It is clear that an operation on that scale could not have been planned and carried out by subordinate members of the party.

As we have seen, documentary evidence and the statements of witnesses establish that the Reichstag was burned with the accord of Hitler, Goering, and Goebbels, and that the trial which followed, as well as the Supreme Court decision intended to legalize the coup d'état of February 28, 1933, were prepared in advance.

Heydrich Behind the Scenes

The international committee that investigated the Reichstag fire examined many documents showing that Reinhard Heydrich was in charge of carrying out that first of the great Nazi provocations. For a time, however, he remained in the shadows because he was not known in Berlin. Outside observers did not suspect him; instead, they focused their attention on SA Gruppenfuehrer Karl Ernst.

After the war, Franz Knospe and Alfred Reischke, two former SS members, declared that Heydrich had directed the operation, and among the SS men who took part in it they named Herbert Packenbusch and Otmar Toifl. Toifl, a technical instructor at the secret SD school in Braunschweig, was trusted by Himmler and Heydrich, but he did not maintain the required secrecy about his part in the fire and he was therefore silenced by death on June 30, 1934.[4]

Defenders of Nazi innocence claim that Heydrich could not have had anything to do with the fire because he was living and working in Munich at the time. It is easy to refute that claim. Existing documents and the statements of witnesses establish that Himmler and Heydrich were in Berlin when the Nazis took power. Lina Heydrich herself has written in her memoirs that her husband was then in Berlin:

> Reinhard did not want to wait in Bavaria for the National Socialists to take power; instead, he wanted to capture the Bavarian fortress from Prussia. He decided to transfer himself and his service to Berlin. A suitable building was found at the corner of Branitzer Platz and Eicheallee, and I also moved into it with all my household equipment.

And she says that during her stay in Berlin with her husband, everything took place "secretly" because "he did not want to stir up a commotion."

Once the provocation had achieved its purpose, Heydrich went back to Munich and, with Himmler, carried out the Bavarian coup d'état on March 9, 1933. On March 13, in a letter to her parents, Lina Heydrich told how Himmler, Roehm, and her husband had gone to see Heinrich Held, the Bavarian Prime Minister, and "negotiated" with him for an hour. She then wrote, "More than two hundred have now been arrested, Communists, Social Democrats, Jews, and members of the Bavarian People's party."[5]

Those men were obviously arrested because they were on a list made up in advance from Heydrich's files. Lina Heydrich is mistaken on one point, however: her husband was not with Himmler and Roehm during the "negotiations" with Held; instead, they were accompanied by Gauleiter Adolf Wagner. Meanwhile, Heydrich, once again operating behind the scenes, was strategically distributing shock troops in the city and conferring with the spies he had infiltrated into the political police. Among them was Heinrich Mueller, who was later to be chief of the Gestapo.

The Gestapo Thesis

The international committee headed by Walther Hofer refuted once and for all the assertion that the Reichstag was burned by a lone arsonist who had no connection with the Nazis. This has been acknowledged by the League of German Historians in its journal, *Geschichte in Wissenschaft und Unterricht.* The editor of that journal is Dr. Karl Dietrich Erdmann, chairman of the Historical Committee of the Institute of Contemporary History, the same committee that in 1964, under the direction of Helmut Krausnick, maintained that the innocence of the Nazis in the Reichstag fire was scientifically proven.

In 1980, the German historian Klaus Hildebrandt wrote in *Geschichte in Wissenschaft und Unterricht,*

> Concerning the question of guilt in the Reichstag fire, it must be recognized that in the *present* state of the controversy the thesis of a single criminal, Van der Lubbe, has clearly been rejected once again in favor of the idea that the fire was planned and executed by the National Socialists.

In his book *Germany 1866–1945,* the American historian Gordon A. Craig endorses the findings of the international committee:

> Despite recent attempts, however, to support the case against Marinus van der Lubbe, the half-witted Dutch vagrant who was tried and executed for the crime, the evidence collected by an international committee headed by Walther Hofer of Berne strongly supports the conclusion that the blaze was set by an SA/SS Sondergruppe under the direction of Himmler's associate, Reinhard Heydrich, and the director of the division of police in the Prussian Ministry of the Interior, Kurt Daluege.

Dr. Otto B. Roegele, director of the Institute of Journalistic Science of the University of Munich, who has studied the Reichstag fire from the viewpoint of propaganda and journalism, has also endorsed the findings of the committee.

Rita Thalmann, a French historian who has a thorough knowledge of Nazism and is the co-author of a book on the "Night of Broken Glass" and the Grynszpan affair, has written a favorable review of the publications of the committee. She stresses that the results of the inquiry conducted by the committee constitute a definitive refutation of all those who try to minimize the crimes of the Nazis.

The version that denies that the Nazis burned the Reichstag is sometimes referred to as "the Gestapo thesis" in the German press, because it was originally presented by former collaborators of Heydrich.

Such former collaborators of Goering and Heydrich who survived the war as Ludwig Grauert, Walter Zirpins, Helmut Heisig, Rudolf Braschwitz, Eberhard Taubert, Melitta Wiedemann, and Paul Karl Schmidt, tried to prove that the beginnings of the Third Reich were innocuous, and thus save something of the "National Socialist revolution." The "Gestapo thesis" of Nazi innocence suited those apostles of exoneration all too well; they did their best to present the Reichstag fire as a fortuitous event and propagate the idea that the Nazis had proceeded without bad intentions or a preconceived idea. By attributing everything to chance, they hoped to put up a smoke screen around the fact that as soon as the Nazis came to power they began turning Germany into a racist state and preparing for world conquest.

One of the several benefits that the Reichstag fire gave to the Nazis was that it enabled Himmler and Heydrich to seize power in Bavaria. Seeing the harshness with which Heydrich treated his adversaries there, Hitler knew he had chosen the right man. Only ten days after the coup, the first of the Nazi concentration camps, at Dachau, was ready to receive at least five thousand prisoners.

According to information supplied by Otto von Heydebreck, the destruction of the Reichstag was an event of historical importance to the Nazis: this was the building in which the betrayal of 1918 had been ratified. Heydrich was proud that he had been chosen to give the signal for the beginning of a new era. The Reichstag fire marked the birth of the Third Reich. The flames ravaging that symbol of democracy lighted the path that the Fuehrer would follow in the future.

The Swastika Flag in Geneva

Soon after the Reichstag fire, Heydrich was given a mission abroad.

In May 1933, the new German government sent a delegation to the disarmament conference in Geneva. The Nazis had a strong interest in giving the impression, especially to the Western powers, that they had no intention of rearming and were ready to support all efforts to relax international tensions.

The head of the German delegation was Ambassador Rudolf Nadolny, but the real representative of the Nazi government was Heydrich, who went to Geneva preceded by his renown as Himmler's close associate and chief of the political police in Munich. He was accompanied by an SS officer named Friedrich Krueger, who later gained a reputation for savagery as a high police official in occupied Poland.

Ambassador Nadolny had acquired great political experience as a collaborator of Friedrich Ebert, first President of the Weimar Republic, and as an ambassador in Sweden and Turkey. He immediately realized that Heydrich, who had been officially sent to Geneva as a police specialist, intended to give himself great importance there. He tried to avoid coming into conflict with him because he knew that Heydrich could make trouble for him once he returned to Munich.

When they arrived at the Hotel Carlton in Geneva, Heydrich sternly said to Nadolny, "Why is the black, red, and gold flag flying above the hotel, and not the swastika flag?" To which the ambassador replied, "The swastika flag isn't the official flag of the state. It's customary to fly only the official flag." But Heydrich retorted, "Don't the Swiss know that we made our national revolution under the swastika flag?"[6]

To Heydrich, it was an intolerable situation that had to be changed. Under cover of darkness, he went up to the roof of the hotel and hoisted a swastika flag he had brought with him in his baggage. The next morning, people in the street were startled at the sight of it. Some of them asked the hotel management what that strange "signal" meant. The news quickly spread all over the city: the Nazis had raised the swastika above the Hotel Carlton! Angry workers organized a demonstration, and Heydrich, afraid that the hostile crowd might invade the hotel, hurriedly took down his flag and put it back into his suitcase.

Soon afterward, there was another disagreeable incident. Heydrich discovered that his statements were being translated by a Jewish interpreter named Hans Jacob. He immediately demanded that Jacob be replaced. And no sooner had the delegates' indignation begun to die down than Heydrich provoked a third incident. He aggressively tried to convince General Temperly, of Great Britain, that the SS, the SA, and the Stahlhelm were only "sports associations" to which no military character could be attributed. He defended this idea with inflexible tenacity until finally the term *defense sports associations* was adopted to describe the organizations in question, which prompted Temperly to remark, "I represent the country where the word *sport* originated, but the expression *defense sports* means nothing to me."[7]

The conference was ill-starred from the beginning. Heydrich's presence in Geneva hindered the diplomatic negotiations. To the people of the city it was a provocation that soon aroused widespread indignation.

"Stones were often thrown at our cars, and we were violently insulted as we passed," reported the interpreter Paul Schmidt.[8] One day he heard Heydrich say angrily,

> What's happening here is incredible! This delegation in Geneva acts as if there hadn't been a national revolution in Germany. Jewish interpreters, black, red and gold flags, reactionary diplomats and hidebound advisers! We National Socialists will have to make a thorough housecleaning, once and for all.[9]

Ambassador Nadolny observed all this with growing anxiety. Finally, he could no longer restrain himself. According to Schmidt, he said to Heydrich,

> In a delegation abroad, there's the same discipline as on a ship at sea. Only the captain decides what will happen. Here in Geneva, I'm the head of this delegation. I therefore can't tolerate any usurpation of authority.[10]

Whether or not Nadolny really spoke to Heydrich in such forceful terms is a secondary question. What is instructive is that Heydrich quickly toned down his behavior, as was reported by participants in the conference. He obviously did not want to draw the attention of the foreign press to himself at such a critical time. And he had no need to do any further "housecleaning" in Geneva, because the conference was soon adjourned till autumn.

Nadolny felt relieved—prematurely, as he later realized, because the new Reich Chancellor had never had the slightest intention of disarming Germany, and Heydrich, informed in precise detail of the Fuehrer's secret plans, had been instructed to make

sure that his directives were strictly applied. Heydrich was held
in such high esteem that his impetuous conduct in Geneva had
no bad consequences for him, even though it went counter to the
interests of the new Reich.

Order to Arrest Thomas Mann

One of the first things Heydrich did after entering the Brown
House was to begin building up files on German intellectuals,
especially Socialists and pacifists. After the Reichstag fire, he
had a large number of those dangerous troublemakers arrested.
Thomas Mann, winner of a Nobel Prize for literature, escaped
arrest only because he was on a lecture tour outside of Germany
at the time. When Heydrich returned from Geneva, he was told
by Himmler to give special attention to "the Thomas Mann case."

Mann's house had already been searched in March 1933, and
his bank accounts had been blocked, on the grounds that he was
a traitor who had fled the country. His friends advised him not to
come back to Germany. He was expelled from the German Rotary
Club, which had previously regarded him as one of its most eminent members. Forty-five notables published a "protest from
Munich, the city of Richard Wagner" in which they accused
Mann of having given a distorted picture of the great German
composer in his writings. The press and radio began attacking
him systematically.

Valentin Heins, Mann's lawyer in Munich, tried to clear him
of the charges against him. He began his efforts with the political
police, addressing a letter to "SS Oberfuehrer Heitrich." This
misspelling of Heydrich's name shows that he was not yet known
to the public. Heins failed to obtain anything from "Heitrich."
He then turned to General von Epp, the Governor of Bavaria. He
sent memorandum after memorandum, not knowing that despite
his high rank General von Epp was powerless to affect the actions
of the political police.

Heins labored in vain to exonerate his client. He asserted that
Mann had never slandered Richard Wagner and that it was not in
the interest of the Reich to make an enemy of a world-famous
writer who had won a Nobel Prize, and he promised that Mann
would return to Germany as soon as it was safe for him to do so.
"We do not have many Thomas Manns to lose," he pointed out.

Heydrich remained intransigent. On July 12, 1933, he wrote a letter to General von Epp explaining the reasons for the measures that had been taken against Mann:

> The writer Thomas Mann, born on June 6, 1875, at Lübeck, formerly living in Munich and now abroad, is an adversary of the National Socialist movement and a partisan of Marxist ideas. He has repeatedly demonstrated this in speech and writing.
>
> Among other things, in 1927 he signed an appeal in favor of the children's home of Red Help, of which he was a member.
>
> That same year, he accepted an invitation from a Polish literary club in Warsaw, and there he requested amnesty for those who had taken part in the revolution of 1918–19.
>
> He described as "nationalistic acrobatics" the triumphal reception given in Munich to the German pilots Köhl and Hünefeld, who had flown across the ocean, and he called the pilots themselves "witless aviators."
>
> In the course of a lecture one evening in 1930, Mann said that the National Socialist movement was characterized by "orgiastic nature worship, radical hostility to humanity, dynamic frenzy, and absolute exuberance," and attributed to it "a certain philological ideology, a Germanic romanticism and a Nordic faith coming from professorial circles, trying to mislead the Germans of 1930 by means of a vocabulary of mystic symbols and wild foolishness, with such words as *racial, national* [*voelkisch*], *communal,* and *heroic,* and adding to this movement an element of enthusiastic cultural barbarism."
>
> In 1931, Thomas Mann became an official of the Association for Defense against Anti-Semitism. He also proved his friendliness to the Jews in his novel *The Magic Mountain,* where he glorifies the methods of ritual slaughter used by Jewish butchers.
>
> In 1932, he signed an antiwar declaration written by a Munich peace group and published in the Communist press.
>
> In October 1932, in a speech to Social Democrat workers in the meeting hall of the Viennese Social Democrat movement, he said it was the first time that he, "a writer born into a bourgeois family," had ever "spoken before an audience of Social Democrat workers." He then continued, "I regard this as an occasion that will mark the rest of my life. What I am going to say will be my declaration of sympathy for your Socialist cause. Socialism is only the decision, in accordance with our duty, not to ignore urgent needs and demands, and to side with those who want to give the

world human meaning." It was reported in the press that "this declaration in favor of Social Democracy by the great German writer was joyfully applauded by the Viennese workers."

This attitude—un-German, hostile to the National Socialist movement, Marxist, and friendly to the Jews—was the reason for the arrest warrant issued against Thomas Mann, but because of his absence he could not be arrested.

In compliance with ministerial instructions, all his assets have been seized.

This letter shows evidence of the persistent efforts to gather information on prominent people that Heydrich began making as soon as he arrived at the Brown House; from the start of his career, he foresaw that he would someday settle accounts with "traitors to the Fatherland."

The Reichstag Fire and the "Worldwide Bolshevik Danger"

While adversaries of the Nazi regime were languishing in the concentration camps created by Heydrich, and German propaganda was trying to prove that the Fuehrer had saved the Reich from an armed uprising by the Communists and the Social Democrats—an uprising which, according to Goering, was to have begun on March 1, 1933, with eight thousand large fires all over Germany—Joseph Goebbels, the Reich Propaganda Minister, went to Geneva to convince the disarmament conference of his country's peaceful intentions. At regular intervals Hitler also sent other messengers abroad to preach peace. This campaign was intended to serve his secret plans.

When Goebbels arrived in Geneva, newspapers all over the world were reporting on the trial, which had opened on September 21 in Leipzig, of the men accused of burning the Reichstag. Outside of Germany, public opinion favored the defendants, especially since Dimitroff was remarkably effective in presenting his own case, without a lawyer.

Before Goebbels left for Geneva, Hitler had secretly made a decision: Germany was going to withdraw from the League of Nations. Goebbels's mission was to use his presence in Geneva as a means of disseminating Nazi propaganda. He held a press conference at the Hotel Carlton on September 28. In speaking to the journalists assembled in the lobby, he complained of other nations' mistrust of Germany, and the campaigns that had been directed against Hitler and his regime. What those nations were forgetting was that if Europe was no longer threatened by the Bolshevik danger, they had only Hitler to thank for it. "If the methods we use to turn back the Bolshevik assault seem too harsh," he said, "just imagine what would have happened if we had lost."[11] The terror that the Nazi regime had been practicing for months was only "certain abuses by uncontrollable elements," and in reference to the Jewish question he said, "It seems incomprehensible to us that other countries refuse to take in the overflow of Jews emigrating from Germany."[12]

When the members of the German delegation to the disarmament conference were on their way back to Berlin, during a stop at Basel they learned that they had unwittingly taken part in a hoax staged by Goebbels: they saw newspaper headlines announcing that Germany was withdrawing not only from the disarmament conference but also from the League of Nations. The interpreter for the delegation later wrote, "I couldn't believe my eyes. I was thunderstruck."[13]

Meanwhile, the trial continued in Leipzig. The Nazis tried to prove that behind Dimitroff, Torgler, and Van der Lubbe were the real criminals responsible for the Reichstag fire: "the Jews of Moscow." Holzhauser, a police official, and Neubuhr, of the SS, claimed to have found in Dimitroff's residence a map of Berlin on which buildings to be burned were marked with an X: the Reichstag, the palace, the Dutch embassy, and others. The court refused to accept that "document" as evidence. Goering and Goebbels later appeared at the trial and swore that the map really had been found among Dimitroff's possessions.

In the atmosphere of tension created by the Nazis' claim that they had saved the nation from an armed uprising, Hitler announced a national plebiscite in which the German people could vote for or against his decision to withdraw from the League of Nations. The press and radio gave sensationalistic accounts of the "revelations" made at the trial. Everything seemed to prove that the defendants had burned the Reichstag as part of a Communist plot.

The results of the plebiscite were a resounding victory for Hitler:

Registered voters	45,176,713
Votes cast	43,439,046
Invalid votes	750,061
Valid votes	42,688,985
Votes of approval (95.1%)	40,588,804
Votes of disapproval (4.9%)	2,100,181

Heydrich said to Hans-Peter von Heydebreck at this time, "The way to the final goal is clear. For a little longer we must go on shilly-shallying with Stalin and letting the English believe we don't want to become a naval power again and that we'd even be willing to help them defend Gibraltar, Suez, Aden, Singapore, and Hong Kong."

Historical Errors

The police official Rudolf Braschwitz was one of the main prosecution witnesses against Van der Lubbe. After the war, mistakenly believing that all compromising documents had been lost because there was no mention of them at Nuremberg, he said that he had always regarded Van der Lubbe as the only one responsible for the Reichstag fire. This statement is contradicted by documentary evidence. It is a lie used in an effort to exonerate the Nazis.

In his major work on World War II, the Dutch historian Louis de Jong, who as a compatriot of the unfortunate Van der Lubbe should have examined Braschwitz's statement with an especially critical eye, unquestioningly accepts it as genuine. He sees Braschwitz as the most important witness for the prosecution, and on the basis of his testimony he concludes that Van der Lubbe burned the Reichstag on his own initiative and by his own means. In Louis de Jong's judgment, the Nazis were not responsible for the fire.[14]

It is significant that the Nazis did not succeed in convincing anyone with their map of Berlin showing buildings that the Communists allegedly intended to burn; not even the court would accept it as genuine. As the result of Dimitroff's extraordinarily

courageous conduct and protests all over the world against the
Nazis' judicial farce (180 witnesses for the prosecution, including
30 policemen), Torgler and the three Bulgarians were acquitted.
Van der Lubbe, however, was sentenced to death, and beheaded
on January 10, 1934.

At the end of 1934, Hitler sent the three Bulgarians to the
Soviet Union. Heller, the police official who had secretly tried to
give the judges evidence that the Jews had incited the Communists accused of burning the Reichstag and were therefore the
real criminals, was assigned to accompany the three men to
Königsberg in an airplane. In Königsberg he asked them to do
nothing more against the Third Reich because he and the
Fuehrer had taken every opportunity to act in their favor.

After the war, this lie and others of the same kind were put
forward by Rudolf Diels, the first Gestapo chief, in his memoirs.[15] He convinced several German historians that the Nazis
had not burned the Reichstag. Those historians still put their
trust in Diels, Heller, and Braschwitz, ignoring documents that
show that they were among the men who staged the farcical trial
and that one of its objectives was to denounce a worldwide
"Judeo-Bolshevik" conspiracy.

In January 1934, when Dimitroff was still in custody even
though he had been acquitted, André Malraux and André Gide
went to Berlin to try to obtain his release. They were received by
Goebbels. After their conversation with him, they were convinced
that Dimitroff had been acquitted only because Hitler felt he was
in no position to confront international opposition. As Malraux
said in 1969, it was in Hitler's interest, since he planned to
attack the Soviet Union later, to convince Stalin that the USSR
had nothing to fear from him.[16]

To further this deception, Hitler sent Rudolf Nadolny, the veteran diplomat who had clashed with Heydrich in Geneva, on a
mission to Moscow. Nadolny's instructions were to propose and
negotiate a plan for collaboration between Germany and the Soviet Union. The resulting semblance of German-Soviet friendship
would last till Hitler obtained an agreement on the respective
sizes of the British and German fleets.

Events during this period clearly show the extent to which
Heydrich had his say in matters concerning the foreign policy of
the Third Reich. In 1931, he had predicted that as soon as Hitler

took power the SS and its secret services would be decisive in the propaganda, diplomacy, culture, economy, and defense policy of the Reich. Himmler, an expert judge of a man's talent as a political policeman, had a high opinion of Heydrich; he was, said Himmler, "an extraordinarily gifted virtuoso who knew how to play on all the registers of the world organ."[17]

Heydrich Is Needed in Berlin

On Hitler's forty-fifth birthday, April 20, 1934, he placed the Himmler-Heydrich team at the head of the Gestapo. This promotion involved a decrease in the power of Goering, who till then had exercised absolute control over the Prussian Gestapo. Hitler could no longer afford to spare Goering's feelings; he needed two men in Berlin who would be ready to apply the harshest methods. Obvious discontent in the party ranks had made a purge necessary, and the Reichswehr did not seem willing to support Hitler unconditionally after the death of aged Reich President Hindenburg.

Special agents in Berlin had reported the formation of a conservative opposition that wanted to institute a regency independent of the Nazis after Hindenburg's death, to prevent Hitler from becoming supreme head of the state. This critical situation offered Heydrich and his secret service an important field of action. As long as the Reichswehr was directly under the authority of the Reich President, it would be a potential danger to the pursuit of Nazi policy and the continuation of police terror.

Going beyond its original role as the Fuehrer's Praetorian Guard, the SS had adopted an increasingly hostile attitude toward the SA. Ernst Roehm, head of the SA, was demanding a "second revolution," by which he meant a new shake-up in the state that would bring him the advantages he regarded as his due. Direct action was out of the question, however: Hitler could count on the support of the Reichswehr, the police, industry, and the bourgeoisie; the SA had almost no weapons; several of its best men had gone over to the SS.[18]

What Hitler feared was that at Hindenburg's death the reactionary elements who had so far been his allies would try to have a regent appointed as head of state. This would be welcomed by part of the civil service, the Catholic leadership, a few Generals, and even the SA. General Kurt von Schleicher, who had long been the political chief of the Reichswehr, had not lost all his influence on the army, and he was considered an outright adversary of the Nazis. There was also Gregor Strasser, who could draw what was called the "left wing of the party" in a direction unfavorable to the regime.

On June 17, 1934, Vice Chancellor von Papen gave a speech at Marburg in which he denounced the Nazis' constant attempts to destroy political tolerance.

Nearly two months earlier—when Heydrich was already installed in his office at Gestapo headquarters in Berlin—Hitler had called a meeting of his closest collaborators to tell them what measures were to be taken in case of an internal crisis. According to his information, some of Roehm's supporters, including SA Gruppenfuehrers Karl Ernst and Georg von Detten, would undertake an "outside action" even before Hindenburg died, in the belief that this would give decisive aid to the plot already hatched by the reactionaries. [19]

Hitler intended to use the drastic methods of the Borgias in settling his score with his adversaries within the party. Speaking to a group of German exiles, Otto Strasser said that long before he came to power Hitler liked to philosophize on the way things were done in the Middle Ages. In those days, the future dictator told the Strasser brothers, people knew how to deal with their enemies: ruthlessly and effectively.

In the Spring of 1934, Heydrich was given two important assignments. The first was to direct the purge that came to be known as the Night of the Long Knives. The second required him to use his special skills abroad: the time had come to organize a coup d'état in Austria. Engelbert Dollfuss, the Austrian Chancellor, was opposed to Hitler's plan to annex Austria to Germany.

The Night of the Long Knives

The massacre took place on June 30, 1934, supposedly to forestall a putsch that Roehm was planning. Today, no one denies that Heydrich was in charge of that operation, worthy of the new era that had just begun. According to official figures, eighty-three people were killed that night. Some of the victims were said to

have committed suicide shortly before or after their arrest. This
dramatic episode in the history of the Third Reich has often been
described, but its real causes have seldom been presented.

Among West German historians, the prevailing idea is that
while Roehm and his supporters may never even have considered
a putsch, Hitler, misled by false information from Heydrich, believed that the SA was planning to overthrow him by force and
that only a massacre of the rebels could eliminate the danger.

This version was given currency after the war by Heinrich
Bennecke, a former SA officer who had maintained close relations with the SS. Bennecke naturally described the events of
June 30, 1934, from his own special viewpoint. He claimed that
it was Reichswehr General Walter von Reichenau, an opponent
of the SA, who had set everything in motion, and that the
Reichswehr and the party leadership, not the SS, were responsible for the massacre.[20]

But it is a fact that the purge was carried out in accordance
with a plan ordered by Hitler and developed by Himmler and
Heydrich. The party leadership, knowing that the SA had decided on a propaganda action that would have repercussions
abroad, wanted to react as quickly and effectively as possible.

The rivalry between Roehm and the Himmler-Heydrich team
had begun when the SS achieved its de facto separation from the
SA. Heydrich had long been gathering information damaging to
the SA leaders, who saw themselves being gradually pushed into
the background while the secret service of the SS took control
of the police in all the German states and placed SS men in all
the important posts. Furthermore, the SA had been forbidden to
obtain the subsidies that would have enabled it to pay the ex-
penses of a secret service. Some of its most capable men had
joined the SS, and others were in frequent contact with Himmler
and Heydrich.

In an effort to allay the growing dissatisfaction of the SA,
Hitler made Roehm a Minister without Portfolio at the end of
1933. This did not pacify Roehm: he felt that his promotion was
actually only a way of shunting him aside, and he saw that all the
main posts were still closed to his friends. In Germany as well as
abroad, the SA was suspected of having burned the Reichstag
and of bestially mistreating those who did not share its views.

Some of Roehm's followers were in disfavor, and even Erwin Villain, leader of the team of arsonists, no longer had Hitler's confidence.

Goering had learned that Villain and his friends, including SA Gruppenfuehrer Ernst, had loudly celebrated their Reichstag success in Köpenick. Villain, who was a doctor as well as an SA Standartenfuehrer, had demanded for himself the post of Reich Health Leader, but Himmler and Heydrich had no intention of placing a friend of Roehm's at the head of the German medical corps. In Köpenick there were rumors that from June 20 to June 26, 1933, Villain and his horde of Brownshirts had killed at least 70 people and tortured 250. According to witnesses, this "Köpenick week" was an act of revenge against those who, in Villain's own town, had dared to say that the Nazis had burned the Reichstag.

Villain had already made a reputation for himself in fights against opposing political groups before the Nazis took power. Now that he had rendered the party such a valuable service as destroying the Reichstag, he was determined not to give up his claim to the highest medical post in Germany. Furious that the promise given to him had not been kept, he physically attacked Dr. Leonard Conti, the candidate for the post backed by Himmler and Heydrich, in a Munich hotel.

The ensuing fight attracted a great deal of public attention. Goering demanded that Villain be tried before a criminal court for his act of violence, but Roehm, Ernst, and other SA leaders strongly opposed this. A court of honor was instructed to look into the matter. Villain told the judges that he was being prosecuted only because he was one of those who knew the truth about the Reichstag fire, and with brutal frankness he described how a group of SA men had secretly gone into Goering's private apartment in the palace to act as special guards. There they had been told that the Communists were trying to burn the Reichstag and that the party wanted them, the SA men, to help spread the fire and make sure the Reichstag was destroyed, because the Communists' act would then bring the Fuehrer millions of votes in the coming elections.

Dr. Helmut Stange, one of the judges of the court of honor, did not forget Villain's startling statements. After the war, he ex-

plained how Villain had come to be included in the list of people
to be killed during the Night of the Long Knives. While the court
was still in session, Petri, one of the SS leaders, came in and
seized the records of the trial by order of the head of the Security
Service.[21] From then on, Villain's fate was sealed.

Heydrich's agents in Berlin kept him informed of everything
that was happening. When SA Gruppenfuehrer Ernst and his
aide-de-camp Walter von Mohrenschildt made secret plans to flee
the country, Heydrich knew it immediately. The SA chiefs had
been in contact with opposition leaders to discuss the formation
of a common political front after Hindenburg's death, if his will
designated someone other than Hitler as his successor.

Ernst and his friends no longer had any illusions about the
SA's chances of regaining its lost power. Increasingly sure of
itself, the SS denounced its rivals as criminals and demanded
their exclusion from the party. Ernst finally made the painful
decision to leave Germany. He used a pretext to disguise his
flight as a pleasure trip: he had been married on September 30,
1933, and now he and his wife announced that they were going to
take a ship at Bremerhaven on June 30, 1934, to begin their
honeymoon. That same day, Mohrenschildt and Obersturmbannfuehrer Daniel Gerth would leave for Rome.

Ernst intended to ask foreign powers to refuse all support to
Hitler's government, and tell them that the SA was opposed to
the policies now being followed by Germany, including the persecution of Jews and Communists. He would take with him secret
documents revealing the truth about the Reichstag fire and the
murder of Dr. Ernst Oberfohren, the leader of a German Nationalist group. Walter von Mohrenschildt and his associate
Daniel Gerth would tell the Italian Fascists about the real plans
of Hitler and his SS. They knew high-ranking people in Rome
who had been viewing the actions of the SS with growing mistrust.

Two weeks before his "honeymoon" was to begin, Ernst gave a
farewell party in his Berlin home. The Gestapo already knew the
actual reasons for his intended departure and had listed him as a
traitor.

Everything was ready for the Night of the Long Knives.
Heydrich had worked out his plan with the thoroughness of a true

staff officer. We can reconstruct the main outlines of that plan from the testimony of trustworthy witnesses. First, we know its pretext: to prevent a putsch by the SA leaders.

The shock produced by the news of the putsch and its repression was intended to be such that everyone, from the man in the street to the Reich President, would be convinced that Hitler had acted out of necessity. The date had been unknowingly set by Ernst and Mohrenschildt when they chose it as the date of their departure. A list of people to be arrested had been drawn up; most of them would be killed in Berlin and Munich.

The various stages of the plan took place on schedule.

Long before June 30, Nazi agents began circulating reports aimed primarily at the Generals, Defense Minister von Blomberg, and State Secretary von Reichenau. According to these confidential reports, Roehm and his supporters were plotting to arrest the Generals and the commanders of the military regions, and then kill them. Roehm, it was said, wanted to get foreign backing in order to bring the Reichswehr under the control of the SA.

The plan called for some of Heydrich's agents to rouse several SA companies out of bed on the night of June 30, tell them that there was a state of emergency, and order them to occupy certain key positions. This treacherous order would enable Hitler to "prove" that the SA had already begun its coup d'état when he intervened.

More reports were circulated: the leaders of the rebellion were abroad, and André François-Poncet, the French ambassador, was involved in the affair. When the financier Schickendanz invited a number of important people to his house for dinner two weeks before the date set for the purge, he had no idea that he was doing Heydrich a great favor. Among his guests were Roehm and Ambassador François-Poncet. It was easy for Heydrich's men to have Roehm's and François-Poncet's cars parked next to each other and photograph their license plates: the "conspirators" were exposed![22]

In preparation for the purge, Hitler sent the most important members of the SA on vacation. Roehm went to Bad Wiessee to rest and take care of his rheumatism. Then, on June 28, Hitler ordered all the other SA leaders to go to Bad Wiessee for a conference to be held on June 30, at which all matters of disagreement would be settled. They suspected nothing: Otto Dietrich, Hitler's press chief, had already announced that the Fuehrer was going to make an inspection trip in the Ruhr.

On the afternoon of June 27, Hitler had a final meeting with Goering, Himmler, and Heydrich to discuss details of the purge.

On June 28, the Fuehrer went to Essen to attend the wedding of Josef Terboven, a veteran Nazi now a Gauleiter, who was marrying Goebbels's secretary. While he was in the Ruhr, Hitler visited the Krupp factories and the Labor Service camp in Buddenberg.

On June 30, at about two in the morning, Hitler boarded a plane at Cologne with Goebbels and Dietrich and flew to Munich, where they landed at 4:30 A.M. At 5:30, he left for Bad Wiessee by car, with an SS escort. At 6:34, he stopped in front of the Hanselbauer Hotel, where Roehm was staying. He hurried to Roehm's room and pounded on the door. When Roehm opened it, in pajamas, Hitler said to him, "You're under arrest." The other SA leaders in the hotel were also arrested and taken, with Roehm, to the Stadelheim prison in Munich.

This was the first act of the bloody purge. In Berlin, an operation directed by Himmler and Heydrich soon followed. On the basis of lists prepared in advance, opponents of the regime were arrested and taken to Gestapo headquarters. Among them was Gregor Strasser.

In Bremerhaven, Karl Ernst and his wife were about to board the ship on which they had booked passage for their "honeymoon" trip. As they were leaving their hotel, they were suddenly surrounded by an SS troop led by a man named Kurt Gildisch. Ernst was put on a plane and flown to Berlin.

At about that same time, another SS troop went into the Berlin home of General Kurt von Schleicher, the former Reich Chancellor. He and his wife, Elisabeth, were shot on the spot. The Nazis later said that this had happened because he had tried to escape.

That same day, Dr. Erich Klausener, the leader of Catholic Action, was found dead in his office. Kurt Gildisch had killed him and disguised the murder as a suicide.

That evening, Hitler released this statement to the press:

As a consequence of the plot that has been discovered, the following SA leaders have been shot: Obergruppenfuehrer August

Schneidhuber, Munich; Obergruppenfuehrer Edmund Heines, Silesia; Gruppenfuehrer Karl Ernst, Munich; Gruppenfuehrer Wilhelm Schmidt, Munich; Gruppenfuehrer Hans Heyn, Saxony; Gruppenfuehrer Hans-Peter von Heydebreck, Pomerania; Standartenfuehrer Count Hans Erwin Spreti, Munich.[23]

Karl Ernst had not yet been shot, as the statement asserted, but Hitler knew that Gildisch had taken him to Berlin in a special plane.

Hitler flew back to Berlin that night and arrived at about ten o'clock. Goering and Himmler were waiting for him at the Tempelhof airfield to report on the purge that had been carried out in the capital.

Heydrich never lost his coolheadedness during those dramatic hours. Before having his prisoners executed, he questioned them one last time: he wanted to know if they had any remaining secrets. And a confession obtained by force might be useful to him someday. He questioned Walter von Mohrenschildt about the Reichstag fire, then had him executed, along with Karl Ernst and his legal adviser, Voss. Mohrenschildt and Voss had intended to go to Rome and tell friends of the party there about the new situation in Berlin and the conflict between the SA and the SS. Gruppenfuehrer Georg von Detten and Oberfuehrer Hans von Falkenhausen were also interrogated in an effort to learn what they knew about the Reichstag fire. They were shot on July 1.

Erwin Villain was not at home on June 30. The SS searched his house in his absence. The next day he voluntarily surrendered to the police and was taken to the barracks of the SS Leibstandarte (Hitler's bodyguard) at Lichterfeld, where he was shot on the night of July 2.

Eugen von Kessel, a retired police captain, and his brother Hans, a journalist, had gathered some documents damaging to the Nazis. Eugen intended to take them out of the country. He was murdered in his home. Hans had gone to Stockholm two weeks earlier and therefore escaped death.

The journalist Otto von Heydebreck, whose brother, Hans-Peter, was killed in the purge, was a friend of former Chancellor Heinrich Bruening and Heydrich had placed him on the list of those who were to die, but he had been warned in time and escaped. Several of his friends took turns hiding him in their

homes. When the wave of murders began to subside, a number of
Generals and high government officials interceded for him with
Hindenburg. He survived, and after the war he revealed many
secrets about Heydrich and the SS.[24]

Another victim of the purge was Father Bernhard Stempfle, the
Catholic priest who had helped Hitler to write *Mein Kampf*; he
knew too much about the Fuehrer's private life and political intrigues. Ernst Roehm was shot in his prison cell, as was Gregor
Strasser. Wilhelm Sander and Otmar Toifl, two SA officers who
had close relations with the SS leadership, were arrested and
made to explain how they came to have inside information on the
Reichstag fire.[25] They were then shot—on the pretext that they
had mistreated prisoners!

After the war, Erwin Villain's widow stated that her husband
and Karl Ernst had been killed because they knew too much
about the Reichstag fire.

One of the main reasons for the purge was that Hitler wanted
to silence those who knew the truth about that fire. He was afraid
they might someday join forces with the conservative opposition
to influence the aged President von Hindenburg, who would then
bequeath legal power to a regency council from which Hitler
would be excluded.

To gain the support of the Reichswehr, Hitler had ordered his
agents to circulate a report that the SA intended to assassinate a
number of Generals. After the war, some of those same agents
claimed that Heydrich originated the false report, that Hitler did
not plan the purge, and that he accepted it only because he
thought he was in danger. But Himmler and Heydrich would
never have dared to undertake such an operation without Hitler's
consent. Hitler knew very well that Roehm and the SA could not
even consider an uprising against Hindenburg, the government,
the Reichswehr, the great industrialists, and the power represented by Goebbels's propaganda—that is, the elements that
dominated the Reich and supported the Nazi leadership.

As has already been mentioned, the official list of victims bore
eighty-three names. The bloodbath showed what Hitler was capable of. He implacably eliminated opponents of his policies and
those who knew too much about his machinations. He was not
deterred by any feelings of personal loyalty: Ernst Roehm, who
had helped to start him on his political career, had to die, as did

Gregor Strasser, whose talent as a propagandist had contributed so much to the Nazis' progress.

On July 2, Hindenburg sent Hitler a telegram thanking him for having "saved the German people from a grave danger" by his "resolute action and courageous personal intervention." Hitler could now count on being Hindenburg's successor.

By the important part he played in the preparation and execution of the purge, Heydrich again showed his cold ruthlessness and his skill in the art of deception. He carefully camouflaged the operation while it was in the planning stage. No one was to say anything that might arouse suspicion, and the killings were to be done at places chosen in advance, where nothing would interfere with them.

In the previous few months, Hindenburg, the Reichswehr, the industrialists, and the intelligentsia had had abundant opportunities to see through Hitler, and they should have turned against his merciless regime after the Night of the Long Knives, if not sooner, but they too hailed him as the strongman who had put down a serious threat to the nation. The SS, the elite corps of the Nazi party, had now come into its own.

In a solemn ceremony, Himmler congratulated Heydrich on having crushed the incipient putsch by traitors to the Fatherland, and in the name of the Fuehrer he promoted him to the rank of SS Gruppenfuehrer, equivalent to General in the Reichswehr. Heydrich clicked his heels, raised his arm in the Nazi salute, and, in his high voice, cried, "Heil Hitler!"

The next day, Himmler promoted Kurt Gildisch to Sturmbannfuehrer ("Major"). This honor turned his head. He went to a bar, drank a hefty amount of brandy, and began loudly telling how he had slaughtered traitors, including Klausener, the Catholic Action leader. Years later, his drunken boasting cost him dearly: a witness recognized him and had him brought to trial. Gildisch admitted that he had killed Dr. Klausener and that he had been ordered to call Heydrich as soon as he had carried out his assignment. It was Heydrich who had told him to put a gun in the dead man's hand, to make his death look like a suicide.[26]

The purge gave Heydrich a chance to prove that he could rise to great occasions. The Fuehrer could now have no doubt that, with a man like him, he could kill hundreds of adversaries with-

out having to worry about legal procedures. Heydrich's authority
had become enormous. He had at his disposal every imaginable
means of wiping out the traces of Nazi machinations such as the
Reichstag fire and the Night of the Long Knives, and he could
put future "revolutionary" actions on the right track from the
start.

He was now more deeply involved than ever in the secret maneuvers of the top Nazi leaders. He had all the documents that
had been seized from the purge victims, as well as records of
their interrogations. He used this information to send hundreds of
people to concentration camps. Some of them, judged to be
"usable," were later released and made to serve the SD.

But this was only one aspect of Heydrich's activity. Having
made his SD the predominant force in the Nazi police, he tried to
become completely independent. He had no intention of simply
furthering the interests of the Nazi leaders. He knew all of them
and was well aware of their weaknesses and the ranks they held
in the Fuehrer's favor. The Night of the Long Knives had shown
them what they could expect if they deviated from the party line.

Since becoming head of the party, Hitler had had two primary
objectives: the annihilation of the Soviet Union, which was a necessary condition for conquering new "living space," and the extermination of the Jews. Roehm, Rosenberg, Goering, Hess,
Himmler, and Dr. Hans Frank (Commissioner of Justice and
Reich law leader), and later Goebbels and Joachim von Ribbentrop, had sworn to devote themselves to those secret goals. It
would take another four or five years to achieve them. The war
being planned would be a lightning war (*Blitzkrieg*) on a single
front, and it would end with a rapid, decisive victory. But the
Fuehrer could not accomplish that alone. He would have to be
helped by Britain and Italy, and he needed a reliable secret service in order to carry on domestic and foreign policies in accordance with his two goals.

The Weimar Republic's diplomats and army officers were important elements in Hitler's camouflage maneuvers because they
were better able than anyone else to gain the confidence of the
British military leaders. The diplomats, headed by Konstantin
von Neurath, would be in agreement with all of Hitler's peaceful
declarations and proposals, and would skillfully make use of
them. The Reichswehr, commanded by General Werner von

Blomberg, would form and train the divisions needed for either exerting political pressure or fighting a lightning war, depending on the needs of the moment. Finance Minister Hjalmar Schacht and his experts had begun financing the production of arms and equipment for the Reichswehr.

It was clear to Heydrich that Neurath, Blomberg, and Schacht were only pieces on an enormous chessboard and that Hitler would make only a limited number of moves with them before replacing them. Hitler had never confided his most secret desires to his ministers, but Heydrich was able to make clever use of the monopoly on information gathering that he had created for himself. He also knew that it was forbidden for the Reichswehr to be involved in politics.

President von Hindenburg died on August 2, 1934. His successor was Fuehrer and Reich Chancellor Adolf Hitler.

The Reichswehr swore allegiance to Hitler. He in turn promised the Reichswehr that it would continue to be the only armed force of the Reich. But he had not given up his intention of creating several SS divisions. These were later to develop into the famous Waffen SS, which was distinct from the apolitical Reichswehr and constituted the Fuehrer's political army, a force for the military execution of ideological plans. Hitler was determined never to have a repetition of what had happened in 1918, when the army abandoned its supreme leader (the Kaiser at that time) and placed itself at the disposal of certain politicians.

When the Night of the Long Knives had ended—and Hitler was gratified to see that it had rid the party of nearly all its internal adversaries—Heydrich's authority within the party increased significantly. Only his closest associates knew that he was personally responsible for the murders of General von Schleicher and his wife, Dr. Erich Klausener, and Gregor Strasser.

The Great Lesson: No More Trials!

Heydrich deeply regretted that Willi Muenzenberg, a "heretic" who fled to France shortly after the Reichstag fire, had left Germany in time to avoid being eliminated in the purge. In Paris,

Muenzenberg and other refugees published a Brown Book in which they denounced Nazi crimes. But they mistakenly asserted that the SA was solely responsible for the Reichstag fire. They made that mistake because they were misled by rumors that Heydrich's agents had been circulating inside and outside of Germany.

Franz Knospe, an SA officer whom Heydrich ordered to take part in the work of collecting and suppressing documents concerning the fire, said after the war that Heydrich had told him to contact a Swedish journalist named Murer and "reveal" to him that Roehm and the SA had burned the Reichstag.

Knospe also stated that Heydrich and Kurt Daluege were furious at the acquittal of Dimitroff and Torgler. And years later, in his wartime headquarters, Hitler complained that the trial had not been conducted harshly enough and deplored the fact that Dimitroff and Torgler had not been made to confess: "But unfortunately the lawyers were as international as the criminals, though less clever, so the trial dragged on for weeks and ended with a ridiculous result."[27]

The Reichstag fire and the trial that followed it taught Heydrich that provocations would have to be handled differently in the future. The mishaps that marked the affair from beginning to end had forced the Nazi leaders to carry out the purge of June 30, 1934. If it had not been for the danger that the truth about the fire might be discovered, they could have used other means to silence the opposition.

When Heydrich had realized the Fuehrer's goals and the order in which he intended to achieve them, he knew that each leap forward would have to be accompanied by a new provocation. And he was certain of one thing: there would never again be a trial of anyone accused of taking part in one of those provocations.

Heydrich had learned from Machiavelli that the people must both love and fear their master. The ruler must preach peace and friendship; if he needs to break his word, he can always find or create some dramatic justification for it. As Machiavelli wrote in *The Prince*, "He who wants to deceive always finds people who are easy to deceive."

Heydrich had not only to guarantee the Fuehrer's safety but

also to make sure that everything he did was accepted by the German people. Heydrich and his secret service would provide Hitler with the pretexts he needed for his criminal acts, without ever letting the people know that they were being deceived.

Official photograph of Heinrich Himmler, intended for display in SS offices.

Official photograph of SS Gruppenfuehrer Reinhard Heydrich, intended for display in SD offices.

Himmler giving a speech on "police law" at the Law Academy in 1935. Seated, left to right: Heydrich; Hans Frank, president of the academy; and Werner Best, organizer of the Gestapo.

Heydrich, on right with fencing foil in hand, shows policemen of the Reich how to practice the favorite sport of the SS.

Himmler and Heydrich during their official visit to Rome in 1936. To the right of Himmler is Luigi Bocchini, head of the Italian secret police. To the left is Ulrich von Hassell, the German ambassador, in the uniform of an SA Gruppenfuehrer.

Heydrich was the designer of the German system of concentration camps. This photograph shows a latrine in a concentration camp.

Bottles of poison and syringes used for giving lethal injections to prisoners in concentration camps.

Concentration camp crematories designed and built by Heydrich's technicians.

In 1938, Gruppenfuehrer Reinhard Heydrich, as a spectator at an athletic competition in the Berlin Olympic stadium.

Himmler, Karl Wolff (his assistant), and Heydrich going to the presentation of a film at the 1935 Nazi party convention in Nuremberg.

Goering's forty-fifth birthday ceremony on January 12, 1938. Lined up to congratulate him (in foreground) are: Himmler, an unidentified officer, and Heydrich.

Heydrich and SS Gruppenfuehrer Arthur Nebe, a high German police official, explaining to a delegation of Spanish policemen the success of the rehabilitation program for political and criminal prisoners in concentration camps.

Heydrich with his wife on May 26, 1942, going to the concert in honor of his father at the Wallenstein Palace in Prague.

Adolf Hitler making his speech on November 8, 1939, in the Buergerbraukeller in Munich. He cut short his verbal attack on England and left with his whole entourage; then, ten minutes later, came the explosion that devastated the room. Reinhard Heydrich was ordered to investigate that "crime against the security of the Reich."

Heydrich's Mercedes convertible after the bomb explosion.

Heydrich's coffin in the mosaic room of the new Reich Chancellery.
Himmler is giving the funeral oration.

Adolf Hitler posthumously awarding the German Order, the highest
distinction of the Reich, to his faithful servant Reinhard Heydrich.

After the war, Heydrich's house on the island of Fehmarn was turned into a residential hotel. His widow still receives his friends there and gives interviews to the press, swearing that he only did his duty as a soldier of the Third Reich. From Fehmarn she writes letters in defense of Heydrich to the editors of large newspapers, now signing them as Lina Heydrich-Maninnen, since she has remarried.

5

The Shady Side
of History

Once the Reichstag fire and its aftermath were behind him, Heydrich turned his attention to other important matters: remodeling the intelligence service, organizing the Waffen SS, and the great issues of foreign policy closely connected with those activities. Now that the "left wing" of the Nazi movement had been destroyed, Hitler was waiting for a favorable occasion to reach an agreement with Britain, so that he could defeat his external enemies when the time came.

At the end of 1934, Heydrich realized that the Fuehrer was placing matters related to foreign policy in the hands of an increasingly large number of trusted men, because the great game was about to begin. Although Neurath was still the official head of German diplomacy, it was obvious that Alfred Rosenberg, director of the party's Foreign Policy Office, had a say in all diplomatic moves. But Rosenberg asked Heydrich's advice on questions involving his main concern—the political strategy best suited to crushing the Soviet Union—because Heydrich was the man who was going to set up the organizational framework for overseeing the various anti-Communist and anti-Semitic groups.

Heydrich's field of activity also extended to the close ties that the secret service had with Joachim von Ribbentrop, whose principal assignment was maintaining friendly relations between the Third Reich and Great Britain. Ribbentrop's constantly repeated message to the British was that Germany had no need for colonies and did not want a predominant position as a naval power, but had to have a strong army capable of warding off the Soviet dan-

ger, which was becoming imminent because of Czechoslovakia, a
Russian tentacle reaching toward Germany.

Goebbels, the Propaganda Minister, was also taking a hand in
foreign policy. According to Nazi doctrine, the "world Jewish
conspiracy" had a pernicious influence on the mass media outside of Germany. To defend themselves against Jewish attacks in
the media, said Goebbels, the Germans had to use psychological
warfare. In his ministry there was a special team that analyzed
foreign newspapers, films, and radio broadcasts to help him plan
his "counteroffensive."

Goering, who considered himself a brilliant military expert,
was working toward the resurrection of German air power. He too
was active in foreign affairs. He was particularly concerned with
foreign military attachés in Berlin and German military attachés
in foreign capitals. He built up an espionage network that later
had special importance because of the decisive part played by
the Luftwaffe (German Air Force) in the war. Through his agents
he was able to feed false information on the progress of German
rearmament to foreign diplomats in Berlin.

Heydrich also did not underestimate the foreign section of the
Nazi party, directed by Ernst Bohle. German citizens abroad and
German minorities in other countries had to be enrolled in the
Nazi cause and made to further the interests of the Third Reich.

Having learned that Hitler was considering replacing the head
of the Abwehr, the military intelligence service, Heydrich wanted
the post to go to his old friend and mentor from his time in the
navy, Captain Wilhelm Canaris. But General von Blomberg, who
as Reichswehr Minister had the Abwehr under his jurisdiction,
favored keeping its present commander, Admiral Patzig.
Heydrich found a way to have Patzig ousted in spite of Blomberg:
he discovered that Patzig had sent reconnaissance planes over
Poland at a time when the German government was trying to
maintain good relations with Warsaw. (Germany and Poland had
signed a nonaggression pact in January 1934.) When Heydrich
revealed this, Patzig was dismissed, and soon afterward Canaris
was made head of the Abwehr.

At the end of 1934, Heydrich undertook the coordination of
the various secret services of the Third Reich, and at the same
time he kept watch on national movements in Austria, Hungary,

Italy, France, and Czechoslovakia. He and Himmler believed that as long as Britain and France supported their allies in East Europe, Germany must not turn away from the friends she had there. Heydrich already had anti-Semitic and pro-Nazi groups at his disposal in several countries, and he could use them as a strike force. The first targets would be Austria and Czechoslovakia.

Direct Action

Heydrich's surveillance of European émigré groups and terrorist movements gave him a special status in all the ministries that dealt with matters concerning the secret services. His SD was the only service that had a clandestine network covering the German minorities and Fascist and Nazi groups in different countries. Such groups had developed chiefly in Austria and Czechoslovakia, but similar tendencies had recently begun to be manifested in Hungary, Yugoslavia, Belgium, France, and Holland.

Since the murder of troublesome people had proved to be advantageous inside the Reich, the strategists of the SD decided to use the same methods abroad. Nationalistic forces had declared themselves ready to carry out actions directed from Berlin, without implicating the Reich. The international situation was propitious for such incidents. Heydrich is reported to have said in July 1934, "Just as Hitler succeeded in bringing the German bourgeoisie to its knees with fewer than a million party members, with a million soldiers we'll force the English and French to accept our Eastern policy."[1]

According to the same source, Heydrich gave advice and money to the Austrian SS officer Albert Rodenbuecher, who was living in Munich at the time, to help him organize a putsch attempt in Vienna in July 1934. The SD also maintained close contact with refugees who came to Germany, Italy, and Hungary to make preparations for seizing power in their respective countries. It is highly unlikely that those terrorist groups, which existed only by means of secret funds from Berlin, Rome, and Budapest, could have undertaken important operations without having at least obtained the approval of those who supplied their needs.

After the Night of the Long Knives, the Nazis' position in Rome was not particularly favorable. And it was even less so in Austria, where Chancellor Dollfuss was diligently seeking friendship with Italy.

On July 25, 1934, the Austrian Nazis attempted a coup d'état in Vienna. Dollfuss was assassinated, but the attempt failed. In Italy, Mussolini became angry (after all, only a month before, Hitler had promised to leave Austria alone) and sent several divisions to the Austrian border. The Germans, however, tried to convince him that the Vienna putsch was a purely Austrian affair: forged documents supporting that contention were secretly sent to Vienna and Rome and fell into the hands of the Austrian and Italian governments. Rudolf Hess and Bormann forbade Austrian Nazi groups to carry on any activities in Germany, though that did not prevent Albert Rodenbuecher from being placed in charge of "aid to Austrian refugees."

When Austria was occupied in 1938, Heydrich continued to present the failed putsch of 1934, as a purely Austrian affair. In the meantime, he had assembled "documentary material" by means of which he intended to open a trial of the Austrian Chancellor, Kurt von Schuschnigg, who had replaced the assassinated Dollfuss. In April 1938, a Commission for the Historical Study of the Uprising of July 25, 1934, in Austria was convened not only to demonstrate that no SS troops from Germany had taken part in the putsch attempt, but also to identify those responsible for the execution of rebels.

In 1934, these rebels had been sentenced to death and executed: Otto Planeta, Friedrich Holzwebwe, August Feike, Franz Leeb, Ludwig Maitzen, Josef Hackl, Franz Saureis, Franz Unterberger, Rudolf Erlbacher, and Franz Ebner. Some of them had died shouting, "I'm dying for Germany! Heil Hitler!" But other conspirators had been promoted after the occcupation of Austria. Paul Hudi, for example, a member of the party since 1920 and one of Heydrich's agents, became a member of the Reichstag in 1938, and, in 1940, an SS Sturmbannfuehrer.

Research has established that in 1934 certain high officials of the Austrian police had made contact with the rebels, in the hope that it might turn out to be to their personal advantage.

Heydrich understandably tried to destroy compromising documents from the years 1934 and 1935, which explains why some Austrian historians now say that the Austrian Nazis attempted their putsch without Hitler's knowledge.

After the insurrection had been crushed, Heydrich must not have been particularly proud of his operation; 153 members of the Austrian Nazi movement had been killed. Others were in prisons and detention camps. Many fled to Yugoslavia, where the police set up a camp for them near Varazdin. There they continued their military training under the swastika flag, and when they had completed it they went to Germany.

Heydrich had learned the unpleasant lesson that it was much easier to carry out a coup d'état in his own country, "from above," than in Austria, where he had been forced to act "from below." According to witnesses, it took him several weeks to recover from that failure.

Heydrich and the Blond Lady of Marseilles

Late in the afternoon of October 9, 1934, sensational news reached Berlin: King Alexander of Yugoslavia and Louis Barthou, the French Minister of Foreign Affairs, had been assassinated in Marseilles.

Some of those who saw Heydrich the next day later said that he had seldom seemed more satisfied. As soon as he received the news, he firmly declared that the Third Reich had nothing to do with the assassination and that from the first reports it appeared that the assassins were Croatian and Macedonian "nationalist revolutionaries." He then told Count Wolf von Helldorf, the police commissioner of Berlin, that as a member of the International Criminal Police Organization he was working on terms of close mutual understanding with the Yugoslavian police.[2]

Meanwhile, the press announced that the assassin, a Macedonian named Veličko Georgijev (actually Vlada Kerin) had been lynched by the furious crowd at the scene of his crime. A few days later, his accomplices were arrested. Among them were the Croatians Milan Rajić, Zvonimir Pospišil, and Mijo Kralj. Kralj had been ordered to throw a bomb but his courage had failed him. Though he knew those who had recruited him—the Ustachi, a Croatian terrorist group—he had no idea who had organized the assassination.

Italy and Hungary supported the Ustachi and had allowed them to form armed troops at Janka-Puszta in Hungary and Fontecchio in Italy. It was widely assumed that the double assassination had been committed with the tacit approval of the Italian and Hungarian authorities, especially since they had long backed the territorial demands of Yugoslavian irredentist circles.

This assumption soon appeared to be untenable, however, because after the Nazi putsch attempt in Vienna neither Mussolini nor Horthy, the Hungarian regent, could have any interest in a political plot of such scope, and their respective countries lacked the means for it. But the Yugoslavian government tried to place full responsibility for the affair on Italy and Hungary, hoping that if they were exposed to international indignation they would stop giving material aid to the separatist émigrés within their borders.

The Yugoslavian accusation had the effect of making Rome turn to Berlin for support. Balugdžić, the Yugoslavian ambassador to Germany, complained to Neurath, the Foreign Minister, because Croatian émigrés had complete freedom of movement in Munich and Berlin. One of them, Mladen Lorković, later became Foreign Minister of the Croatian satellite state during the war.

After the assassination, nearly all partisans of the Ustachi in Germany were arrested and questioned, and written records of their statements were kept. Berlin had to take this action because inquiries in France had indicated the possibility that some of those who had participated in the assassination might have come from Germany.

One of the organizers was identified: Eugen Kvaternik. He had traveled to Marseilles under the name of Eugen Kramer, with the assassins, and then had gone to a hotel in Aix-en-Provence with "a blond lady" using the name of Maria Vondraček. On the morning of October 9, 1934, the two assassins, Georgijev and Kralj, had visited her in the hotel, and she had given them two bombs and two pistols, a Mauser and a Walther. Immediately afterward, she and her husband, Jan Vondraček, also known as Peter, had disappeared from the hotel.

Georgijev and Kralj, however, had taken a bus back to Marseilles, where they were to kill King Alexander and Louis Barthou that afternoon. When the time had come for Kralj to throw his bomb, he could not bring himself to do it, according to his declaration after his arrest, because it would have killed many innocent bystanders.

The Yugoslavian police reported that Eugen Kvaternik spoke perfect German, as well as several other languages, and had close friends in Munich and Berlin. His father, a farmer Austrian officer, was sympathetic to the German Nazis. It was known that Kvaternik and the blond lady spoke German to each other and that their French was poor.

Identification of the blond lady was the key to the mystery surrounding the group of assassins. She was neither Italian nor Croatian and she spoke German with a Slavic accent. Vladeta Miličević, the chief Yugoslavian investigator, refused to consider the possibility that the double assassination had been organized in Germany. The Yugoslavian secret service was convinced that the blond lady was a member of the Ustachi and that the man with her was Ante Pavelić, who was later to be head of the Croatian state created by the Germans during the war. This conviction prevented the affair from ever being totally cleared up.

The Yugoslavian government decided to have an investigation carried out in Berlin. If the blond lady was German, the Nazis were lucky that the investigation was conducted by Miličević, who knew much more about good food and drink than he did about work of that kind. He concluded that the blond lady was a Croatian "in the pay of Italy." The Nazis were secretly delighted to see Italy getting most of the blame for the assassination.

Hitler gave the Yugoslavian government firm assurances about its territorial integrity, and Goering went to Belgrade to attend the funeral of the murdered King. In conversation with Juraj Demetrović, the Yugoslavian Minister of Industry and Commerce, Goering promised an improvement in trade relations between their two countries, as well as vigorous prosecution of Ustachi members in Germany.[3]

In the course of his investigation, Miličević worked with Count Wolf von Helldorf, the Berlin police commissioner. They had known each other since the year before, when they had met in

Vienna at a convention of the International Criminal Police Organization. Like many other Serbians, Milićević believed that to maintain the unity of the Yugoslavian state Hitler and Mussolini had to be played off against each other.

Helldorf took him to the Adlon Hotel on Prinz-Albrechtstrasse, where they conferred with a tall, blond police official. After the war, Milićević no longer remembered that official's name; he described him as an extremely well-mannered man who took a great interest in the investigation. When he was shown a photograph of Heydrich, he immediately recognized him as the man he had met on Prinz-Albrechtstrasse. But he said that he had had nothing more to do with Heydrich afterward and had conducted his investigation only with Helldorf, who was executed ten years later, after being accused of taking part in the attempt to kill Hitler on July 20, 1944.

In 1947, Milićević had some interesting things to say about his conversation with Heydrich. When Milićević permission to question at least a few of the Croatian terrorists who had been arrested, Heydrich had replied that unfortunately he could not grant his request because German administrative procedure required such interrogations to be authorized by the Attorney General or a legally qualified court. He then asked Milićević why he believed that Kvaternik was one of the organizers of the assassination. Milićević told him that Kvaternik had gone from Marseilles to Aix-en-Provence with the blond lady who had given German pistols to the assassins. After remarking that anyone could get German pistols in order to put the police on a false trail, Heydrich expressed contempt for terrorists who would use a woman as their agent.

Finally, Heydrich gave Milićević some "valuable documents" and introduced him to two pretty women. The documents convinced Milićević that Heydrich trusted him and had been frank with him, and the expression of contempt for terrorists who used a woman as their agent convinced him that Heydrich would never do such a thing himself. If the two pretty women convinced him of anything, we do not know what it was. In any case, after the war he was still certain that Heydrich knew nothing about the blond lady.

That mysterious woman, described as being about thirty and

attractive, had a false Czechoslovakian passport in the name of
Maria Vondraček. After Germany created the Independent State
of Croatia during the war, relatives of Mijo Kralj stated that the
organizers of the assassination had told them that the blond lady
was a German. Kralj and Pospišil died in prison, from unex-
plained causes, soon after the Germans occupied France. According to a statement made to me by Joseph Paul-Boncour, the
royal family's lawyer at the trial following the assassination, the
conspirators' guards told him that their prisoners had referred to
the blond lady, who spoke German with a Slavic accent, as being
an associate of Alfred Rosenberg. "But she probably knew a
Slavic language thoroughly," Paul-Boncour said. "At any rate,
she was in contact with one of the Ustachi leaders, Eugen
Kvaternik."

Kvaternik's relations with the Brown House were well known.
He often went to Germany, and after the creation of the Independent State of Croatia he became one of its highest police officials—with the Nazis' consent, of course. It is certain that
before the assassination Kvaternik was in close contact with SS
Gruppenfuehrer Gottlob Berger, a confidential agent of Himmler
and Heydrich. After the war, Otto von Heydebreck stated that
Berger knew the blond lady personally, that she frequented émigré circles, and that she was considered to be among the anti-
Comintern activists. It has also been reported that she was an
agent of Heydrich's SD and that Goebbels provided her with a
cover. Berger is said to have been the most important liaison
agent between the SS and the East European émigré groups, and
to have worked with Rosenberg and Goebbels.

After the war, many of the policemen involved in the investigation tried to learn the identity of the blond lady who was the key
to that act of terrorism. Here is what Police Inspector Alexandre
Guibbal wrote about her:

Yes, it was that "blond lady" who attracted the most attention
from the public, and perhaps from the court. . . . It was said that
she radiated the famous Slavic charm, that the leaders of the plot
used her to fascinate the assassins, and that because of her charm
she was the one chosen to smuggle in the weapons for the assassination, concealed in her luxurious luggage, all of which

helped to stir up the interest taken in her by fans of detective films and spy novels.[4]

Ivan Paprika, a Yugoslavian linguist, has studied all the documents on the Ustachi and reached the same conclusion as the French historian Jean-Baptiste Duroselle: only the Nazis could have had any interest in eliminating Louis Barthou and King Alexander. Paprika published a series of articles on the subject in the Zagreb newspaper *Fokus*, in April-May 1978. He is firmly convinced that the whole affair was directed from Munich and that its main objective was to eliminate Barthou; the murder of King Alexander was only incidental. According to Paprika, the German secret service created an alibi for itself by casting suspicion on the Croatians and Macedonians.

Only Vladeta Miličević's statements contradict the supposition that the blond lady was German. In his version, Jan or Peter Vondraček was actually a member of the Ustachi named Antun Godina, and Maria Vondraček was his wife, Stana. This, said Miličević, was discovered in Italy in 1937, through an amateur photographer named Bubalo who had taken pictures of the Godinas. Bubalo did not claim that Stana Godina was the blond lady of Marseilles, but the Yugoslavian investigators came to that conclusion on the basis of photographs he showed them.

Miličević's version did not seem completely credible even to him; he admitted that "they [Stana and Antun Godina] were not in the files of the Yugoslavian police." Furthermore, the investigators had no photographs of the blond lady that they could compare with Bubalo's photographs. How could Miličević have recognized her when he did not know what she looked like?

The assassination of King Alexander and Louis Barthou came at a good time for the Third Reich, considering that only three weeks earlier, on September 18, 1934, the Soviet Union had become a member of the League of Nations, and that Barthou, the French Foreign Minister, had been working openly to achieve a Franco-Soviet alliance.

But while Hitler was apprehensive that French diplomatic efforts to form close ties with the Soviet Union might eventually succeed, for the moment they were useful to him because they allowed him to claim that France was willing to ally herself with bolshevism in order to save the Versailles Treaty, which gave him a pretext for rearming Germany and persisting in his denunciation of the treaty.

An entry in Alfred Rosenberg's diary dated June 8, 1934, shows the anxiety aroused in the leaders of the Reich by Barthou's efforts, but also a certain optimism concerning the advantages that the Reich might gain from the new French strategy:

> Then the Fuehrer again spoke for a long time about the situation in foreign policy. It has become less tense, after a difficult period: Barthou has not presented a complaint in Geneva about our rearmament and he has obtained no moral and judicial sanction for aggression. He does not think that France would risk aggression without such a sanction. With regard to the new Franco-Russian rapprochement, the Fuehrer is satisfied, now as before, contrary to the Ministry of Foreign Affairs, as he pointed out. France has compromised herself.[5]

Why was Hitler satisfied when the Ministry of Foreign Affairs was not? Because the professional diplomats feared that Barthou's efforts might lead to the encirclement of the Reich and the annihilation of their plans to regain territory lost in the World War, whereas Hitler had prepared a countermeasure to prevent that: he would change the course of Yugoslavian policy.

Conservative forces in the German government were alarmed by the news that King Alexander had concurred with Barthou's views on European security; with a Franco-Soviet alliance, Germany would be dangerously hemmed in.

Heydrich immediately turned his attention to the problem. He and the experts working with him realized that the Little Entente—the alliance among Yugoslavia, Czechoslovakia, and Romania, in which Yugoslavia held the predominant place—had to be destroyed.

The change that took place in Yugoslavian foreign relations after the double assassination showed that those who organized the plot had judged the situation realistically. Milan Stojadinović's government inaugurated a policy of friendship with Hitler and Mussolini. The Little Entente was no longer a barrier to Germany's annexation of Austria.

I do not mean to imply that the assassination in Marseilles was entirely the work of the German secret service. The hypothesis published after the war—that the operation was set up by Goering and the German military attaché in Paris—seems unsatisfactory to me. It is highly unlikely that such a mission would have been assigned, especially in writing, to an ordinary military attaché.

The criminologists who took part in the investigation of the assassination all ruled out the possiblity that the deaths of King Alexander and Louis Barthou could have been useful to Mussolini, but they assumed that the German secret service must have been delighted at being able to use the Ustachi and Macedonian conspirators as scapegoats.

In a letter to Vladeta Milićević dated November 5, 1956, Joseph Paul-Boncour, the former French Foreign Minister who had defended the interests of the Yugoslavian royal family at the trial, accused both Mussolini and Hitler of being accomplices in the assassination. This prompted me to request another interview with Paul-Boncour. It took place, in Milićević's presence, at the Hôtel Plaza-Athénée in Paris.

I asked Paul-Boncour to tell me his specific reasons for believing that Hitler was involved in the conspiracy. He replied that when Milićević had conducted his inquiry in Berlin, he had told him that the Italian secret service would not have taken part in that operation without express authorization from Berlin. After the publication of his memoirs, he had occasion to read the reports of certain men who had been imprisoned with Pospišil and Kralj. According to them, the two criminals had shown marked sympathy for Germany and none at all for Italy. And after the fall of France in 1940, it was not the Italians who concerned themselves with the conspirators' fate: Heydrich's representatives in occupied France carefully examined the trial records and special emissaries tried to find all documents relating to the assassination. Paul-Boncour then came to the conclusion that an international inquiry was needed, because only such an inquiry could establish that the Ustachi and the Macedonians had perhaps been instruments of Hitler, Rosenberg, and Himmler.

In response to this reasonable opinion expressed by an experienced statesman who had been present at the trial and had access to all its documents, Milićević said he was still firmly convinced that only Mussolini and Ante Pavelić had directed the operation.

Certain clues seem to indicate that Mijo Kralj did not die in the Fontrevault prison but was freed by the Germans and went back to Croatia, though the members of his family were not able to confirm this. They did state, however, that the blond lady was German.

In the absence of conclusive evidence, this statement must be treated with skepticism, but it cannot be ignored. All sorts of hypotheses have been formulated about Kvaternik, Pospišil, Rajića, and Kralj, the four Croatians implicated in the assassination, but in examining those hypotheses no one has ever found any trace of a "Croatian heroine." The blond lady, however, is often mentioned as being in contact with Rosenberg, Heydrich, and Berger, regarded as the organizers of the assassination, and we know that those three powerful Nazis afterward took an interest in the development of the situation in Croatia. Certain people who went to Croatia to study the affair were told that during the war the blond lady was seen in Zagreb with several SS officers. We cannot rule out the possibility that after the creation of the Independent State of Croatia she visited Kvaternik to talk over their past exploits.

When, after publishing his book, Milićević learned of the reports and rumors mentioned above, he admitted that he might have been mistaken and that perhaps the blond lady was German. It is certain that Heydrich gave Milićević an ambiguous answer when he asked if Kvaternik had taken refuge in Germany, and that he refused to let Milićević have any contact with the arrested members of the Ustachi whom he wanted to question about the blond lady.

An Operation in Czechoslovakia

The Black Front, an anti-Nazi organization headed by Otto Strasser, who had fled from Germany in 1931, had a secret radio transmitter in Czechoslovakia which could be heard all over Germany and constantly broadcast news of Nazi crimes. It was Strasser who revealed, for example, that Ernst Oberfohren, a

prominent German Nationalist in the Reichstag, had been murdered by the SS in Kiel on May 7, 1933. Strasser had learned of
the murder from Oberfohren's brother, who was living in Califor-
nia but received information from Kiel. Bruno Frei, who had just
published in Strasbourg a report on the murder of Eric Jan
Hanussen, became one of Strasser's sources. The clandestine radio station in Czechoslovakia announced that Hanussen had been
murdered by Wilhelm von Ohst and an SS detachment. For the
moment, Strasser gave only that one name, but he promised his
listeners that when he finished his inquiry he would name each
member of the detachment.

Since Strasser's broadcasts were, of course, monitored by
Heydrich's SD, they aroused growing concern among the Nazi
leadership, and especially among those who were specifically
named as murderers. Moreover, a British newspaper, the
Manchester Guardian, began taking an interest in the information
broadcast by the secret transmitter. This came at a particularly
bad time for the Nazis because Ribbentrop was about to conclude
the Anglo-German agreement on naval power that Hitler wanted.

Heydrich was ordered to draw up a plan for putting an end to
the activities of Otto Strasser and his group in Czechoslovakia.
The operation was intended to convince the British that the
Czech government was granting asylum to anti-German revolutionaries, terrorists, and Communists, and even supporting them
financially. The plan was for one of Strasser's associates to be
abducted in Czechoslovakia and brought back to Germany, and
his abduction would be disguised as a voluntary return. There
would then be a trial at which he would make such a complete
confession that a large number of Communists, Jews, and members of the Black Front could be arrested. The main purpose of
the trial would be to discredit the Czech government and its secret service.

Heydrich was already prepared for that false trial; he had
"witnesses" who would swear to whatever he wanted, and "evidence" that American Jews were financing the secret radio station in Czechoslovakia. He was well informed on the activities of
Strasser's group because he had two agents in it: Hildenbrand
and Adam, who used the names of Fritsche and Mahr, respectively.

Heydrich had never been able to lure Otto Strasser back into Germany. Strasser was a wily adversary who avoided all traps and saw through all subterfuges. The Nazis had decided not to abduct him and bring him back by force because they knew they could not convincingly present his return as voluntary or make him give a confession that would be satisfactory to them. Early in December 1934, the Fuehrer summoned Heydrich and told him to abduct Rudolf Formis, Strasser's closest collaborator.

Formis had been a highly respected radio technician in Stuttgart before he left Germany and went to Czechoslovakia. The SD had gathered abundant information on him, including the fact that he had a weakness for athletic-looking young women. Heydrich intended to take advantage of that weakness. He wanted to leave nothing to chance; he had to succeed, because a failure would stir up hostile criticism abroad, which might be seriously prejudicial to the negotiations with Britain. Military conscription was to begin in Germany no later than the spring of 1935. Time was pressing.

Meanwhile, Strasser's revelations were attracting more attention in other countries. Heydrich wondered how long it would be before newspapers and radio stations all over the world began simply repeating the news they heard from the secret transmitter in Czechoslovakia, without questioning its accuracy. Strasser was pretending to broadcast information to a resistance organization within Germany, which did not yet exist, and the governments of nearby countries were beginning to take him seriously.

After the war, Strasser said that he had regularly received news from inside Germany, but that those who gave him that news were agents sent by Heydrich to spy on him. Emissaries from Berlin constantly came to Strasser claiming to bring him "secret material" but actually trying to involve him in a scheme of espionage and counterespionage directed from a distance. He was aware of this: "For a long time I played the game, so that I at least knew what was upsetting Heydrich."[6]

Those voluntary assistants offered him not only information but also money. Saying they were friends of the Black Front, many of them claimed to be Jews living in Germany who wanted to help opponents of the regime. But Strasser, an ex-Nazi who knew Nazi methods well, was not taken in. After the war, he said:

Even now, I don't know if Alfred Raeschke, my brother Gregor's secretary, who often came to Prague, was sent to me by Heydrich or if he made those trips on his own initiative. It may be that he was carrying out missions given to him by Heydrich, out of loyalty to him. In any case, he told me in January 1935 that his friend Franz Knospe, an SA Sturmfuehrer, had heard Heydrich say that the men who burned the Reichstag belonged to the SA. Knospe had repeated what he knew to a Swedish journalist named Murer. Years later, I studied the question and concluded that Raeschke had told the truth. But he also told me that in December 1934 Knospe had found some of Van der Lubbe's personal documents in the home of one of Daluege's spies, named Brauser. And he said that Heydrich had made plans for a trial by which he thought he could prove that SA Gruppenfuehrer Ernst had had Eric Jan Hanussen killed because of a dispute over money. Our broadcasts always bothered the Nazis, of course, but they reacted violently when we discussed Germany's preparations for war and talked about the people who had been murdered: Oberfohren, Hanussen, my brother, Schleicher, Klausener. That must have been what made them decide on the abduction.[7]

The transmitter was about thirty miles south of Prague. To the Nazis it was a constant source of irritation and worry. What disturbed them most was Strasser's weekly review, in which he reported on the rapid progress of German rearmament and said that it would soon reach the point where Hitler could issue an ultimatum to one of Germany's neighboring countries. This was alarming news. Without being a Jew or a Communist, Otto Strasser had come to be regarded as one of the most dangerous adversaries of the Nazi regime.

Once Heydrich's agents had determined the location of the transmitter, it was easy to identify Rudolf Formis as the technical director of the installation. With a minimum of help and money, Formis had set up a functioning radio station in the Zahori Hotel, at Dobris.

He was not unknown to the Nazis. On February 15, 1933, while Hitler was making a radio speech in Stuttgart, the broadcast had been stopped by a "technical accident." The engineer on duty was Rudolf Formis. After giving a plausible explanation, he had left Stuttgart and joined Otto Strasser in Czechoslovakia.

Since the Nazis considered him an expert technician with strong political convictions, they believed him to be responsible for the installation of a series of clandestine stations in other countries besides Czechoslovakia.

Hitler told Heydrich that he must abduct Formis before the end of January 1935. Strasser had announced that on January 30, the second anniversary of Hitler's seizure of power, he would broadcast new information on the Reichstag fire, the purge of June 30, 1934, and other machinations of the Third Reich. The Nazis could hesitate no longer. The operation, under Heydrich's personal control, had to be carried out as quickly as possible.

Heydrich's plan called for two of his agents, a man and an attractive young woman, to go to Dobris, ostensibly to do some skiing. The woman would strike up an acquaintance with Formis and allow her relations with him to become increasingly intimate. To facilitate this, her companion would go away for a few days. During that time, he would return to Berlin and make a progress report; the SD wanted to be informed of Formis's behavior before taking the next step. Then the agent would go back to Dobris, accompanied by another agent who would help with the abduction.

Heydrich assigned the mission to three agents in whom he had great confidence. He had known one of them, Alfred Naujocks, since his days in Kiel. Naujocks was an experienced man in such matters. In 1926, at the age of only fifteen, he had already belonged to the central espionage bureau of his native city. Werner Groethe, the second male member of the team, was also from Kiel, where he had been Naujocks's mentor to some extent. The female member was Edith Kersbach, a blond physical education teacher. She was a Berliner, but since Formis might be wary of anyone from Berlin, she would claim that she, too, was from Kiel, and to guard against slipups, Naujocks would give her a detailed description of the city.

The Czech police, Otto Strasser, and the Czech historian Miroslav Ivanov have given me information on the Formis affair, and I have also studied the reports of journalists who investigated it after the war. On the basis of all those elements, the general course of events can be reconstructed, though there are still a number of uncertainties that I attribute to the fact that after the

war the three agents tried to diminish their responsibility for Formis's death as much as possible. There is every reason to believe
that they were ordered to kill him if they failed to abduct him,
but if they had admitted that in 1945 they would have been risking a death sentence for murder.

Before they left for Czechoslovakia, Heydrich gave Alfred
Naujocks and Edith Kersbach a map showing them how to get to
the town of Pribram, and from there to the village of Dobris and
the Zahori Hotel. Their equipment also included two compasses,
a pair of binoculars, a camera, a first-aid kit containing bottles of
chloroform, two pistols hidden in hollowed-out books, calling
cards bearing their assumed names and fictitious addresses, and,
of course, false passports.

On January 12, 1935, they left Berlin in a comfortable Mercedes, license number IP 48 259, with skis attached to its roof.
They were now a pair of lovers going off to Czechoslovakia to do
some skiing.

They spent the night in Dresden. The following night, they
slept at the Wilson Hotel in Prague. Naujocks registered as
"Hans Mueller, businessman, Kiel, born September 20, 1911."
They spent the next night at the Paroplavky Hotel in Stechovice.
Late in the afternoon of January 15, they arrived at the Zahori
Hotel in Dobris.

When they went into the hotel dining room that evening, they
found only one other guest there: Formis. They began talking
with him. Sometime later, Naujocks left the dining room, saying
he was tired from his trip. Formis and Edith Kersbach remained
behind, absorbed in conversation.

Naujocks and Kersbach spent the next day skiing. That evening, they again had dinner with Formis. The next morning, they
went back to Stechovice. Naujocks said he had to spend a few
days in Prague, and he seemed unwilling to leave his fiancée at
the Zahori Hotel while he was gone. But since there was a shuttle
bus between the Zahori in Dobris and the Paroplavky in
Stechovice, Formis would be able to develop his budding ro-
mance with her.

Now thoroughly acquainted with the hotel and the village, and
confident that relations between Formis and Kersbach would
steadily become closer, Naujocks took a Lufthansa plane back to

Berlin on January 17 and reported to Heydrich.

Heydrich was satisfied with the first results of the operation. The next day, Naujocks left with Werner Groethe, who was using the name of Gerd Schuster. Heydrich had given them their final instructions: if Formis did not let himself be lured to Stechovice, where his abduction could take place without attracting attention, they would have to abduct him at the Zahori Hotel, no matter what the consequences; and if they were unable to abduct him, they would have to kill him and destroy the transmitter.

On January 18, Naujocks and Groethe arrived in Prague, took the car that Naujocks had left in a garage at 40 Stepanska Street, and drove to Stechovice. From January 19 to 22, they patrolled between Stechovice and Pribram, near Dobris. During that time, they observed Formis and Kersbach together, but she never succeeded in drawing him to Stechovice.

On the afternoon of January 23, Naujocks and Kersbach officially returned from Stechovice and took rooms at the Zahori Hotel. Groethe stayed out of sight. He was to wait till darkness fell, then climb up to Kersbach's room on a rope ladder that Naujocks would attach to the window.

Formis greeted the couple warmly, and they spent the evening together. At about 10:15, the three of them went up to the second floor, where their rooms were. They shook hands and told each other good night. Suddenly everyone in the hotel heard a scream from Kersbach, followed by several shots. Naujocks and Groethe ran to the owners of the hotel, threatened them with their pistols, and made them go into the cellar.

Formis was later found on the second floor, dead, with two bullets in his head and two in his chest. The police investigation showed that the murder weapon was a 7.65-millimeter pistol.

According to one version, Groethe was waiting in Kersbach's room, ready to chloroform Formis while Naujocks and Kersbach held him. They intended to carry him to the car as soon as he was unconscious, then head for the border. But this plan failed because Formis turned out to be strong as an ox and defended himself so vigorously that he could not be chloroformed.

After the war, Naujocks gave another version: Formis had shot first, and his attackers had killed him in self-defense. Groethe corroborated this version.

As for Kersbach, she claimed she had come to Czechoslovakia only for pleasure and had known nothing about the abduction plan.

Although the various versions differ in details, the essential points remain unchanged: Heydrich had worked out a plan to abduct Formis and, to Hitler's great regret, it had failed. With Formis dead, there could be no trial aimed at discrediting Strasser and the Czech government.

Heydrich had not foreseen that after meeting Edith Kersbach in the Zahori Hotel, Formis would talk to his friend Strasser about her. After the war, Strasser recalled that when he told Formis he ought to be cautious with that young couple from Kiel, Formis had replied naively, "Don't worry, they're harmless. They're not even involved in politics, much less the Gestapo. You see the Gestapo everywhere. Those two are here to ski, that's all. Edith is an expert skier—and she's very pretty, too."

The hotelkeeper, who, of course, knew that Formis had radio equipment in his room, noticed the young German woman's advances to him and told Strasser about them. Strasser warned Formis again, this time so urgently that Formis began to have doubts and promised to be careful. That was why Kersbach never succeeded in luring him to Stechovice, where the abduction was supposed to take place.

According to the account that Naujocks gave after the war, he knocked on the door of Formis's room and asked to borrow a bar of soap. Formis opened the door but immediately sensed danger and drew his pistol. After a struggle, Naujocks and Groethe subdued him. Then Groethe killed him. Naujocks and Groethe set fire to the transmitter with phosphorus and ran out of the hotel.

Günther Deschner, one of Heydrich's biographers, says that when Naujocks came back to Berlin the first time, after leaving Kersbach in Czechoslovakia, Heydrich told him to be sure to bring Formis back alive and destroy the transmitter with phosphorus.

But everything went wrong. While they were struggling with Formis, the bottle of chloroform broke. Formis managed to get out his pistol and lightly wounded Naujocks three times. Groethe killed Formis with a bullet in the head. The two SD men had time to burn the transmitter with phosphorus and escape from the hotel. After an eventful trip, they crossed the border and reached Berlin at about noon on January 24. In his Berlin office, Heydrich flew into a rage against Naujocks for botching his mission like an amateur and using methods "like those in a gangster film."[8]

While the Nazis were trying to neutralize their enemies in foreign territory, Hitler's government carried on a pretense of friendship. Czechoslovakia, a victim of that hypocrisy, joined with the Reich in organizing a series of shared cultural and sports events. The Prague government had to be extremely cautious with Germany because Hitler was accusing the Communists and Jews of fomenting disturbances in Czechoslovakia, and it did not take much imagination to realize that those accusations might be a prelude to something very serious.

To the Czech police, the Formis case was clear: German agents had killed a political adversary and then escaped. In response to this view, Berlin claimed that Formis had provoked the incident himself by starting a political discussion with German tourists who became outraged at his attacks against the German Reich.

The Czech bourgeoisie were interested mainly in restoring order; they wanted all those political refugees to stop making trouble, and they were resentful of Otto Strasser in particular for having abused their hospitality after being granted asylum in their country. If he was punished for it, it would serve him right.

Since there was no denying that a murder had been committed, the wheels of justice finally began turning, though with a great deal of creaking and grinding. But the judges' first concern was to make their contribution to German-Czech friendship: Otto Strasser had to pay the penalty for breaking the law. For having illegally used a radio transmitter, he was sentenced to four months in prison. The court of appeals upheld the sentence and gave as its reason that "the character of the accused gives no reason to expect an improvement." This shows that the court had accurately appraised Strasser's character: he built another clandestine transmitter as soon as he was out of prison. "I had to warn the world of the danger of war, no matter what the cost."[9]

After the war, Strasser tried to find Naujocks and Groethe and have them put on trail. His efforts not only failed but also aroused opposition that made life difficult for him. That man who had fought against the murderous Nazi regime from abroad was refused the old-age pension to which he was legally and morally entitled. Meanwhile, the men who had killed Formis were still free.

From my long conversations with Otto Strasser about his period of exile, it became clear that the murder of Formis had far-reaching consequences: after it occurred, the Czech government began paying closer attention to Nazi propaganda and the subversive activities of the German minority in the Sudetenland, and quickly discovered Hitler's real intentions with regard to Czechoslovakia.

But while Strasser's broadcasts warning the world against the coming war were heard by the secret service of the Czech Army, the agents of that service who came to him, pretending to be amateur radio operators, tried to discourage him: his warnings were based on nothing but "gloomy ideas"; France stood firmly beside her Czech allies; Hitler would never dare to attack the Maginot Line and the fortifications along the German-Czech border. Strasser later remarked on that subject, "Czech industry and finance were making a lot of money from those fortifications, and no one wanted to foresee a war of movement in which planes and tanks would be dominant."[10]

In 1935, Strasser, turning his back on his Nazi past, was vitally concerned with awakening the world to the danger of the war planned by the Reich and making government leaders see through the pretense of friendship that Hitler was maintaining in order to lull his future victims. Strasser had become as great a threat to the Nazis as Hermann Rauschning, former President of the Danzig Senate, who also saw catasrophe approaching. Strasser, Hermann Rauschning, and Konrad Heiden were certain that Hitler was preparing for armed conflict. All three had belonged to the Nazi party; they knew that the Reichstag fire, the Night of the Long Knives, and the murder of Formis were alarm signals along Hitler's path to a second World War.

During a chance encounter with Frantisek Moravek, head of the Czech military secret service, Strasser told him that there were other provocations still to come, that the Night of the Long Knives and the murder of Formis had been only trial balloons:

The Nazis will stage an operation along the lines of the Reichstag fire each time they want a pretext for inflicting exemplary punishment on their enemies. The murder of my friend and the destruction of our transmitter were a provocation against Czechoslovakia, intended to make the Czech bourgeoisie turn against the anti-Nazi refugees.

Moravek accepted what Strasser had said and asked, "In your opinion, who encourages Hitler to have such ideas?"

"I think Himmler is too stupid for that," replied Strasser. "Hitler's 'evil spirit' is Heydrich."

Moravek then asked Strasser a personal question, "What makes you live so dangerously? Someday you may find yourself in a very unpleasant situation!"

"You're probably right. But each of us does what he can for his country."

This answer pleased Moravek.

"'Each of us does what he can for his country'—well said!"

Opposition from Switzerland

The German journalist Berthold Jacob had gone into exile after the Reichstag fire. Since then, he had been in Switzerland writing as a commentator on military matters. The Nazis considered him dangerous because he denounced their preparations for war. Heydrich began devising a plan to bring him back to Germany and have him tried for treason.

In March 1935, several of Heydrich's agents made contact with Jacob in Basel and convinced him that they were anti-Nazis. He got into a taxi with them; by the time he realized he had fallen into a trap, it was too late: the car had crossed the German border at Lörrach.

On March 12, Jacob was taken to Heydrich's office on Prinz-Albrechtstrasse in Berlin. Heydrich believed he could make Jacob confess to espionage activities in Germany before his exile, and that this could be used as propaganda to help convince the public that military conscription was needed in order to strengthen the country's defenses against hostile foreign powers.

But the Swiss—unlike the Czechs, who had not protested the

murder of Formis two months earlier—had no intention of letting the Nazis get away with that act of gangsterism. They reacted so vigorously that the affair threatened to have serious repercussions, and finally, on September 18, Hitler allowed the abducted journalist to go back to Switzerland.

After this disappointment, Heydrich intensified his spying on German exiles living in Switzerland. He sent some of his best agents there, including several women who pretended to be convalescents and sent back detailed reports of their observations.

Baron von Neurath, the German Minister of Foreign Affairs, eventually succeeded in convincing his Swiss counterpart that the "border incident" involving Jacob had been the result of conflict between certain minor officials and that the German government had played no part in it.

Activities of the SD and the Abwehr Outside of Germany

In 1935, Heydrich began dealing more extensively with problems related to foreign policy. He knew that Hitler and his General Staff had drawn up plans to be applied after the outbreak of war. The conversion of the German economy was already under way. Technical institutes were working on the development of substitute products to make the munitions industry independent of foreign sources of supply.

Funds allotted to the SD were increased. The number of its part-time agents was to be doubled within the next three years. The Fuehrer ordered Heydrich to expand the activities of his Department III (foreign affairs). The Nazis wanted to exploit the opportunity to recruit informers among anti-Semites and Fascists in foreign countries. This was the starting point of a gigantic organization that extended to the German minorities in Poland, Czechoslovakia, Romania, the Soviet Union, and Yugoslavia, and to the Swiss, the French, and the German-speaking people in Luxembourg. In Belgium the Flemings were to be transformed into a fifth column, though that term had not yet been coined. (In 1936, during the Spanish Civil War, General Emilio Mola said that four columns were marching on Madrid and that a fifth column, composed of people sympathetic to the insurgents, was already inside the city.)

In the name of certain minorities in various countries, Fascist groups had begun asking Germany to support their efforts for independence as soon as Hitler came to power. Heydrich was given the task of coordinating the activities of foreign Fascist movements, German minorities, European peoples dissatisfied with their fate, and the anti-Bolshevik movement among Russian emigrants. These elements demanded the establishment of a new order in Europe. Not only were they a fertile source of informers for the Nazis, but some of them had formed terrorist groups that were waiting for a chance to act. Heydrich was to be ready, when war began, to install puppet governments devoted to the Reich.

He and his staff studied ways to begin exporting anti-Semitism when the time came for it. They planned a series of provocations that would have effects all over Europe and favor the political aims of the Reich. For the moment, however, anti-Semitism was not yet ready for export.

The Nazi leadership felt that the Ministry of Foreign Affairs and its diplomatic corps were not suitable for such operations. Although Hitler continued to use the officials he had inherited from the Weimar regime, he asked them only to pursue their normal relations with foreign countries. It would have been a mistake to replace those experienced diplomats. They were trusted abroad and could still be useful in persuading other countries to adopt policies favorable to Germany's economic needs.

By 1935, it had become necessary for the SD to deal not only with matters of foreign policy but also with problems related to the coming war. The work had to be divided between the two secret services, political and military, and their efforts had to be coordinated.

This had already been discussed in the autumn of 1934, when Hitler decided that the Abwehr must be reorganized. As we have seen, the head of the Abwehr at that time was Admiral Conrad Patzig, who had completely failed to grasp the implications of Hitler's rise to power. He saw no need to concern himself with the police, and he came into conflict with Heydrich because the latter was spying on members of the officer corps.

On January 2, 1935, Wilhelm Canaris became head of the

Abwehr. Nazi insiders knew that Heydrich had persuaded the Fuehrer to appoint Canaris. To Blomberg, the Reichswehr Minister, the move was an encroachment on his administrative authority. Furthermore, he did not like having to deal with a man who was able to approach Hitler directly, because of his relations with the SS. Blomberg also realized that Hitler's decision to place Himmler and Heydrich in Gestapo headquarters had deprived Goering of all real power and made him lose de facto control of the Gestapo. And now Himmler and Heydrich were also going to have a strong influence on the Abwehr. Blomberg considered it almost sacrilegious.

On January 17, Heydrich and Canaris came to an agreement that established the basis of collaboration between the political and military secret services. In December 1936, this collaboration was codified by a more detailed agreement that came to be known as the Ten Commandments, negotiated by Heydrich's assistant, Werner Best, and representatives of the Abwehr. It defined the areas in which each of the two services would have jurisdiction. The Gestapo would be concerned primarily with acts of treason, the Abwehr with military espionage in foreign countries.

Foreign diplomats, representatives of the press, businessmen, and foreigners held in suspicion would be under the surveillance of Heydrich and his men. The struggle against all enemies of the state, in Germany and abroad, was now Heydrich's responsibility. The Abwehr would assist him when necessary. The Reichswehr recognized that the activities of the SD extended beyond the borders of the Reich.

The increase in foreign operations required a corresponding increase in the personnel of the SD. Special groups were thoroughly trained in carrying out abductions, murders, coups d'état, and other kinds of plots. Heydrich reorganized his Department III in order to collaborate as well as possible with the Abwehr, in spite of the formal agreement marking off their respective fields of activity. This reorganization was on the model of the Abwehr, as is shown by the three sections that Department III now included:

Section III/1, foreign intelligence; that is, espionage in other countries. Heydrich sent abroad agents who used means other than the "classic" methods of the Abwehr. These means included death threats and other kinds of pressure.

Section III/2, counterespionage, or defense against foreign activities in Germany. This section had the function of protecting the authorities of the Reich, camouflaging the munitions industry, and neutralizing enemy agents sent into the country or recruited among Germans.

Section III/3, sabotage abroad. This was the most important section of Department III, capable of carrying out complex actions to place foreign governments or prominent foreign individuals in disadvantageous situations. Its agents were also trained to be ready for sabotage in war.

As head of Section III/3, Heydrich appointed Heinz Jost, a young lawyer and a fanatical Nazi who had joined the party in 1927. By 1933, he had become the police chief of Worms. After the Night of the Long Knives, he had joined the SS at Heydrich's request. However, relations between Heydrich and Jost did not always go smoothly, because Jost proved to be ruthlessly ambitious and "showed no gratitude to the man who had promoted him."[11]

Thus, at the beginning of 1935, Heydrich transformed his offices on Prinz Albrechtstrasse and Wilhelmstrasse into "fortresses of the revolution" that enabled him to deal with matters of foreign policy, both legally and illegally. Although he still remained in the background, he was in a position to shape world history. Canaris quickly realized that he was playing second fiddle to his former pupil. It was a situation that caused many difficulties, but never any open conflict.

It was at this time that Heydrich began to feel a need for a publication that would convey his own ideas, as well as the Fuehrer's, to the Nazi elite. He founded an SS newspaper called *Das Schwarze Korps* ("The Black Corps") and chose as its editor Gunther d'Alquen, son of an Essen businessman, formerly a leader of the Hitler Youth and now an SS officer. At first Heydrich thought that a printing of fifty thousand copies per issue would be enough, but soon, seeing that there was a greater demand than he had expected for his tirades against the Jews, Christians, Freemasons, and Bolsheviks, he increased the number of copies to nearly a hundred and ninety thousand, and

the number of pages from eight to twenty. (Two years later, in
1937, printings had risen to half a million copies, and at the
beginning of the war they were up to 750,000.)

Foreign diplomats and reporters in Germany read *Das
Schwarze Korps* for the insights it gave them into the powerful SS.
Heydrich knew he had an instrument by which he could serve the
Fuehrer's cause in Germany and abroad.

In the summer of 1935, he realized that open manifestations of
anti-Semitism would impair the propaganda advantages that
Hitler expected from the Olympic games to be held in Berlin the
following year. Fanatics had just broken the windows of Jewish
shops in Munich once again. In *Das Schwarze Korps* Heydrich
laid down the line to be followed for the time being: "The Jewish
question, one of the most serious problems facing our people,
will not be solved by terror in the streets."

He was already thinking of more effective methods. The Final
Solution would come later, at a better time and place, and in an
atmosphere of war.

The "Nazi Olympics"

Heydrich was a sports enthusiast. He therefore wanted to make
the Berlin Olympics of August 1936 an extraordinary event, as
much for himself as for the Reich.

Thomas Mann, winner of a Nobel Prize for literature, had fled
from Germany in 1933 and had been denouncing Hitler's Reich
ever since. Heydrich still regretted Mann's escape, and now,
while a new Olympic stadium was being built in Berlin for a
hundred thousand spectators and athletes from fifty-two countries, Mann's brother Heinrich, also a writer (author of *The Blue
Angel*, which became a famous film), attacked the coming Olympics: "Athletes who go to Berlin will be nothing but the gladi-
ators, prisoners, and buffoons of a dictator who thinks he is
already master of the world."[12]

The Nazis hoped to silence this and similar opposition to the
Berlin Olympic games by presenting them as a great demonstration of international solidarity in favor of peace and mutual understanding among nations. But many remembered that only two
years earlier the Nazis had murdered Engelbert Dollfuss, the

Austrian Chancellor; only one year earlier, in September 1935, the anti-Jewish Nuremberg Laws had gone into effect; on March 7, 1936, German troops had reoccupied the demilitarized zone of the Rhineland; since the beginning of the Spanish Civil War, in June 1936, the Luftwaffe had been fighting on the side of Franco's forces and transporting weapons to them.

In the United States, Spain, Holland, Norway, Sweden, France, and Britain there were public demands for a boycott of the 1936 Olympic games. Those "Nazi Olympics," as they were called, had only one purpose: to mask the Nazi dictatorship and its preparations for war. The Third Reich had used German sports as a political instrument from the beginning, and Heydrich himself was a member of the Olympic committee. He had worked to bring a large number of German athletes into the SS.

Hitler had ordered Heydrich to turn the Olympics into a Nazi festival and see to it that everything went smoothly. Heydrich and Goebbels worked out the strategy to be followed. The first step they took, long before the opening of the games, was to send the best German athletes as "goodwill ambassadors" to countries where criticism of the Nazi government was particularly strong. The famous boxer Max Schmeling, for example, was sent to America for this purpose.

During the games, newsstands were instructed to stop displaying *Der Stuermer*, the vile anti-Semitic sheet, and replace it with foreign newspapers and photographs of Hitler in civilian clothes. Plans were made to take national delegations to visit schools, factories, and social service institutions. Each time a group of foreign athletes arrived, they would be greeted with flowers and drumbeats by members of the Hitler Youth.

Heydrich ordered the most loyal and best-educated Nazi sports officials to come to Berlin from all over Germany. Wearing brand-new black uniforms and generously supplied with pocket money, they were to show the city to visiting female athletes. And male athletes would be given the same treatment by pretty young women who spoke their language. The goal was to leave all visiting foreigners deeply impressed by the friendly warmth of the welcome they had been given in Nazi Germany.

The opening of the 1936 Olympics in the new stadium was marked by a splendid ceremony. The Fuehrer of the Third Reich appeared with the President of the International Olympic Committee, the Belgian Count Henri de Baillet-Latour, and his German colleague Theodor Lewald. When the 4,269 athletes from 52 countries came into the stadium, they all gave the stiff-armed Nazi salute to Hitler.

It was not only members of foreign delegations who succumbed to the illusion that things had taken a turn for the better in Germany. Karl Diem, one of the organizers of the games, proudly pointed out that athletes of all races were taking part in the games on an equal footing. The world would have to recognize that there was no racial discrimination in Germany. The German women's fencing team had a Jewish member: Helene Meyer. The German men's hockey team also had its Jewish alibi: Rudi Ball. The Nuremberg Laws seemed to have been forgotten.

Pierre de Coubertin, the founder of the modern Olympics, who had worked energetically to prevent a boycott, was now convinced that his efforts had been justified: Hitler was sincere in his offers of peace and friendship.

No participant in the games saw an anti-Semitic sign or a concentration camp. During that period, the political prisoners who ordinarily worked on farms in striped uniforms were kept out of sight. Houses were adorned with swastika flags. There was nothing visible to suggest the slightest lack of harmony between the German people and their government.

The Olympic games were a triumph for Hitler, Goebbels's propagandists, and Heydrich's SD. The final ceremony, held at night, crowned their victory. The crowd was overawed when more than fifty gigantic searchlights were turned on around the stadium, creating the illusion of a luminous dome above it.

The triumph was shared by the German athletes themselves: they won thirty-three gold medals, and nine more medals overall than their American competitors.

"Our success in the Olympics has shown that the year 1933 also marked the beginning of a new era for German sports," Heydrich told the German fencing team.

In their elegant black uniforms and high, shiny, boots, with the death's-head emblem on their caps, the SS had given a convincing performance in their role as guardians of world peace. No one suspected then that three years later they would be engaged

in mass murder. If they were questioned about German concentration camps, they answered calmly, in accordance with
Heydrich's instructions, "Yes, we have concentration camps, but
only for Communists and criminals." And that reply was generally accepted.

Heydrich was one of the few who already knew the ultimate
aim of that Olympic operetta. As head of the SD, he was responsible for maintaining absolute secrecy around German rearmament. In 1936, he had the special assignment of taking all
necessary measures to make sure that the receptions given by
Hitler, Goering, and Goebbels to celebrate the Olympic games
were isolated from the reality of the Third Reich.

Hitler was working to build a solid Anglo-German friendship.
He regarded it as a necessary condition for the acceleration of
German rearmament, and he hoped it would prevent British military intervention in the coming war. A number of key men in
British politics were invited to Berlin for the Olympics. Among
them was Sir Robert Vansittart, Permanent Undersecretary of
State for Foreign Affairs. A magnificent reception in his honor
was held in the new Reich Chancellery. One of the other guests
was the Duke of Hamilton, a friend of the royal family. Rudolf
Hess, who favored a preeminent position for British power in the
world, was introduced to the Duke and tried to win his friendship. Five years later, when Hess made his wartime flight to
Scotland, he landed near the Duke's home and asked to be taken
to him.

Goering also had his guest of honor—Lord Londonderry, for
whom he gave an Anglo-German hunting party at his estate forty
miles from Berlin. In the evening, after the hunt, Goering turned
the conversation to the subject of Germany's efforts to build an
air force and tried to convince his British listeners that the Reich
wanted only enough air power to protect itself from an attack by
the Soviet Union.

So that the Italian friends of the Reich would not feel slighted,
Goebbels gave an Italian night on Peacock Island, near Berlin.
Prominent members of Berlin society mingled with Goebbels's
Fascist guests in an elegant fete lighted by Chinese lanterns.

Ribbentrop did his part to win friends for Germany by giving a
garden party at his house in Dahlem, one of Berlin's finest resi-

dential districts. He paid special attention to his British guests, who already knew him by reputation: his success in the Anglo-German naval agreement of June 18, 1935, had shown that he could be a shrewd negotiator.

Alfred Rosenberg, head of the Nazi party's Foreign Policy Office and editor of the party newspaper, the *Voelkischer Beobachter*, did what he could to honor the most prominent foreigners. At each reception he became the central figure around whom the others gathered, because they all wanted to be favorably mentioned in such an influential newspaper as the *Voelkischer Beobachter*. Rosenberg was regarded as the party's official ideologue and as a strong advocate of maintaining the power of the British Commonwealth and destroying the Soviet Union. To him, the Olympic games were an early skirmish in the battle that the West would have to fight and win against bolshevism.

But all those diplomatic and propagandistic efforts did not prevent a certain anxiety from arising within the German government after the Olympics. Sir Robert Vansittart was reported to have said that a new war was inevitable, that the Third Reich was obviously in the midst of a formidable rearmament, and that the war would have incalculable consequences because it would soon spread far beyond the borders of the countries first involved in it.

Heydrich recorded these prophetic statements by Vansittart in the SD files. Paul Schmidt, the Reich's leading interpreter, later expressed a similar view: "The next war will not be limited by national boundaries. Fronts will be formed within each people, because it will not be a war of nations, but of conflicting views of the world."[13]

Still hoping to achieve an agreement with Britain that would prevent her entry into the war, Hitler ordered Ribbentrop, the new German ambassador to London, to intensify the policy of friendship pursued during the Olympics. But it was an effort doomed to failure because the British realized that the great spectacle had been staged only to divert the world's attention from German rearmament.

Heydrich had another plan in mind: in two years there would be another athletic competition in the Berlin stadium, this time between a European team and an American one. The political symbolism would be clear: European solidarity against America.

But the Spanish Civil War and Germany's annexation of Austria prevented this plan from being carried out.

Thirty years later, I questioned Werner March, one of the builders of the Berlin Olympic stadium, about what the architects, the organizers of the games, and the whole German people had been thinking when they enthusiastically took part in the great Hitlerian illusion. "The Olympic games? You mean the Heydrich games!" he said. "The architects, the athletes, and the German people believed in peace. Only after the games were under way did we clearly realize that we had been shamefully deceived."[14]

When I asked March what he meant by calling the Olympic games the "Heydrich games," he replied that he had not invented the expression: it had first been used by an official of a German sports organization who often conferred with Heydrich during preparations for the Olympics. Everyone knew that Heydrich also had a say in the design of the stadium. "Heydrich knew a great deal about staging spectacles, but nothing about architecture. He was presumptuous and overbearing. It was as if we were building the stadium for his personal use."

As head of the secret police, Heydrich was better able than anyone else to interpret and transmit the Fuehrer's wishes. With his skill in manipulating individuals, groups, and institutions, he turned the 1936 Olympics into a vast enterprise of dissimulation.

Not all Germans were taken in by it, however. In Berlin, anti-Nazis tried to open the eyes of the foreign athletes and tourists. Thousands of leaflets addressed to them were distributed in the streets at night, especially in the vicinity of the stadium. One of those leaflets, published by "the free unions, Social Democrats, and Communists of Berlin," contained the following:

For the opening of the Olympic games, new trials directed against unions and Social Democrat, Communist, and Catholic workers have begun. Heavy prison and concentration camp sentences [are imposed on those] who have dared to fight for the right to be free and improve their living conditions. . . . Demand that you be allowed to visit prisons and concentration camps so that you can talk with people who have taken a stand for freedom and are now being tortured and martyred because they fought for peace, freedom, justice, and their own welfare.[15]

It came as no surprise to Heydrich that there were people in Berlin who opposed the Nazis, but it enraged him to know that they were still able to express their opposition. Holding up one of the leaflets, he shouted to a group of Gestapo men gathered at headquarters on Prinz-Albrechtstrasse, "Only the Jews are capable of turning out such lies! And the Jews smuggled these filthy sheets into the Reich! We'll make them pay for that!"[16]

Heydrich was already secretly developing his plans for annihilating the Jews. The process of psychological preparation for that project was still far from being completed, and the SD and the Gestapo did not yet have the necessary means at their disposal. The Jews and the world in general did not yet suspect that the Reich intended to eliminate all "non-Aryans" in Europe. For the moment, the Nazis wanted to avoid hostile reactions from the colonial peoples and the Japanese allies of the Reich.

The Wilhelmstrasse Center of Criminal Operations

In April 1934, Heydrich had gone to Berlin from Munich to take over offices at Gestapo headquarters on Prinz-Albrechtstrasse and SD headquarters on Wilhelmstrasse. This move enabled him to put into practice a number of projects that had been only theoretical possibilities while he was in Munich. Since ordinary government functionaries could not be expected to commit murders, acts of sabotage, and illegal arrests, such things had to be done by a special group composed of completely reliable people always ready to accomplish any mission assigned to them, using whatever means were necessary.

As soon as Hitler had come to power, preparations for war had begun in earnest, and the SD had been given a new field of activity. From then on, it had little concern with individual arrests, seizing illegal publications, and crushing Communist cells; the Gestapo took care of all that. The SD had great, historically important missions to fulfill, the kind of missions that Heydrich had been dreaming of for years.

"The Security Service [SD] is concerned only with great matters of worldwide scope," Himmler said in a speech to a group of

Wehrmacht officers in January 1937.[17] (The Reichswehr had become the Wehrmacht in September 1935.) He told them that Switzerland and Holland had been lost to Germany for centuries, and that Austria was not part of Germany because in the past no one had waged the necessary propaganda campaign or done the work of consolidating national sentiment. Wehrmacht officers, he said, must know the full extent of the Comintern's secret plans, the influence exerted by the churches and the Jews, and the identities of people in other countries who stirred up public opinion against the German nation. "Such are the things that are studied scientifically here [at SD headquarters], in the manner of a military General Staff—and that comparison is exact. These studies will continue for many years. . . . In most cases we are still only at the beginning."[18]

Heydrich also reigned over Gestapo headquarters, but it was at SD headquarters on Wilhelmstrasse that he worked to achieve his great objectives. He envisaged transforming the Nazi state into an SS state in which the SS would control every major aspect of German domestic and foreign policy, and he continued to elaborate his plans for eliminating all adversaries of the Reich, with the ultimate aim of enabling Germany to conquer greater "living space" and dominate Europe.

The SD also had a special department whose function was to carry out such operations as the Reichstag fire, the purge of 1934, and the murder of Formis. The offices on Wilhelmstrasse had a staff of two hundred people, nearly all of them university graduates: jurists, linguists, economists, propagandists, historians, experts in various scientific fields (physics, chemistry, medicine), and specialists in military matters, sports, graphic arts, and religions, including Judaism. And there were specialists in activities that were the exclusive province of the SD: arson, forgery, abduction, murder. Finally, the SD formed armed groups that would be at Hitler's disposal as soon as war began. These "operational groups" would specialize in massive arrests and killings of the Jews and intelligentsia of conquered countries.

Heydrich, like all members of his staff, wore the black SS uniform with a red armband bearing a black swastika on a white background. Whenever the Fuhrer appeared in public, he was accompanied by SS men, including Sepp Dietrich, the commander of his bodyguard. Even Rudolf Hess and Martin Bormann wore the SS uniform on many occasions.

After the Night of the Long Knives, it was clear to informed observers that of all Hitler's henchmen Heydrich was the one most to be feared. Ernst Hanfstaengl, who for many years was Hitler's foreign press chief, said to me in a postwar interview:

> Heydrich openly showed contempt for everyone who rose above the mass of Nazi leaders. He simply regarded them as opportunists who were being cynically used by Hitler. To him, they were only pawns. Many of the Nazi leaders overestimated their influence on Hitler—Ernst Roehm was an outstanding example of that. But Heydrich always knew what his Fuehrer was thinking. It was ultimately the judgment of his SD that decided questions of promotion in the state and the armed forces, even when appearances were saved and everything seemed to happen only by Hitler's will.

Himmler let Heydrich take responsibility for getting rid of any "pawns" that became bothersome. Heydrich always had information that could be used against such people: for years he had been keeping secret dossiers, locked in his personal safe, on everyone who held a position of any importance in the Third Reich.

With Hitler, said Hanfstaengl, Himmler was as servile as Goebbels, but Heydrich only pretended to be servile. He was too intelligent to let himself be manipulated. Although he played the part of the devoted servant, it was actually he who manipulated Himmler.

Hanfstaengl also said that the temple of national socialism rested on three pillars: the party, the SS, and the SD. In 1935, the party functioned as an administrative and propagandistic organization that laid down the line to be followed by the state but was controlled by the SS. The SS had a secret General Staff, the SD, headed by Heydrich. Himmler had chosen Heydrich because he saw in him the qualities he needed: intelligence, a talent for intrigue, quick understanding, courage, strength of will, and total ruthlessness in carrying out a decision once it had been made.

The SD had spread its network of agents all over Germany. In 1935, it had about a thousand full-time employees, plus twenty

thousand part-time agents; by 1938 those numbers had increased
to three thousand and fifty thousand, respectively. That army of
SD collaborators was not Heydrich's only source of information,
however: he also had the Gestapo and the many SS members who
held important posts in the party and the state.

In 1935, to take only the case of Berlin, Heydrich already had
files on a hundred thousand of the city's residents, primarily
Communists, Social Democrats, Christians, Freemasons, Jews,
and "reactionaries." Among the "reactionaries" were aristocrats
whose spouses were either Jewish or politically suspect. The files
contained all sorts of information, down to such details as
whether or not the subject decorated his windows during Nazi
holidays.

Although they held no political office, Himmler and Heydrich
had gained decisive power in the Third Reich. There were few
political and military leaders whom they could not oust whenever
they chose—with Hitler's consent, of course. No single government ministry had a clear overall idea of how the state was being
transformed and how preparations were being made for war, but
the SD was kept fully informed of everything; it acted according
to secret directives from Hitler.

Industry, the army, and the universities were in a state of euphoria induced by propaganda: the Versailles Treaty had been
abolished, "parliamentary anarchy" was a thing of the past, Germany had become a power to be reckoned with in international
politics. Hitler's government had reinstituted military conscription on March 16, 1935. His supporters believed that he
was going to satisfy German territorial demands. What did it matter that opposition political leaders had either fled the country or
were in concentration camps, and that the Jews were victims of a
systematic discrimination enacted into law on September 15,
1935? To business and professional people, the exclusion of Jews
from large areas of the economy had at least a practical advantage: fewer competitors. No one knew that the driving force behind that new policy was the SS. Some Germans dreaded its
influence but, at the same time, profited from the results of its
activities. The Fuehrer handed out money and property to old
and new aristocrats. The feudal caste of the Third Reich saw him
as the new Kaiser.

Himmler was courted by people who knew it was advantageous

to be on good terms with him. He gave high ranks in his SS to all the great dignitaries of the Third Reich, thus constituting what would later be called his "circle of friends."

The SD's Economic Experts

Since he was concerned with everything related to preparing Germany for total war, Heydrich extended his SD into the realm of the economy. To head that new branch he chose Otto Ohlendorf, a peasant's son who had studied political economy and law, and had soon found the path that led him into the SS. At the Kiel Institute of World Economy, he had specialized in the transformation of the German economy in the event of war.

In his work for the SD, Ohlendorf received his instructions directly from Heydrich, who had a perfect understanding of the Fuehrer's wishes. Heydrich and Ohlendorf both knew that the output of German industry had to be rapidly increased to the point where it would enable Hitler to achieve his political and military objectives before other countries could build up superior forces to oppose him. They were guided by three basic Nazi ideas:

1. All the laws and activities of the Third Reich were governed by racial doctrine. This meant that the German economy had to be "Aryanized" and that its various branches had to be directed by Nazis of proven loyalty and ability.

2. The Fuehrer's plans for conquering "living space" in Europe had to be carried out within a relatively short time, while he was still at the peak of his physical and mental condition.

3. The German economy had to be adapted to producing the weapons Hitler would need for his lightning war in different parts of Europe.

By the end of 1937, munitions production had made such progress that Hitler was able to tell his generals that in the following year he would begin taking action to achieve his goals of conquest. His diplomatic moves and propaganda campaigns with regard to Austria and Czechoslovakia clearly show that he was following a well-established plan. And he was firmly resolved to invade Poland in the near future, believing that he could succeed so rapidly that France and Britain would decide against trying to defend a country that had already been conquered.

In their efforts to shape the German economy into an instrument of Hitler's planned aggression, Heydrich's economic experts had to resolve difficulties that arose not only from differences of opinion but also from rivalries among industrialists, and they dealt with such diverse matters as agricultural production, utilization of manpower, manufacturers' associations, allocation of raw materials, technical institutes, construction of housing, bringing women into the work force, and education.

Within the framework of preparation for a war of expansion, Heydrich himself was concerned primarily with the economic, political, and ethnic transformation of conquered territories and the ways in which their populations would be treated. He referred to his aims as "the solution of the Czech problem," "the solution of the Polish problem," and "the solution of the Russian problem." One of his basic principles was that members of the dominant social class in each conquered country had to be eliminated, by either killing them or sending them to concentration camps. He and his experts also developed plans for annihilating other large parts of those populations by means of famine, forced labor, deliberately induced epidemics, and the use of lethal chemicals. They saw the coming war as an opportunity to rid Europe of "inferior elements." By using the most efficient means of achieving that purpose, they would be sparing precious German blood.

The Jewish Question

The flood of reports sent to SD headquarters by Heydrich's agents all over Germany was so great that the offices on Wilhelmstrasse would have been submerged if more offices had not been set up in other buildings, often houses that had been confiscated from Jews.

Department II of the SD had the task of keeping records on adversaries of the Nazi state and maintaining surveillance of those who were not already in concentration camps. "Defensive measures" were taken as soon as Heydrich gave the word: the person involved was immediately arrested and taken to the nearest camp. Catholic and Protestant clergymen were automatically under suspicion because, through their sermons, they had the opportunity to criticize the regime, directly or indirectly. Freemasons were also suspect, especially those who had attained high rank in their lodges, and close watch was kept on writers and artists of all kinds.

But it was the Jews who received the SD's most careful attention. Heydrich had divided them into several categories: assimilated Jews, Eastern Jews (immigrants from countries east of Germany), Orthodox Jews, Zionists, and Jews who had fought in the World War.

In 1935, Heydrich began greatly increasing his activities against the Jews, regarding them as the most important enemy within Germany. According to the plan adopted by Hitler, Himmler, and Heydrich, the "solution of the Jewish problem" would take place in several stages, beginning with a census of the Jewish population in order to establish a sharp demarcation between Germans and Jews. During this period, Jews would still be allowed to emigrate. Eastern Jews and the "lower levels" of other categories would be expelled from Germany by force, preferably to countries of Western Europe. The French historian Rita Thalmann has stated that the Nazis expected the emigration and expulsion of Jews to stir up anti-Semitism in the countries where they took refuge.

Department II had special sections for assimilated Jews (Section II/112–1), Orthodox Jews (Section II/112–2), and Zionists (Section II/112–3). A fanatical anti-Semite named Adolf Eichmann began working at SD headquarters in 1935 and soon became an adviser on Zionist matters.

In late 1937, as Hitler prepared to begin his territorial expansion the following year, Heydrich strengthened his anti-Jewish apparatus and set up the framework of the future extermination program. Documents from this time show that he instructed the director of Section II/112 to take anti-Jewish measures devised in accordance with a "scientific system." From a report by that director, dated October 5, 1937, we know that twelve people in his section were working primarily on the Jewish question. Functionaries in other sections were doing the same. The number of people engaged in such work all over Germany has been estimated at

four hundred, not including the three thousand part-time agents
who acted as informers and supplied information to those bu-
reaucrats of racism.

In his report on the activities and organization of Section
II/112, its director wrote, "The special file of Section II/112 is up
to date with regard to new entries. This was confirmed by SS
Hauptsturmfuehrer Hartmann after his inspection." Elsewhere,
this report shows that the Gestapo and the SD collaborated on the
census of Jews. Thousands of documents were exchanged between the two headquarters as the anti-Jewish organization was
steadily extended and developed. The report also shows that specialists on the Jewish question were given military and athletic
training. High officials, such as SS Oberscharfuehrer Dannecker
(who later persecuted the Jews in France), SS Scharfuehrer
Eisenmenger, and SS Unterscharfuehrer Hagelmann, regularly
took fencing lessons. This was Heydrich's favorite sport, and he
wanted future soldiers in the war of extermination to be good
fencers.

The same report states that "there are no Jewish informers
available in the upper and lower sections," but there was an
informer in Palestine: a certain "Dr. R." was already in
Jerusalem. The SD took an active part in the Gestapo's operations and supplied information to the party and the state. According to the report, SS Untersturmfuehrer Wisliceny attended the
twentieth Zionist congress in Zurich from July 30 to August 12,
1937. On September 26, Hauptscharfuehrer Eichmann left for
Palestine.

Officials of the anti-Jewish section engaged in diverse activities. They spied on members of Mussolini's entourage during
his visit to Germany; they maintained close and frequent contacts
with other state offices, including the Reich Bureau of Genealogi-
cal Research and the Race and Settlement Bureau; they collaborated with *Das Schwarze Korps;* they furnished material to the
Propaganda Ministry for its exposition, "The Eternal Jew," which
was to take place in Munich.

Heydrich had not yet finished constructing his instrument of
persecution and annihilation. His Jewish file was still in-
complete, and he had to broaden his network of spies and informers. The anti-Jewish section counted on the support and

collaboration of the whole SD. Training of its leaders, which was done mainly at the SD school in Bernau, where Dannecker and Eichmann taught courses, had only just begun.

On January 19, 1937, Heydrich sent an order to all departments and sections of the SD: every six months, beginning February 15, they were to draw up detailed reports on all their activities, among which were naturally included surveillance of hotels, embassies, legations, and commercial representatives.

A report dated August 28, 1937, subtitled "Struggle against Jewry," reveals that the entire SD was using a wide variety of means to attack Jews in all economic, cultural, and social areas. Because the SD wanted as much information as possible on all eminent Jews, including those living abroad, the Jewish press was regularly monitored; Jewish organizations were under surveillance by Heydrich's agents; spies attended all Jewish meetings. SD agents were particularly interested in Jews who tried to disseminate "their concepts" among non-Jews. "To a large extent, these concepts correspond to the Jewish mentality," says the report of August 28.

It is clear that by 1937 the SD was seriously working on plans for a total "settling of accounts" with the Jews in Germany and other countries.

The Nerve Center of the Third Reich

The experts who worked for Heydrich's SD had to prove specialized knowledge in at least one technical field before being accepted. Physical characteristics were also taken into account: preference was given to men with blond hair and a height of at least 1.7 meters (5 feet 7 inches), and a special committee examined the degree to which their appearance was "Aryan." Candidates were first accepted on a trial basis.

"Honorary collaborators" (part-time agents) also had to prove their competence. They worked everywhere, from factories to universities and government ministries. Their zeal in informing on their colleagues entitled them to be regarded as "political soldiers."

Scientists working for the SD reported on all the latest developments in science and technology.

SD headquarters was the nerve center of the Third Reich.

Heydrich's training as a naval officer enabled him to follow the growth of the munitions industry and the results of the research institute created to aid it. He was especially interested in metallurgy, torpedoes, submarines, aircraft engines, and rockets. (An experimental rocket program had been under way since 1931 in the Berlin suburb of Kummersdorf.)

Hitler now knew that he had the German people behind him. In 1933, and even in 1934, he had felt it necessary to "condition" them by elections and plebiscites, but there was no longer any need for that. His achievements, particularly the elimination of unemployment, had won him the support of the masses. He had a formidable army at his disposal. Germany had regained her place as a great nation.

As head of the secret service of that powerful state, Heydrich had a broad range of responsibilities. Besides the routine work of the SD, the Gestapo, and the criminal police, which he personally directed, his field of action extended to people who had become troublesome for one reason or another and had to be not only removed from their posts but also silenced forever. Such operations did not always succeed. In February 1937, Ernst Hanfstaengl, a longtime friend of Hitler and Goering, was told to go to Spain in a special plane. When the plane was flying at high altitude, the pilot pretended to have run into a storm and urged his passenger to jump out with his parachute. Hanfstaengl refused, knowing very well that the parachute would not open. Once the plane landed near Leipzig, Hanfstaengl was able to escape to Switzerland, by way of Munich. After the war, members of Goering's entourage claimed that the incident had been only a practical joke—a rather macabre one, considering that Hanfstaengl had never made a parachute jump.

In 1970, Hanfstaengl told me that Heydrich had felt it was necessary to kill him because he knew nearly all of Hitler's plans and might leave Germany when war became imminent. Before the plane ride, the SD had supplied Hanfstaengl with false papers, supposedly to enable him to pass through the Republican lines in Spain. "If I had jumped," he said, "the newspapers would have reported the next day that I had died while performing a mission for the Fuehrer. With the false papers on me, and the unopened parachute, it would have been a perfectly camouflaged murder. Everyone would have believed I had been on my way to Spain."

The Spanish Civil War posed problems of secrecy and espionage that came under Heydrich's authority. While German fliers were testing their planes and weapons in Spain, Heydrich was able to study the fighting methods of the Republicans and the international brigades, one of which was commanded by Heinrich Rau, a German Communist. In 1936, a large number of Heydrich's agents went to Spain; it was in their reports that he first came upon the term *fifth column*. Spain gave his agents valuable experience in warfare, propaganda, and provocations. He planned to have them trained to serve as a German fifth column in other countries.

In the late nineteenth century, the Pan-German movement had arisen in Germany and Austria. Its goal had been to unite all German-speaking peoples, and it had supported the idea of the "drive to the East," following the example of the eleventh-century Teutonic Knights. It had soon developed its own terminology: "lands of the German people in the East," "Germans abroad," "frontier Germans," "Germanized," "assimilable foreigners," "unassimilable foreigners." "Aryans" who did not speak German could be assimilated, but not "non-Aryans." The term *anti-Semitism* was used only in relation to the Jews, since the Arabs had to be regarded as allies, at least for the time being.

Himmler and Heydrich believed that the German minorities in other countries were of great importance to the Third Reich and its plans for expansion. They would compose the fifth column, providing propagandists, spies, military and paramilitary units, and recruits for the Waffen SS. Heydrich therefore extended his network of agents to Germans in the Baltic States, the Soviet Union, Bolivia, Czechoslovakia, Yugoslavia, and, of course, the Fuehrer's native country, Austria.

Those minorities would also provide shock troops who would attack the Jews, at first by propaganda, then by physical violence.

With the help of Germans in other countries, the Reich's natural allies Britain and Italy, anti-Semites all over the world, and a vigorous campaign of anti-Communist propaganda, Himmler and Heydrich believed they could create a climate favorable to a German conquest of Europe. In their view, the Spanish Civil War had already forced conservatives in all countries to choose between fascism and communism, and in the coming years the European bourgeoisie, like the German bourgeoisie in 1933, would have to choose between national socialism and communism.

Meanwhile, there were still critics of the Nazi regime to be silenced. Among them was Martin Niemoeller, a former submarine commander who had become a Protestant pastor and was now preaching peace and freedom in his sermons. He was arrested and charged with inciting his congregation to resistance against the state. But the Nazi leaders soon realized that the case could create great difficulties for them in other countries. If they had really wanted Niemoeller to be convicted, the SD would have fabricated such convicing evidence that even the most unbiased judge would have given him a severe sentence. Foreseeing that a conviction would turn the Christian world even more strongly against him, Hitler preferred a verdict that could support the claim that German courts were impartial: Niemoeller was acquitted. But despite his acquittal, he was kept in a concentration camp until the end of the war.

The time was not yet ripe for a massive persecution of Catholics. Mussolini, because of his relationship with the Italian royal family, would have protested. But to Heydrich the doctrine of racial equality propagated by the churches was as dangerous as Marxism.

Seen from the outside, the Third Reich seemed calm in 1937, but that was only a deceptive appearance. The SD was working more zealously than ever. In his gigantic witches' cauldron, Heydrich continued to brew the poisons that would rid the Reich of its enemies.

The term *witches' cauldron* is appropriate: Heydrich, like Himmler, was drawn to the concept of witchcraft because witches and sorcerers rejected established religions and found new ways of intimidating people by using supernatural forces. After the war, one of Heydrich's collaborators, Dr. Werner Best, told the Israeli historian Shlomo Aronson that Heydrich had been greatly pleased to discover a seventeenth-century witch among Himmler's ancestors. This is confirmed by a letter from Heydrich to Himmler, dated January 9, 1939, now in the Berlin Document Center.

Best contributed ingredients of his own to the witches' cauldron. His specialty was describing the SD's criminal acts in a neutral administrative style that gave them a semblance of legality. After the war, he tried to present Himmler as having been a kind of romantic who wanted only to revive "the Germanic heritage" and was obsessed with such superstitions as astrology and graphology.

Heydrich adopted some of Himmler's strange ideas. He and the other SS leaders, including Best, went on the annual nocturnal pilgrimage to the grave of the tenth-century Emperor known as Henry the Fowler, at Quedlinburg. The pilgrims considered themselves a new Germanic elite, the "Germanic nobility of the Nordic race." Each of them tried to find some kinship between himself and an Emperor, a Duke, or a hero of Germany's past. Best liked to think that he was descended from Arminius, chief of the Cherusci, an ancient German tribe, as Carlo Schmid has reported to the author. (While he was an administrative official in occupied France, Schmid maintained close relations with Best, who confided some of his dreams and desires to him.)

But the SD was not staffed primarily by romantic, superstitious mystics. Most of the men in it were desperadoes working with ruthless efficiency to put their racist ideas into practice. For them, esoteric doctrines were only tools. Out of the thirty thousand occultists, clairvoyants, and fortune-tellers in Germany, Heydrich had only a few hundred arrested: those who foretold a future that was not to the liking of the Nazi leaders. There were some who refused to placed their "art" in the service of the Nazi state. The astrologer Bruno Noack died in a concentration camp because he had predicted an early death for Heydrich.

6

A Shake-up in the Wehrmacht and the Beginning of the War

The Fritsch-Blomberg Affair

In late 1937, Field Marshal von Blomberg, the Minister of War, and General von Fritsch, Commander in Chief of the army, had not yet become fully aware of the harsh realities of Nazism. They both expected to take part in decisions that would determine Germany's fate. At a conference with Hitler on November 5, they criticized his plans for conquest. The SD immediately began looking into the private lives of these two eminent soldiers. In his safe, Heydrich had dossiers on them that could now be expanded.

Fritsch and Blomberg noticed a considerable increase in the number of men shadowing them. They unsuspectingly interpreted it as an additional security measure.

On January 12, 1938, the evening newspapers and the Berlin radio reported that Field Marshal von Blomberg had married Margarete Gruhn, with Hitler and Goering as witnesses. The announcement surprised nearly everyone, including Colonel Alfred Jodl, head of the Home Defense Department, who wrote in his diary, "The Marshal has married Fräulein Gruhn quite unexpectedly." Two weeks later he wrote, "On January 26 at noon, after asking me for my word of honor not to repeat it, General Keitel told me that the Marshal has been dismissed; he is leaving today."

This news spread rapidly because it seemed so momentous that

175

many of those who learned it could not keep the promise of secrecy they had given. It became known that a few days after
attending Blomberg's wedding the Fuehrer summoned him and
asked him to resign, for the sake of the Wehrmacht's honor, because documents had been discovered that showed that his wife
had been registered as a prostitute in several small towns. Blomberg vehemently replied that the charge against her was nothing
but baseless slander. Hitler remained adamant. He added that
the criminal police had photographs showing her in indecent situations. Blomberg asked to see them, and Hitler promised to have
them shown to him. But neither he nor his wife was ever able to
see those photographs. "It was all a machination by Heydrich,
and he must have been acting on orders from Hitler," Blomberg's
widow said to me in 1970.

At about this same time, General von Fritsch was also summoned to the Reich Chancellery, where Hitler greeted him very
coldly. He had decided, he said, to relieve Fritsch of his command because the criminal police had documents and trustworthy
testimony proving that he had homosexual tendencies. Like
Blomberg, Fritsch vehemently denied the charge, and again the
Fuehrer was adamant: Fritsch had to resign, but he would be
allowed to defend himself before a court of honor presided over
by Goering.

On February 4, 1938, came the official announcement: Blomberg and Fritsch had resigned "for reasons of health." That same
day, Hitler also announced that he was creating the High Command of the Armed Forces (Oberkommando der Wehrmacht, or
OKW), which would supersede the War Ministry. "From now
on," he said, "I personally take command of the armed forces."

In political and military circles everyone speculated on what
had happened. Not only Hitler's enemies but also his friends in
Rome, Budapest, and Sofia waited for an explanation of these
mysteries.

Those best informed believed that, with German rearmament
nearly completed, Hitler was about to make far-reaching decisions in foreign policy and wanted to remove men of limited ability from the key posts they had held till now. After dismissing
Fritsch and Blomberg, Hitler also dismissed some of their friends
and supporters, and this opened up new possibilities of promotion to their ambitious subordinates.

The shake-up of January 26, 1938, has become known as the Fritsch-Blomberg affair. It shows all the marks of a Nazi provocation, and once again only one man was capable of staging it: Reinhard Heydrich, chief of the SD.

What was behind that conspiracy against two high-ranking officers?

Heydrich routinely gathered information on all important political and military figures. When it was learned that Field Marshal von Blomberg, fifty-eight, was closely involved with a young woman of twenty-six, Margarete Gruhn, SD agents began carefully noting all his visits to her, and Heydrich soon had a complete report on all her relatives, friends, and acquaintances.

At the beginning of December 1937, Goering told Blomberg that he was willing to intercede with Hitler for him if he wanted to marry his mistress. In mid-December, the Fuehrer summoned Blomberg, gave him a friendly reception, congratulated him on his decision to marry, and said that he and Goering would be witnesses at the wedding. It would be advisable, he added, to have the wedding soon, no later than January, to put an end to the ridiculous gossip that had begun to circulate. Blomberg explained that the gossip had arisen only because his fiancée was of "modest origin": her father was a gardener and her mother ran a massage parlor. Hitler showed great understanding and sympathy; no one was a saint, he said, and he himself was of "modest origin."[1]

When he attended the wedding on January 12, Hitler seemed to be in an excellent mood, and he expressed satisfaction at seeing a Field Marshal marry a young woman of the people. After the reception, the newlyweds left on a honeymoon trip that took them to Leipzig and Dresden. It was in Dresden that they first learned of the scandal that had already shaken Berlin: Frau von Blomberg's "past" had been discovered.

Before Blomberg was summoned for his interview with Hitler, General Wilhelm Keitel, whose son was engaged to Blomberg's daughter by a previous marriage, was confidentially informed that Blomberg was in a very difficult situation. Curt Hellmuth Mueller, an official of the criminal police, had seen a vice-squad report on Margarete Gruhn, as well as photographs of her with a young man in which both of them were naked.

Such a discovery would normally have been transmitted imme-

diately to either the SD or the Gestapo, but Arthur Nebe, head of
the criminal police, who was under Heydrich's command, over-
stepped his authority and placed the potentially explosive dossier
on the desk of Count Wolf von Helldorf, the Berlin police chief.
Nebe and Helldorf then passed it on to Goering, again bypassing
Heydrich.

One explanation of this, put forward after the war, is that Nebe
and Helldorf did not want Heydrich to see the dossier because
they were afraid he might use it as the basis of an intrigue against
the Wehrmacht. It would be hard to imagine a less plausible
explanation. The two policemen knew very well that as soon as
Goering learned about the alleged scandal he would go straight to
the Fuehrer and report it to him. If there was one man who cov-
eted Blomberg's post as War Minister, it was Hermann Goering.
But even if that had not been the case, he would have had no
choice but to inform Hitler. Nebe and Helldorf, Heydrich's subordinates, would not have bypassed him on their own initiative.
Since they went directly to Goering, we must assume that
Heydrich had instructed them to do so, wanting to avoid the suspicion that the scandal involving Blomberg had been contrived by
the SD.

Although Blomberg was his friend and the father of his son's
fiancée, General Keitel saw his marriage to a woman with a dis-
graceful past as a violation of the military code of honor. He
proved his loyalty to the Fuehrer by telling him everything he
knew about the matter. Hitler thanked him for his frankness and
assured him that he would dismiss Blomberg. He would have to
take over the Wehrmacht himself, he said, and when he reorganized it he would not forget a General who had shown such
fidelity.

From the beginning, there were many skeptics who suspected
that Blomberg's downfall had been the result of a deliberate maneuver to discredit him. Propagandists countered these suspicions by depicting the Fueherer as having been taken completely
by surprise, and claiming that there had been tears in his eyes as
he looked over the documentary evidence against Blomberg's
wife. But the suspicions remained.

As for General Keitel, he was described by the propagandists
as having been motivated only by his deep patriotism when he

denounced Blomberg to the Fuehrer. His display of loyalty soon bore fruit. When Hitler created the OKW, with himself as Supreme Commander, he made Keitel his Chief of Staff. He promoted him to Field Marshal in 1940, and in 1943, gave him an estate worth 740,000 marks. Since Keitel never dared to express an opinion that differed even slightly from the Fuehrer's, he came to be called "General Yes-Yes," and then "Marshal Yes-Yes."

Blomberg's dismissal, officially announced on February 4, 1938, was followed by another announcement: "The Fuehrer and Reich Chancellor has elevated the Commander in Chief of the Luftwaffe, General Hermann Goering, to the rank of Field Marshal."

This was not the only change that took place in the aftermath of Blomberg's downfall. Baron Konstantin von Neurath, the Foreign Minister, was replaced by Joachim von Ribbentrop. The German ambassadors to Italy, Japan, and Austria were called back to Germany. A short time earlier, Hjalmar Schacht, the Minister of Economics, resigned; he was succeeded by Goebbels's friend Walther Funk, a journalist who specialized in economic matters and had been an official of the Propaganda Ministry.

Unfortunately, there are still historians who maintain that the Fritsch-Blomberg affair happened only by chance, but that once it had happened, Hitler cleverly took advantage of it to reorganize the Reich and thus seal Germany's fate. This view is supported by the testimony of witnesses who claimed that Hitler was astonished when he learned of the Blomberg scandal. And then there is the friendly letter that Hitler wrote to Blomberg after the scandal, expressing gratitude for the services he had rendered during "five years of reconstructing our nation and its Wehrmacht."

Other witnesses, such as Erich Schultze, a friend and confidant of Heydrich, have said that although Heydrich had been keeping Blomberg under surveillance as a matter of routine, he, too, was surprised by the scandal, because he had known nothing about Margarete Gruhn's "past" or the existence of the compromising photographs. Schultze's testimony, given after the war, contains one detail that lends it a semblance of credibility. According to his story, in December 1937, he sent a note to his

maid, who lived on Eisenacherstrasse, in the same building as
Margarete Gruhn. A few days later, he met Heydrich, who gave
him a suspicious look and said, "What business do you have on
Eisenacherstrasse? Are you involved with Blomberg's mistress?"
And that, still according to Schultze, was how he himself had
learned that Blomberg had a mistress. Conscious of his duty, he
decided to go to Blomberg at his ministry and notify him that
Heydrich was keeping him under surveillance. Then it occurred
to him that he himself might be under surveillance, so he tried to
meet Blomberg in such a way as to make it seem accidental, but
without success. Next he asked Ludwig Mueller, a Protestant
bishop who was a friend of Blomberg, to deliver the message for
him. By this story, Schultze wanted to show that he had exposed
himself to real danger in order to help a man who was being
watched by the SD.

There are many other examples of such desperate seeking for
alibis by people who were once close to Heydrich and now want
to exonerate him and themselves; they admit having known about
acts of persecution, but deny that they knew the reasons behind
them.

But we have contrary testimony from a man who was able to
observe Heydrich's intrigues closely: André François-Poncet, the
French ambassador in Berlin. In 1960, he said to me:

> Anyone could see that Himmler and Heydrich were pulling the
> strings. We found it strange that the officer corps let themselves
> be taken in by that outrageous tragicomedy. But it seems incredi-
> ble to me that historians are not ashamed to tell false stories and
> try to make us believe that everything happened because of mis-
> takes or excessive zeal on the part of insignificant policemen.

Schultze's story does not explain why Heydrich unprotestingly
let that dangerous affair be taken out of his hands, or why Nebe
and Helldorf did so without fearing punishment or even a repri-
mand. And would not Heydrich himself have incurred severe
censure if, in spite of all his surveillance, he had failed to discover the scandalous background of the woman who was about to
become one of the first ladies of the Reich by marrying Field
Marshal von Blomberg?

In 1974, Blomberg's widow, then living in Berlin, said to me:

Naturally there are no original photographs. The whole thing was concocted by Heydrich, and there was nothing we could do about it. Hitler had ordered Heydrich to create a pretext for getting rid of my husband, by any means necessary, because my husband was completely opposed to Hitler's war plans. My husband even knew who had faked the photographs: a retoucher who worked for Heydrich, named . . .

I now know that man's name and SS number, but for understandable reasons I give here only his initials: K.M.

According to Frau von Blomberg, K.M. was an amateur painter who had become an expert at falsification in the workshop organized by Heydrich. She assumed that he added her head to the body of a woman photographed in a pornographic scene. She was firmly convinced that Hitler would never have made such a pretense of friendship and understanding in his farewell to her husband if there had been the slightest shred of truth in the "evidence" against her. Furthermore, she said, if there had been any truth in it, the SD would have found it out very early, and in that case her marriage would not have taken place.

Only one conclusion is possible: there are no originals of the pornographic photographs of Margarete Gruhn. Statements made by Frau von Blomberg after the war tally with the explanations that her husband gave to several of his friends. We can now be certain that the "Blomberg case" was a machination by Heydrich and that Helldorf, the Berlin police chief, was only an instrument of the SD, perhaps unknowingly.

The writer Hans Bernd Gisevius told me, at the request of his friend Arthur Nebe, that the evidence against Frau von Blomberg was genuine and that her past immorality was the sole reason for her husband's dismissal. But, confronted with my objections, he finally had to admit that maybe Nebe had been deceived, or might not have told him everything.

Considering the importance of the provocation, Nebe could not have told the whole truth to Gisevius, because it concerned a deliberately fomented crisis in which Heydrich was personally involved. If Nebe had so much as hinted at the deception on which it was based, he would have exposed himself to brutal consequences.

As long as no experts have examined the photographs and

guaranteed their authenticity, it cannot be credibly said that Hitler reorganized his government, the Wehrmacht, the diplomatic corps, and the whole German state because he was shocked at the sight of some pornographic pictures. But even if the photographs were shown to be genuine, it would not prove that Hitler, Himmler, and Heydrich had not known about Frau von Blomberg's past before her marriage. If they had not, it would be hard to explain why Hitler took no action against Heydrich for having been so lax in his duties as not to have discovered Margarete Gruhn's background before Blomberg married her.

For Otto von Heydebreck, the Berlin journalist who was always well informed, there was nothing mysterious about the Blomberg affair, and his belief that it had been staged by Heydrich was confirmed by Colonel Hans Oster, an Abwehr officer and an opponent of the Hitler regime who knew the truth from conversations with his chief, Admiral Canaris. During that period, Canaris often consulted with Heydrich about the annexation of Austria, which was imminent. Oster soon discovered that not only Heydrich but also Canaris had built up a dossier on Blomberg and his mistress. Heydrich convinced the Fuehrer that a certain reluctance could be discerned in the army and that it might cause a grave crisis. "That supposed crisis in the Wehrmacht was 'eliminated' by faked photographs," Blomberg told Otto von Heydebreck in 1943.

Canaris had noticed that just before Blomberg's marriage Heydrich had been summoned to talk with Hitler more often than usual, without Himmler. Because of his friendship with Heydrich, Canaris knew what was being planned. He confided in Colonel Oster and asked for his opinion. Oster passed the information on to Heydebreck.

Heydebreck's story gains credibility in the light of what Hitler said to a gathering of high-ranking officers at the War Ministry on February 4. Accompanied by his new army commander, General Walther von Brauchitsch, he entered the meeting hall at two in the afternoon. While the officers stood up and turned to the Fuehrer, Heydrich slipped into the last row; he did not want to miss that historic event. Hitler began by announcing that he was going to explain the reasons for the changes that had taken place in the Wehrmacht. He would treat the Blomberg and Fritsch af-

fairs with all due discretion, so as not to give other countries an
unfavorable image of the German state and the Wehrmacht, even
though those affairs had resulted from thoroughly exceptional circumstances. Ordinarily, he said, Fritsch would have been his
choice to take over Blomberg's post, but that would not be possible as long as Fritsch's situation had not been completely cleared
up. Although Fritsch had assured him of his innocence, there
were still unresolved questions in the matter of two Hitler Youth
boys whom Fritsch had taken into his home.

Hitler's meaning was clear: Fritsch would not become the head
of the OKW, and the Ministry of Justice would investigate the
accusations against him.

Coming back to the Blomberg case, Hitler said he was convinced that the former War Minister had deceived him. Everyone
knew that Blomberg always lost his head in a crisis. It would be a
mistake to think that he had been largely responsible for German
rearmament. He did not even deserve to be an honorary Colonel
of his regiment. He would not be deprived, however, of the re-
muneration to which he was legally entitled.

In the course of his speech, Hitler stated that he had no intention of placing the SS above the Wehrmacht or of putting
Himmler in command of the Wehrmacht.

General von Manstein asked if an army officer would later be
made commander of all the armed forces. Hitler replied that the
way was open for such a measure and that it would be taken at
the appropriate time.

After this session at the War Ministry, Hitler took his special
train to Berchtesgaden, where, on February 12, he was to meet
with Kurt von Schuschnigg, the Austrian Chancellor, to discuss
undecided questions between their two countries.

On the day of the meeting, Hitler took the offensive as soon as
his conversation with Schuschnigg began: "I am determined to
put an end to all this. The German Reich is a great power and
will not allow anyone to intervene if it settles its border problems." Within three days, he said, Schuschnigg must reshape his
government and appoint Dr. Arthur Seyss-Inquart, a Nazi, as
Minister of the Interior. Hitler also demanded revocation of a
decree forbidding the Nazi movement in Austria, and amnesty for
all arrested Nazis.

Heydrich had personally prescribed the way in which

Schuschnigg and Guido Schmidt, his Foreign Undersecretary, were to be treated. The treatment was effective: on February 16, at two-thirty in the morning, Schuschnigg formed a new government, exactly as Hitler had ordered him to do. Heydrich's agents immediately began putting pressure on him. On March 11, Seyss-Inquart, who was ready to cooperate fully with Hitler, became the new Austrian Chancellor. All German military and political demands were accepted. On March 12, at five in the morning, Heydrich and Daluege went to Vienna and began making preparations for Hitler's arrival.

Heydrich saw to it that the German troops about to cross the Austrian border would be given a friendly reception. General Schilhawksy, the Austrian Army commander, had no choice but to obey the orders he received from the Germans. At eight in the morning, motorized Wehrmacht troops set off for Austria. At one-fifteen in the afternoon, Hitler crossed the border at Braunau. On March 14, he went to the Hotel Imperial in Vienna to confer with Himmler, Heydrich, and Daluege. The next morning, he greeted the crowd gathered in front of the Hofburg.

Schuschnigg was placed in "protective custody" and was not freed till the end of the war.

In 1934, before the putsch attempt in Vienna, Hitler had brutally eliminated Ernst Roehm and his friends. Before the annexation of Austria, he did not need a great purge because he knew his officers had no choice but to accept his policy of expansion. He had only to get rid of Blomberg and Fritsch, in a "delicate" way. The officers remained silent. Blomberg was undoubtedly telling the truth when he said to Otto von Heydebreck in 1943, "If I hadn't given in then, I'd now be where your brother is." (He was referring to the murder of Heydebreck's brother in the purge of 1934.)

On February 5, the *Voelkischer Beobachter* wrote with regard to the restructuring of the state, "The Fuehrer's decisions, which were disclosed today, are a milestone in the administration of the National Socialist state because they spring from the unchanging spirit of the party."

Thus the faked photographs in the Blomberg affair and the false testimony against Fritsch served only Hitler and enabled him to achieve his purposes. As he said in a speech at

Königsberg on March 25, 1938, he had confronted his adversaries with two alternatives: "either an orderly solution or a disorderly, revolutionary eruption."[2]

The Fritsch affair, which took place during the same period as the Blomberg affair, also bears Heydrich's imprint. Hitler wanted to take total control of the Wehrmacht in order to pursue his policy of expansion. This meant that General von Fritsch had to be removed from his post as Commander in Chief of the army. Heydrich, who was experienced in such matters, soon devised a plan.

Fritsch greatly underestimated the power of the SS and the Gestapo. Perhaps he also thought the Nazis were grateful to him for having created a new officer corps. If so, he was soon to realize his mistake. The fact that he was a childless bachelor made him a good target for an accusation of homosexuality. To find an accuser, the SD had only to draw on its "pool of witnesses." A cooperative criminal named Hans Schmidt declared to the police that on a certain day General von Fritsch had paid him a thousand marks for a homosexual encounter. And it was proved that on that same day Fritsch had withdrawn a thousand marks from his bank account. Preparing this bit of evidence was no problem for Heydrich. He simply had Fritsch trailed till he went to his bank. Schmidt's declaration could then be supported by the testimony of an impartial bank teller and the records of Fritsch's account.

When Fritsch denied the accusation, Hitler ordered the formation of a court of honor with Goering presiding. But Goering, ordinarily so devoted to his Fuehrer, was apparently unwilling to lend his full support to the provocation set up by Heydrich. Ludwig Krieger, the court reporter, told me after the war that Goering attacked Schmidt so harshly that the witness soon found himself in the position of the accused. Goering finally said to him, "Enough! Tell the truth now!" Schmidt replied, "If I tell the truth . . ." He stopped, afraid to go on, but Goering pressed him: "What will happen if you tell the truth?" Schmidt moved the edge of his hand toward his neck to convey the idea that his head would be cut off. Furious, Goering shouted to Heydrich's representatives, "Gentlemen, go and find a better witness!"

The court of honor acquitted General von Fritsch for lack of acceptable evidence. But he was not reinstated as Commander in Chief of the army.

The trial took place at the time that Hitler entered Vienna as a liberator. He had never had any intention of letting men like Blomberg and Fritsch share in such a triumph.

After Fritsch's acquittal, many Wehrmacht officers mistakenly believed that it had been a costly failure for Heydrich and that his power would now be greatly reduced. According to Otto von Heydebreck, who was able to follow the trial closely, Goering explained the acquittal by saying that Schmidt refused to repeat before the court what he had told the Gestapo. But actually Schmidt had never met Fritsch. Heydrich also had an explanation: his subordinates had confused General von Fritsch with a certain Captain von Frisch, whom the police had been watching because of his homosexual activities.

Surprisingly, this version of the facts was accepted by a number of historians after the war. But if Fritsch had really been a victim of mistaken identity, his rehabilitation would have had a different ending: in the Polish campaign he was "authorized" to lead a regiment as its "honorary" commander and, as expected, he died heroically for the Fuehrer and the Fatherland.

After the war Franz Josef Huber, a former Gestapo policeman who had worked for Heydrich, stated the following version of events. One evening in 1938, he went into the office of his colleague Josef Meissinger, who was also working on the Fritsch case. Meissinger was not in his office at the time. On his desk, Huber found records of a bank account in the name of Captain von Frisch. Realizing that General von Fritsch had been confused with Captain von Frisch, Huber explained the mistake to Himmler and Heydrich. Meissinger was then "punished" for his mistake: he was sent to the German embassy in Tokyo as a police attaché.

It is scarcely plausible that a policeman who had shown his incompetence by making a serious mistake involving the Commander in Chief of the army would have been given the responsibility of an embassy attaché, especially in a country as important to the Reich as Japan was at that time. Meissinger, however, was dead when Huber told his story, and therefore could not contradict it. Huber also put other distorted accounts into circulation.

Although he was the son of an anti-Nazi, Huber was able to win Heydrich's confidence. Incontrovertible documents have established that several complaints concerning the past activities of Huber and his father were "buried" after they reached Heydrich's desk. Huber's attitude after the war clearly showed his continued loyalty to Heydrich. His stories contributed significantly to the formation of legends designed to exonerate Nazi criminals. According to him, Heydrich was only a professional policeman like so many others, rigorous in his work but incapable of the machinations attributed to him by adversaries of Nazism. All of Heydrich's collaborators who survived the war presented that same view of him.

Unfortunately, many historians give credence to Heydrich's collaborators and ignore the testimony of his victims. That, in my opinion, is the reason for the cloud of vagueness and uncertainty that still surrounds his personality.

In the annexation of Austria, Heydrich served Hitler not only by eliminating opposition within the Wehrmacht but also through the activities of his fifth column in Austria. And it was he who decided on the "special treatment" to be applied to Chancellor Schuschnigg.

One of Heydrich's first acts after the annexation was to begin prosecution of those who had accused him of organizing the putsch attempt of July 25, 1934, and the assassination of Chancellor Dollfuss. Then came a shake-up of the Austrian police and the beginning of persecution of the Jews. He had a concentration camp built at Mauthausen. Austrian democrats were the first victims sent to that camp, just as German democrats had been the first to go to Oranienburg and Dachau.

Next, Czechoslovakia

Soon after Austria had been incorporated into the Reich, Heydrich turned his attention to preparations for the dismemberment of Czechoslovakia.

Before taking any action, Hitler tried once again to influence Britain. On September 26, 1938, he received Sir Frederick Maurice, the head of a British association of World War veterans, as a gesture intended to show his solidarity with those who wanted peace. That same day, a personal letter to Hitler from

Prime Minister Neville Chamberlain was delivered by Sir Horace Wilson, the British ambassador in Berlin. At the Sportpalast that evening, Hitler gave a speech on the world situation. Standing before his audience in a uniform that included high black boots, he said with regard to the Sudetenland in Czechoslovakia, "This is my last territorial demand."

After that solemn promise, he invited to Munich the Prime Ministers of Britain, Italy, and France to discuss putting an end to talk of war. As the result of his threat to go to war against Czechoslovakia if the Sudetenland was not returned to Germany and his reiteration of his "last territorial demand" promise, the Munich Pact was signed on September 29, 1938. Czechoslovakia was to give up the Sudetenland by October 1.

When Chamberlain and Edouard Daladier, the French Premier, returned home, they were acclaimed as angels of peace.

But Hitler had actually brought about the Munich Pact because he did not want to attack the Czech fortifications unnecessarily and because he wanted British and French assent to his "drive to the East." He had no intention of abiding by the terms of the pact. His plans for expansion had long since been laid. Two more parts of Czechoslovakia had to be annexed: Bohemia and Moravia. That would strengthen the German war economy and extend German territory to the southern border of Poland. It had to be done before Britain and France had time to build up their armies and develop their aircraft industry.

When the Reich began proclaiming that even after the occupation of the Sudetenland there were still too many Germans left in Czechoslovakia, the euphoria that had followed the Munich Pact was replaced by bitter disappointment. The Nazi propaganda machine was again set in motion: this time, Prague was the center of the Jewish conspiracy. Hitler claimed that thousands of Soviet agents were active in Czechoslovakia and that at any moment that strategically located country could be transformed into a springboard for Soviet aggression.

This was a clear indication that Hitler had decided to move against what was left of Czechoslovakia. But he needed a pretext. Once again Heydrich was instructed to devise a provocation. Britain and France had to be prevented from actively opposing Hitler's plan to annex Bohemia and Moravia and turn Slovakia into a "free state," that is, a German satellite.

The experts on "the Czech question" assembled by Heydrich went to work. The fifth column installed in Bohemia and Moravia was ordered to provoke a series of tense situations that would support German allegations of a Czech, Soviet, or Jewish conspiracy. A plan to assassinate the German ambassador in Prague was considered, then abandoned, because it would probably have been recognized as the work of the German secret service.

Experience had taught the Nazis that each provocation needed a period of preparation. World public opinion had to be conditioned. Hitler first turned to France. German diplomats made it known that the Third Reich had no claims with regard to Alsace-Lorraine. Before the occupation of Czechoslovakia, Ribbentrop, the Foreign Minister, would go to Paris to demonstrate the goodwill of the German government. But Jews in all countries were highly skeptical about that goodwill. Hitler tried to turn their skepticism to his own advantage by citing it as evidence that the Jews wanted war.

The world anxiously kept its eyes on Germany and waited to learn what Hitler would say in his speech commemorating the fifteenth anniversary of the unsuccessful putsch attempt of 1923. There was also speculation on what the consequences of Ribbentrop's scheduled visit to Paris would be. Then, suddenly, an obscure young man appeared on the world stage and seemed to strike a powerful blow against Hitler's peace efforts.

Herschel Grynszpan, seventeen, was an unemployed German Jewish refugee in France. On the morning of November 7, 1938, he bought a pistol, went to the German embassy in Paris, and fired five shots at Ernst vom Rath, the third secretary of the embassy, who, unknown to Grynszpan, was suspected by the Gestapo of being an anti-Nazi.

German propaganda immediately seized on this event as a pretext for denouncing the international Jewish conspiracy against peace. On November 9, Ernst vom Rath died of his wounds. Hitler gave him a posthumous promotion.

The night of November 9–10 has become known as the Night of Broken Glass (in German, *Kristallnacht,* "Crystal Night"). It was the worst explosion of Nazi anti-Jewish barbarity that had so far occurred. Nearly all synagogues and more than seven thousand Jewish shops were smashed or burned. Ninety Jews were killed and some twenty thousand were sent to concentration camps. From then on, Hitler openly claimed the right to take whatever steps were necessary to prevent Jews from engaging in their "seditious activities." In view of the murder committed by Grynszpan, an "instrument of world Jewry," the agreement signed at Munich six weeks earlier was null and void.

Immediately after the murder, suspicions that it was the outcome of a plot by the German secret service were voiced in Paris. The French government tried to stifle rumors that might be a new source of conflict with Germany.

Shrewd observers were struck by the fact that the murder had taken place just when Hitler's plans for expansion were becoming clear to everyone. Some of them wondered if Grynszpan had fallen into a trap set by provocateurs who took advantage of his hostility to Nazism. Several known facts seemed to indicate that he had been in contact with messengers from Germany and had received financial aid from them. It was also known that his political and religious convictions were well suited to making him the victim of a machination.

The theory that the murder had been provoked by German agents was not expressed publicly because the French authorities were unwilling to admit the possibility that such a thing could have happened in spite of the close watch kept on the foreigners by the police and the secret service. Some of the lawyers defending Grynszpan, wanting to combat the Nazi propaganda that presented him as an instrument of world Jewry, maintained that he had acted for purely personal reasons. This gave rise to the claim that the murder had resulted from a quarrel between two homosexuals. It is an absurd idea, contradicted by the fact that the two men had never seen each other before the murder, but it was nevertheless adopted by certain interpreters of history after the war.

Heydrich undoubtedly discussed the murder with his wife, and although Lina Heydrich has become an expert in the art of minimizing the crimes of her husband and the regime he served so devotedly, her account of Grynszpan's act shows how advantageous it was to the Nazis:

At the German embassy in Paris, the Jew Herschel Grynszpan had shot Secretary Ernst vom Rath and fatally wounded him. For all those who wanted a quick and radical "solution" of the "Jewish problem," this murder had obviously come at the right time. Goebbels, especially, seemed to need such an opportunity.[3]

She "can prove" that her husband had nothing to do with the murder, because on the night of November 9, 1938, they "went to bed early" and were awakened by the man on guard duty, who said Heydrich had to "call his office immediately," and added, "The synagogues are burning!" Heydrich left and was gone for several hours. When he came back, he said to his wife:

They've demolished everything, destroyed and looted all the shops. The Wilmersdorf synagogue is still burning. And the worst of it is that Goebbels is behind it. It's supposed to have been a spontaneous action, but no one will believe us if we say that. From now on, any lessening of aggression against the Jews will be out of the question. But why did Goebbels do that?[4]

Since the war, there have been other attempts to make Goebbels solely responsible for that barbaric pogrom. This interpretation is bolstered by a story that Heydrich's assistant, Werner Best, put in circulation, obviously hoping that all documents concerning the Night of Broken Glass had been lost in the chaos at the end of the war. Best "remembered" that Himmler and Heydrich were not in Berlin that night. They had both gone to Munich, with Best, for a swearing-in ceremony of SS recruits. Heydrich had dinner with friends in a room of the Vier Jahreszeiten Hotel. He was "totally surprised by what Goebbels had done," said Best. "I was with him when a synagogue a few meters away from the hotel burst into flames."[5]

Other former SS men have made statements supporting this version. Heydrich is depicted as having sent Gruppenfuehrer Karl Wolff to Himmler with a request for information on what was happening. Wolff did not find Himmler until 11 P.M., in Hitler's private apartment on Prinzregentenstrasse. Like everyone else, of course, Hitler was greatly surprised. "When I questioned the Fuehrer," Wolff said at Nuremberg, "I had the impression that he knew nothing about what had taken place."

Was Wolff's "impression" accurate? Or had Hitler again shown his talent as an actor, as he had done during the Reichstag fire?

According to the postwar SS version, if Grynszpan had not killed a German embassy official in Paris, Goebbels would have had no reason for reacting as he did. And the SS leaders had no responsibility for the Night of Broken Glass. On the contrary, they tried to limit the damage. A great deal of glass was broken but, thanks to the SS, a large-scale massacre was avoided.

So much for that wondrous story in which the SS was innocent of everything. The truth is that the Night of Broken Glass was organized and directed by Heydrich. A Teletype that he sent to all Gestapo posts at 1:20 A.M. is sufficient to show how far he was from being taken by surprise. The Teletype deals with six points, presented in the usual bureaucratic style. I will mention only two of them here. The burning of synagogues was authorized, provided there was no danger of fire spreading to nearby buildings. And "for the execution of police security measures, assistance may be requested from the criminal police, members of the Security Service, available troops, and the SS in general."

The text of this Teletype reveals that the Night of Broken Glass was a gigantic operation designed to foment attacks against Jews, the burning of synagogues, and the destruction of Jewish shops. Heydrich knew in advance how it was to be presented, as is shown by the beginning of his Teletype: "Because of the murder in Paris of Embassy Secretary vom Rath, demonstrations against the Jews must be expected all over Germany in the course of this night, November 9–10, 1938."

On November 12, there was a meeting attended by Heydrich, Minister of the Interior Frick, Finance Minister Schwerin von Krosigk, Minister of Justice Guertner, and Propaganda Minister Goebbels, as well as a large number of officials from various ministries. Goering, at Hitler's order, was to report on "the consequences of the demonstration." Looking solemn, he addressed the assembly:

> I have received a letter from [Martin] Bormann, the Fuehrer's deputy, written by order of the Fuehrer, stating that from now on the Jewish question must be treated in accordance with an overall plan, with a view to a final resolution. Yesterday, the Fuehrer again confirmed, by telephone, that I must centralize decisive measures.

In a letter to Goering on November 11, Heydrich had detailed the results of the Night of Broken Glass: 815 shops, 29 department stores, and 717 homes set afire or destroyed (these were preliminary figures, expected to be only a fraction of the final totals), 191 synagogues set afire and 76 others completely destroyed. "About 20,000 Jews were arrested, plus 7 Aryans and 3 foreigners. The latter were arrested only for their own security. There were 36 killed and also 36 seriously injured. Those killed and injured were Jews."

After that night of horror, more than twenty thousand Jews—the exact number will never be known—were sent to concentration camps. Events and their context clearly show that Heydrich had not merely reacted to the murder of an embassy official in Paris, but had launched an operation that marked the beginning of a precisely planned program.

During this same period, Hitler ordered Heydrich to make secret preparations for the partition of Czechoslovakia and the occupation of Bohemia and Moravia. Nazi propaganda continued harping on its two main themes: Soviet agents were at work in Czechoslovakia, and the German minorities in Bohemia and Moravia were being persecuted by Czech extremists.

Heydrich's fifth column set about increasing the tension. By the beginning of March 1939, Bohemia and Moravia were in turmoil. Hitler invited President Emil Hácha of Czechoslovakia to come to Berlin for a meeting in which they would try to find a "peaceful solution."

On March 14, Hácha arrived in Berlin with his Foreign Minister, Chvalkovsky. Hitler did not receive them until after one o'clock in the morning. Like Schuschnigg, they were subjected to a relentless barrage of insults and threats. Hácha's resistance finally collapsed. At 3:55, he signed a document giving Germany complete control of Czechoslovakia.

On the morning of March 15, German troops entered Czechoslovakia. At eight o'clock that evening, Hitler arrived at Hradcany Castle in Prague. Himmler and the other top men of the SS were there to greet him. Hitler immediately conferred with Generals Keitel, List, and Blaskowitz. The next day, he issued a decree establishing the Protectorate of Bohemia and Moravia.

Everything had taken place according to plan. Military pressure and a series of dramatic provocations had resulted in the incorporation of Bohemia and Moravia into the German Reich.

After the annexation of Austria and the occupation of Bohemia and Moravia, Heydrich began making plans, with the consent of Hitler and Himmler, for the creation of a gigantic organization that would encompass the functions of the SD, the Gestapo, and the criminal police. It later came into being as the Reichssicherheitshauptamt, or RSHA (the Reich Central Security Office).

It was during this period that the euthanasia program began. All people "unfit to live"—those who were crippled from birth, permanently disabled, insane, feebleminded—were to be discreetly killed. This program cost thousands of lives before it was discontinued as the result of protests from all over Germany. In spite of government terror and propaganda, the German people refused to tolerate the murder of the physically and mentally handicapped.

During the time of its application, the euthanasia program created experts in mass murder, as was demonstrated in testimony at many trials after the war. Its purpose was to improve the health of the nation and increase the number of doctors, nurses, and hospital beds available for treating wounded soldiers. This Nazi version of euthanasia was a logical consequence of Nazi racial theories. The planned extermination of the Jews was also seen as a means of preserving the health and integrity of the German nation. Schoolchildren and university students were taught that the German nation would have disappeared in less than three centuries if the Nazis had not taken measures to maintain its racial purity.

The Gleiwitz Incident

Late in the afternoon of August 9, 1939, a Ju 52 military plane landed at the Neustadt airport in Upper Silesia and Reinhard Heydrich got out of it. Emmanuel Schaeffer, the local Gestapo chief, was waiting for him. Heydrich put his coat and briefcase on the wing of the plane and told Schaeffer that he had come for a secret matter of the greatest importance. From Heydrich's next sentence, Schaeffer knew that he was not exaggerating: "The Fuehrer needs a pretext for war."

The two men got into a car and went to Gleiwitz, a town near the Polish border.

Heydrich had already worked out the general plan of the provocation. He had come to Gleiwitz only to study the terrain and determine the extent to which the collaboration of the Gestapo and the border police would be needed.

His plan called for supposedly Polish troops to seize the Gleiwitz radio station, about four miles from the border, and broadcast a speech insulting to the Fuehrer and the German nation. The false incursion would have to be staged so convincingly that other countries, particularly Britain, would acknowledge that Hitler could not let such an outrageous violation of German territory go unpunished.

A German border post near Hohenlinden would be attacked, and armed Polish groups would enter a village near Kreuzburg. At first Heydrich had thought of trying to maneuver Polish soldiers into crossing the border and fighting against a specially trained German force, but he had decided it was unlikely that Polish troops would fall into such a trap. He therefore intended to use 150 Germans who came from the border region and spoke Polish. Wearing Polish Army uniforms, they would simulate an incursion into Germany.

Supplying them with uniforms was no problem. Members of the large German minority in Poland had been drafted into the Polish Army. For some time, many of them had been deserting and fleeing into Germany, where their Polish uniforms were collected and kept by the Abwehr.

To make the provocation—known as Operation Tannenberg—completely convincing, corpses would have to be found at the site of the attack. Heydrich had decided to use a dozen prisoners from the Sachsenhausen concentration camp: they would be dressed in Polish uniforms, brought to the site, and killed.

Although Heydrich kept general command of Operation Tannenberg, he entrusted its execution to his subordinate Heinrich Mueller, head of the Gestapo.

Once the invasion of Poland had begun, SD groups behind the German lines would track down enemy intelligence agents and liquidate Jews and other "parasites." The SD and its fifth column in Poland had already provided valuable information on the Polish armed forces, fortifications, munitions depots, and rail centers. This information would greatly facilitate the advance of the attacking forces: Army Group North, led by General Fedor von Bock, and Army Group South, led by General Gerd von Rundstedt. Hitler always gave preference to SD reports over those that came from the Abwehr.

Heydrich usually discussed strategy not with military leaders but with Ohlendorf, his economic adviser, and Canaris, head of the Abwehr. The three of them agreed that Germany's military situation would have been much less favorable if other European countries had concentrated on developing air power and armored forces. Heydrich was fascinated by everything that concerned the design and production of weapons. In his opinion, the success of a lightning war depended on superiority in both weapons and intelligence work.

Poland was expected to succumb to an avalanche of decisive blows within a few days. The Polish Army, with thirty-eight infantry divisions, two motorized brigades, eight or nine hundred tanks, a thousand planes, and a million men, had taken up positions along a border seventeen hundred miles long. A good part of it was composed of cavalry units that would be useless against planes and tanks.

Hitler had massed seventy-five divisions on the border, including six armored and eight motorized divisions; he had twenty-five hundred tanks, about the same number of planes, and a million and a half men. Polish planes and tanks were thus outnumbered by nearly three to one, but the decisive factor was to be the mobility and firepower of the German ground forces.

When Heydrich came to Gleiwitz to reconnoiter the terrain, he knew that the Fuehrer would give the order to attack in about two weeks. Besides Heinrich Mueller, his staff for Operation Tannenberg consisted of SS Obersturmbannfuehrer Otto Hellwig, SS Standartenfuehrer Hans Trummler, SS Oberfuehrer Otto Rasch, SS Sturmbannfuehrer Alfred Naujocks (whom we have already encountered in the operation against Strasser and Formis), SS Oberfuehrer Herbert Mehlhorn, and SS Brigadefuehrer Heinz Jost, plus several technicians.

Heydrich decided that Hellwig would lead the group of "Polish aggressors" at Hohenlinden. Trummler was placed in command of the border policemen who would resist the incursion. The attacks on the Gleiwitz radio station and the village near Kreuzberg would be executed by Naujocks and Rasch, respectively. Admiral Canaris had agreed to furnish the Polish uniforms and military equipment. Mueller would bring the prisoners, who were given the code name of "canned goods," from the concentration camp. Mehlhorn would make sure that the different phases of the operation were properly coordinated.

The Polish-speaking Germans were taken by truck to the police school at Bernau, near Berlin, on August 16, 1939. Among other things, they were taught Polish military regulations and even Polish songs. On August 20, the 150 "Polish soldiers" went through maneuvers on the school's drill field, though the exact details of the operation had not yet been revealed to them. We know about their training from statements made by those of them who survived the war. But with regard to the actual operation, they were much less talkative: under the laws of the Federal Republic of Germany, they could have been tried for complicity in the murder of prisoners. None of them, of course, admitted to having taken part in the killing of the "canned goods" at Gleiwitz.

After the war, conflicting accounts of the operation were given. I will summarize here the conclusions of the official inquiry conducted by Attorney General Alfred Spiess.

Spiess confirmed the part played by Heydrich in the preparation and execution of the provocation, under the code name of Operation Tannenberg. Mueller was placed in charge of carrying it out; he was to direct it from a command post in the Gestapo office at Oppeln.

The operation, composed of three different actions, took place in accordance with Heydrich's directives:

1. To attack the Gleiwitz radio station, Naujocks formed a group of six or seven men, all members of the SD. Between 8:00 and 8:30 on the night of August 31, they occupied the station, and an appeal to "the champions of freedom" was broadcast in Polish. Then came an announcement in German spoken with a Polish accent: "Attention! Attention! This is the Association of Polish Insurgents. The Gleiwitz radio station is in our hands. The hour of freedom has struck!" The men wore civilian clothes and appeared to be a band of saboteurs who had suddenly burst into the station and overwhelmed its personnel.

2. The SS men in Polish uniforms, shouting to each other in Polish and singing Polish songs, captured the border post at Hohenlinden and destroyed it. Then, other SS men, dressed as members of the German border police, "counterattacked" the "Polish aggressors" and "arrested" them. The next day, they all went back to the police school at Bernau.

3. A simulated attack on the forester's lodge at Pitachen was carried out between 8:00 and 10:00 P.M. by SS men in civilian clothes. "They loudly spoke and sang in Polish as they went through the forest. When they reached the forester's lodge, they began widly shooting into the air. The kitchen of the house was destroyed, and half a bucket of cow's blood was spilled in it."[6] The men returned to Bernau that same night.

To make the false aggression as convincing as possible, Heydrich had ordered that several "Polish" corpses be left behind. "The transportation and killing of the prisoners was assigned to a special group, called the 'canned goods group,' which kept completely separate from those who made the simulated attacks at Gleiwitz and Hohenlinden."[7]

According to an agreement between Heydrich and the Gestapo post at Gleiwitz, a farm-equipment dealer named Franz Honiok, from Hohenlinden, was to be one of the "aggressors" killed in the operation. In 1921, Honiok had fought against the Germans and vigorously demanded Polish nationality. The operation would be more convincing to the local people if they recognized one of the dead bodies as that of a man who could plausibly be considered as having taken part in the attack.

On August 30, in great secrecy, Franz Honiok was arrested and imprisoned at Oppeln. On the night of August 31, an SS Untersturmfuehrer, wearing a doctor's white coat to deceive his victim, gave him an anesthetizing injection. While Naujocks's group was attacking the Gleiwitz radio station, a limousine brought Honiok to the scene. He was laid on the ground, still unconscious, and at about 8:30 an SS man killed him with a bullet in the head.

After the attack, the bodies of the prisoners who had been killed were photographed by the police. The next day, these photographs, presented as proof of the "Polish attack," were shown to foreign journalists in Berlin.

Attorney General Spiess was unable to learn the names of those who brought the prisoners, those who killed them, or the man who anesthetized Franz Honiok. From what we know today, it is well established that all the different actions of the provocation were agreed upon beforehand between Heydrich and Mueller.

The Nuremberg tribunal ascertained that the dead men in Polish uniforms found at Hohenlinden had shaved heads, which clearly indicates that they had come from a concentration camp.

Operation Tannenberg involved 350 participants, 40 officials and agents, and at least 2,000 inhabitants of the border region who had to be indirectly made ready to accept the idea of a Polish incursion into German territory. The border guards had to be alerted, but also prevented from intervening. The operation had to be planned in such a way that it could not degenerate into a real skirmish in which several SS or SD men might lose their lives. All the details were worked out under Mueller's supervision.

A photographer with special training in criminal investigation was taken to the scene of the Gleiwitz "attack" by Gestapo policemen. After the war he gave this account of his visit:

As soon as I came into the radio station I saw control panels on one wall and a big table with a microphone on it. In front of the table, a man lay on the floor, facedown, with his arms outstretched. Three or four meters away was another man who, like the first one, lay facedown on the floor with his arms outstretched.[8]

The photographer saw no trace of blood anywhere, which shows that the corpses had been brought into the room only to be photographed there.

Mueller had an additional duty: to orient the inquiry. A special commission whose members were officials of the criminal police and the Gestapo quickly concluded that the attack had been carried out by Poles.

On August 17, Admiral Canaris had notified General Franz Halder, chief of the Army General Staff, that a pretext for war was going to be created, and Halder wrote in his diary the names of the three men who were planning the operation: Himmler, Heydrich, and Trummler. There can be no doubt that the General Staff was informed of that provocation and approved of it, and also approved of the idea that Poland would be crushed within three weeks.

The German ambassador to London showed the same willingness to accept a spurious pretext for war. Evidently unaware that the Fuehrer already had far better advisers to give him ideas, he wrote:

If a Polish provocation should be staged, such as the bombardment of a German village by a mentally deranged military commander, or the bombing of a German locality by a Polish pilot, it would be crucially important with regard to the attitude of Britain, first, that the incident be unquestionably proved to world opinion, and second, that the British public have time to form a precise idea of the incident and of the exclusive guilt of Poland.

But world opinion was not deceived. At 4:45 on the morning of September 1, 1939, the German invasion of Poland began. On September 3, Britain and France declared war on Germany. Hitler's attempt to wage war on only one front, as a prelude to world conquest, had failed. He also suffered a psychological defeat as far as the German people were concerned, because he had assured them that in view of Germany's military superiority Britain and France would not let themselves be drawn into war, and would accept the invasion of Poland after it had ended in a German victory. Britain and France rejected any idea of peace negotiations with the German government. Hitler had to acknowledge that he had underestimated them.

In that new situation created by a war that might spread all over the world, the German intelligence services would become even more important. Hitler needed an all-encompassing security organization. Thus was born the RSHA. And its chief, of course, was Reinhard Heydrich.

A Miraculous Escape?

For once, it was announced in 1939, Hitler would not go to the Buergerbräukeller in Munich on November 8 to give a speech commemorating the anniversary of the putsch attempt that had taken place there in 1923. His deputy, Rudolf Hess, would speak in his place. Observers wondered about the reason for that change. In diplomatic circles, the choice of Hess to give the speech was interpreted as a signal to the British, who were still rejecting all peace overtures, because it was known that Hess had always advocated a policy of maintaining friendly relations with Britain and supporting the continued existence of her empire.

The German-Soviet nonaggression pact had been signed in August. Hitler had regarded it only as a means of being able to launch the first phase of his plan for expansion without having to fight a war on two fronts. But now that Britain had declared war on Germany and refused to discuss peace, Goebbels was directing his propaganda against British plutocrats and warmongers, as well as international Jewry; they had all conspired to provoke this war, he said, and were trying to spread it to other countries.

A large part of the German people, imbued with patriotic sentiments, approved of the war against Poland. The Nazi propaganda machine had finally convinced them that it was time to punish the Poles for their repeated provocations against peaceful Germany. The war against Britain and France, however, worried a great many Germans. It was easy to foresee that the enormous industrial power of the United States would eventually be placed at the disposal of the Western democracies. Hitler, of course, expressed satisfaction with the German-Soviet pact and the desperate situation in which Britain and France had been placed by the military superiority of the Third Reich and the determination of the German people. Goebbels made strenuous propaganda efforts to arouse the Germans' fighting spirit. The increase in war production was cited as proof that the nation was united against those who, in Britain, France, and the United States, were making huge profits from the war. The Western countries had said at the beginning of the war that they were not fighting against the German people but only against Hitler and his tyrannical regime; Nazi propaganda presented this as an attempt to separate the people from their Fuehrer.

What was Hess going to say in Munich about the pursuit of the war? This question was raised not only in Germany but also abroad. Then suddenly the press and radio announced that the Fuehrer had changed his plans and would go to Munich on November 8 as usual.

All over the world there was speculation on what he would say in his speech. Perhaps he would give some indication of his military plans. In view of the "phony war" that was stagnating on the western front, many observers wondered if Hitler would ever be able to launch a lightning offensive when the forces on both sides were evenly matched. The Maginot Line seemed to be an impassable barrier. The Wehrmacht had gained experience in the Polish campaign, and it was well equipped with modern planes and tanks, but a large part of the German officer corps recalled the failure of the offensive in 1914 and feared great losses.

Hitler and his General Staff knew that Britain and France had no plan of attack, that they had considered only defensive strategy against all German military initiatives. To the Nazi leaders this was a great advantage, because they continued to believe in a war of movement led by planes and tanks.

Heydrich's spies had reported to him that the French had prepared no antitank defenses within their country. And French fortifications along the border held no secrets for him. "Wherever the French have buried a cannon in concrete, we'll overrun it with ten or twenty tanks," Ohlendorf had assured him. He and Ohlendorf were well aware that the success of the German offensive depended largely on their ability to deceive the enemy with regard to the place and direction of the main assault.

On the night of November 8, 1939, after giving his speech at the Buergerbräukeller in Munich, Hitler left immediately, rather than staying awhile to talk with his old comrades from the early days of the Nazi movement, as he usually did on these occasions. The Nazi leaders who had come with him—Heinrich Himmler, Alfred Rosenberg, Martin Bormann, and others—also left; only a few guards and the organizers of the ceremony remained behind. Ten minutes later, at 9:20, a bomb exploded, killing several people and injuring many others.

That night, Christian Weber, a party veteran and not a member of the SS, was in charge of security. This meant that Heydrich and his SD, who ordinarily looked after the Fuehrer's safety, could not be held responsible for what clearly appeared to be an assassination attempt.

The combination of these two circumstances—Hitler's early departure and Heydrich's having turned over the security measures to someone else—prompted several Wehrmacht officers to think and say that the apparent attempt on the Fuehrer's life might have been only a provocation, like the sham attack on the Gleiwitz radio station.

Anyone who carefully examines the incident will reach the conclusion that it was a propaganda operation designed to convince the German people that the British had tried to win the war by an ignoble plot to assassinate the Fuehrer and other important German leaders.

The bomb blast killed seven people The number of wounded was first announced as about sixty, then reduced by almost half.

Diplomats and journalists in Berlin realized that the Nazi propaganda machine now had enough material to fuel it for several months. Goebbels began constantly denouncing the British as a mob of murderers who wanted to deprive the Germans of their Fuehrer after he had united them into a true national community. The *Voelkischer Beobachter* said that it was "only by a miracle that the Fuehrer escaped safe and sound from that attempt on his life, which was also a blow struck against the security of the Reich."

If Hitler and the men with him had stayed in the Buergerbräukeller a few minutes longer, a significant part of the Nazi leadership would have been killed or wounded. The bomb had been hidden in one of the pillars supporting the ceiling, and the power of the explosion reduced the room to a heap of rubble. The newspapers were filled with photographs showing the devastation of the Buergerbräukeller.

It seemed strange to many observers that in all the vituperative propaganda there was not one reproach against the SS, the organization charged with protecting the Fuehrer, for having failed to take adequate security measures. It was Himmler himself, in fact, who was ordered to form a special commission to investigate the crime.

Arthur Nebe was named to head the commission. Actually, however, the investigation was conducted by Heydrich. Nebe, a former Weimar official who had earned an international reputation as a criminologist, was only a figurehead.

Despite all efforts to prove that the crime was a British atrocity, public opinion in Germany and abroad viewed it as a provocation of the same kind as the Reichstag fire, the Night of the Long Knives, and the attack on the Gleiwitz radio station. Hitler needed such a machination to reinforce his myth, inflict a psychological defeat on the British, and unite the German people for the planned offensive in the West. And the idea of a provocation continued to gain credibility, not only because there had been no criticism of Himmler and Heydrich but also because a whole series of events, before and after the bomb explosion, indicated that it had been the outcome of an operation coordinated by high German authorities.

On November 21, 1939, Himmler, Heydrich, Mueller, Nebe, and the criminologist Franz Josef Huber were congratulated on having cleared up the mystery. The next day, the *Voelkischer Beobachter* announced on its front page, "The German people have learned with deep satisfaction that the perpetrator has been arrested."

The perpetrator was said to be a carpenter named Georg Elser, who had acted on orders from two officers of the British Intelligence Service operating in Holland: Major R. H. Stevens and Captain S. Payne Best. Photographs of Stevens and Best, designated as Elser's accomplices, were published in the newspapers. Gunther d'Alquen, editor of *Das Schwarze Korps,* wrote an article that was published in the *Voelkischer Beobachter* on November 22, under the title "The Discovery." It praised the special commission for having reconstructed the whole crime after painstakingly gathering and analyzing a multitude of details.

According to the commission, Georg Elser had begun preparations for his crime in late August, under the direction of the British Intelligence Service. Otto Strasser, who now lived in Switzerland, had served as the go-between. Also involved were Sir Robert Vansittart and Eduard Beneš, the former President of Czechoslovakia, both sworn enemies of the Third Reich. Elser had made a complete confession.

The press reported that on the night of the assassination attempt Elser had been arrested at the Swiss border by German guards who happened to see him outside a window of their building, listening to a radio news broadcast. For weeks before the crime, he had repeatedly gone into the Buergerbräukeller at night and hollowed out a cavity in the pillar, concealing his work each time by replacing the outside material. Then he installed his time bomb in the pillar so cleverly that it escaped detection. But German border guards arrested him because of his suspicious behavior as he was about to leave the country. Two postcards with pictures of the Buergerbräukeller were found in his pocket. The commission took this as undeniable proof of his guilt. "Pictures of the Buergerbräukeller in the perpetrator's pocket—isn't that a little too much?" Otto von Heydebreck asked Oster, Canaris's collaborator.

It is understandable that Heydrich did not inform his colleague Canaris of the Buergerbräukeller operation, because it was a state secret. Furthermore, he knew that Canaris was surrounded by men who, though they were devoted to Hitler and wanted a German victory for patriotic reasons, did not carry their patriotism so far as to approve of murder.

During meal I had with him at Vichy in 1956, Charles de Gaulle said to me:

> Since coming to power, Hitler had built up the forces he would need for his lightning wars, and it was to be expected that he would create pretexts for each of his interventions in Europe; that is, that he would provoke incidents to give himself the right to take the offensive. After the Munich bomb explosion and the incident on the German-Dutch border in which two officers of the British Intelligence Service were abducted, it was obvious that Hitler was trying to make us feel aversion and contempt for the British.

At that time, de Gaulle was living in retirement at Colombey-les-deux-Eglises and liked to recall his days as an army tank commander. Since 1935, he had been convinced that any future military conflict could only be a war of movement, but in 1937, when Germany had six armored divisions, France had none at all.

De Gaulle continued:

> Hitler tried to wear us down with his "phony war." He wanted us to make enormous efforts that would turn out to be useless. He

hoped to demoralize Britain and convince "the man in the street" that he would have to suffer the consequences of bombings and the submarine blockade. In May, before the German offensive and after the attack on Norway, the German secret service succeeded in deceiving us by making us believe there was about to be an offensive against the Balkans and the Soviet Union.

From the beginning, de Gaulle had thought that Hitler was using not only his secret police but also a secret military strategy, diplomacy, and propaganda. Those four secret activities of the Nazi state influenced even Hitler's main adversaries and helped to turn proud officers into cowards and traitors. "The Germans were very clever in that respect," said de Gaulle. "They used anticommunism, anti-Semitism, and antiplutocracy whenever it seemed opportune to them."

Otto von Heydebreck also knew the importance of air power and armored divisions; before he had ever heard of de Gaulle, he shared his ideas. He, too, had seen through Hitler's secret diplomacy and propaganda, and he knew that Heydrich was pulling the strings of all those puppets. Immediately after the Munich bomb explosion, he set about clearing up its details. As a correspondent of the *Basler Nachrichten*, he was able to learn many things, not only from his Swiss colleagues but also from certain diplomats. He was the first to explain—confidentially, of course—that the Nazis had implicated Otto Strasser in the affair to make it seem more plausible and to intimidate the Swiss, who, according to the Nazis, were guilty of tolerating the intrigues of German refugees.

"The fact that the assassin tried to take refuge in Switzerland completed the deception by giving the impression that the Germans might invade Switzerland. In Germany, Otto Strasser was denounced as a left-wing nationalist who used a secret radio transmitter and was therefore quite capable of organizing an assassination attempt,"[9] said Fritz Heberlein, a friend of Strasser. Oster learned from Canaris that Germany would demand extradition of Strasser, claiming that he had emissaries constantly going back and forth between Zurich and Munich.

Strasser and Heberlein told me that agents pretending to be secret supporters of the Black Front (the anti-Nazi organization

created by Strasser) had offered to help them carry out a great
operation against Hitler. They wanted Strasser to meet with some
important conspirators at the Swiss town of Kreuzlingen, near the
German border. But Strasser, who knew that the Nazis had abducted the pacifist Berthold Jacob in Switzerland, refused their
offer. As soon as news of the Munich bomb explosion reached
him, Strasser said, "It's another version of the Reichstag fire.
They're going to accuse me of it and try to have me extradited."
And that was what happened. When the extradition request was
made, Strasser fled to France with the help of friends, including
Fritz Heberlein.

The Abduction at Venlo

Theo Hespers, a Catholic Youth leader who had taken refuge in
Holland, had remained in contact with anti-Nazi Christians in the
Ruhr. The SD succeeded in infiltrating them and making use of
them after discovering their identities.

Hespers knew of an anti-Nazi named Captain Schaemmel, but
had never seen him. Schaemmel sent word to Hespers that he
was coming to Holland and wanted to meet with him to discuss
important actions.

When Captain Schaemmel turned up in Holland, he presented
himself as a specialist in munitions transport. Seeming extraordinarily well informed about the war plans of the Third Reich, he
nevertheless claimed that he belonged to the opposition within
the army because he was against the war. His General, he said,
had ordered him to make contact with officers of the British Intelligence Service. He and his group wanted to overthrow Hitler's
barbaric anti-Christian regime.

Schaemmel was so convincing that he soon gained the confidence of Major Stevens and Captain Best, two perfect representatives of proper British society; like Schaemmel, Best wore a
monocle, and he and his companion had polished manners. They
both believed that young Captain Schaemmel hated the crude
dictator who now ruled his country. Seeing him not only as a
member of the anti-Hitler opposition but also as a valuable informer, they gave him a radio transmitter so that they could keep
in touch with him. He introduced his General to them: the Gen-

eral spoke with an Austrian accent, which increased the British officers' confidence still more.

The conspirators met several times at different places in Holland. There was to be a meeting on November 8, 1939, at which Schaemmel would give some important information to Stevens and Best, but at the last minute the two Germans changed its time to the next day and its location to the Café Bacchus in the town of Venlo, on the Dutch-German border. Schaemmel explained that it had to be in a border town because he would have very little time that day, but that his information was vitally important. Stevens and Best had the impression that the General was ready to go into action. And that night, when they heard on the radio that there had been an attempt to assassinate Hitler in Munich, they believed it had been the work of Schaemmel and his agents.

At about four o'clock in the afternoon of the next day, Stevens and Best drove up to the Café Bacchus in Venlo. Schaemmel was already there. No sooner had their car stopped than another car rushed toward it from the German side of the border. Men leapt out of the second car and quickly subdued Stevens and Best. Lieutenant Klop, a Dutch intelligence officer who was with the two Britons, tried to draw his pistol and was fatally wounded. The driver was also wounded. The attackers took possession of the car and drove it into German territory with all its occupants.

That crime has come to be known as the Venlo incident. Hitler presented the capture of Stevens and Best as proof that Britain had organized the Munich assassination attempt from Holland, with the help of the Dutch.

The abductors were agents of Heydrich, led by Alfred Naujocks, whom we have already seen at work in the Formis and Gleiwitz affairs. As a reward for his success, Naujocks was allowed to keep the British officers' car.

After the abduction, Stevens and Best learned that Captain Schaemmel was actually Heydrich's assistant Walter Schellenberg, and the General was his adviser on psychological matters, the psychiatrist Max de Crinis. De Crinis later boasted that he had correctly sized up the two British officers from the start: he had told Heydrich that they were gullible and could easily be drawn into the trap being set for them.

During the time when Heydrich was making preparations for the abduction, he was able to transmit false information to London, through Stevens and Best. He wanted to convince the British that there were powerful anti-Nazi currents in Germany, especially in the Wehrmacht and the Abwehr. It was true that many of Canaris's agents were not Nazis, but he had hired them because they had good connections in other countries and he believed that for this reason they could be valuable to the cause of the Third Reich.

Although I have great respect for Otto von Heydebreck's knowledge of the Third Reich, I cannot share his opinion that Canaris was surprised when he learned of the Munich bomb explosion. Heydrich and Canaris were still working closely together at that time, and continued to do so even during the great offensive in the West.

Two Useful Operations

The Munich bombing and the abduction that followed it had the desired diplomatic and military consequences. Hitler's myth was considerably reinforced. He was going to punish France for having helped Britain on the Continent, and the abduction would serve as a pretext for violating the neutrality of Holland, Belgium, and Luxembourg.

In his memoirs, Walter Schellenberg wrote that on the night of the explosion Himmler called him at Düsseldorf, convinced that the British had tried to kill Hitler, and ordered him to bring Stevens and Best into Germany as soon as possible. Having already been in contact with them, and having made an appointment with them for the next day, Schellenberg obeyed Himmler's order.

If this account were true, it would indicate that neither the explosion nor the abduction was a Nazi provocation. But its falsity can be shown by raising a few questions. Why did Schellenberg make his appointment with Stevens and Best at a place that was only a few feet away from the Dutch-German border? Why would Himmler have given the order for the abduction, rather than Heydrich, who had been directing the contacts between "Captain Schaemmel" (Schellenberg) and the two British

officers? Is it plausible that Hitler, who till then had been seeking a separate peace with Britian, would have decided on the
spur of the moment, before the investigation into the Munich
bombing had even begun, to have Himmler order such a serious
action as the abduction of British officers in the territory of a
neutral country?

Two more questions can be raised. In the Munich bombing,
did George Elser play the same part as Marinus van der Lubbe in
the Reichstag fire and Franz Honiok in the simulated attack on
the Gleiwitz radio station? At a time when the Nazis wanted to
vilify Britian, did Stevens and Best find themselves in the same
position as Dimitroff and Torgler six years earlier, when the
Nazis wanted to begin a massive persecution of the Communists?

The Nazis always staged a provocation before each great political, diplomatic, or military move, either to justify it or present it
as a reprisal. Van der Lubbe provided an opportunity to per-
secute the Communists and establish the Nazi dictatorship. Margarete Gruhn provided an opportunity to crush the opposition just
when Hitler was preparing to carry out plans that he had made
long before. Herschel Grynszpan killed a German embassy secretary in Paris when Goebbels was proclaiming that Prague was the
center of an international Jewish conspiracy. Honiok and the
"canned goods" attacked the Gleiwitz radio station when Hitler
wanted a decisive pretext for putting an end to "Polish provocations" by invading Poland.

Georg Elser was never tried for the Munich bombing, and after
his arrest, he was given relatively lenient treatment. At the
Sachsenhausen concentration camp, he had two rooms in a separate building. There he was allowed to play his zither, and he
even had a carpenter's bench and tools. He was also able to have
contacts with Stevens and Best, as described in the latter's book,
The Venlo Incident, published in 1950. If certain details of the
situation seemed implausible, we can conclude that Elser did not
succeed in making himself clearly understood. And by the time
Best wrote his book, he no longer had perfectly precise memories
of everything that had happened.

After the war, those who wanted to minimize the double crime
at Munich and Venlo tried to discredit Best's testimony by exaggerating certain implausibilities and apparent contradictions in

his account of Elser's story. But Elser talked with others besides Best and Stevens, including a Bible scholar who reported to Pastor Martin Niemoeller everything that Elser had said. Elser also confided in Josef Kojecki, a Czech journalist known in the Resistance as Nikolas, and each time he went to the infirmary he talked with Milivoj Pandurović, a Yugoslavian diplomat who reported those conversations after the war.

Although Best's account differs from those of Niemoeller, Kojecki, and Pandurović in some respects, they all agree on the main points: because of his Communist background, Elser was chosen to play the part of the would-be assassin; it was not he who put the bomb inside the pillar; the Gestapo took him to the Swiss border, where he was "arrested," according to the plan, so that he could later be accused of having committed the crime at the instigation of Otto Strasser and the British Intelligence Service.

Elser told his fellow prisoners that in the summer of 1940, at Sachsenhausen, the Gestapo had presented him with a new written version of his confession in which he admitted having made the time bomb and hidden it in the pillar. Then he had been ordered to make another bomb like the first one, in the little workshop in his cell, to convince Best and Stevens that he was capable of making such a device.

When Pandurović asked him why the Nazis had used him rather than someone else, he replied, "They chose me because I was a Communist and one of my friends had gone to Switzerland." Pandurović asked if the friend was Otto Strasser. No, said Elser, he was a childhood friend who later returned to Germany for a visit and was killed in an accident that was never completely cleared up. He added that if he had really committed the Munich bombing he would not have been so stupid as to have pictures of the Buergerbräukeller in his pocket when he reached the Swiss border.

He attributed the fact that he was still alive to the Nazis' intention of presenting him to the public as an alibi for the Gestapo. He compared his case with the Reichstag fire and the Gleiwitz attack; it was, he said, a dirty trick played by Himmler and Heydrich. Before and after the bombing, the Gestapo had had him interrogated by SS men who promised him enough money to buy the little house he wanted, as a reward for his contribution toward wiping out the plutocrats. This was confirmed by Walter Usslepp, his SS guard. Elser had asked him to tell the world what had happened to him, because he knew that eventually he would be killed. Usslepp, who was disgruntled at having been made a guard at Sachsenhausen because of a minor offense, became friendly with Elser and later told his story, as Elser had asked him to do.

Martin Niemoeller saw Elser for the last time in the shower room of the Dachau concentration camp. Elser seemed greatly depressed, because he expected to be liquidated before the end of the war. And he was right. On April 5, 1945, Heinrich Mueller, head of the Gestapo, sent a letter to the commandant of the Dachau camp ordering him to have Elser put to death and announce that he had been killed in an air raid. The order was obeyed.

The military writer Wilhelm von Schramm, who has thoroughly studied operations on the western front, concludes that Hitler owed his rapid victory to his secret service, which deceived the enemy so effectively that the German offensive in May 1940 was opposed only by scattered forces. Before the beginning of the offensive, a diversionary maneuver drew French armored units away from the main point of attack. A week later, in the Sedan sector, the French commander no longer had anything but rifles with which to oppose the German tanks. Schramm says that the officers of the Wehrmacht were deeply impressed by Hitler's ability as a strategist. This was confirmed to me by Otto von Heydebreck in his account of a conversation he had with Canaris after the French campaign. "The Fuehrer is a genius," said Canaris. "But our victory was possible only because our secret service was able to adapt itself perfectly to the Fuehrer's intuition."

Heydebreck told me that Britain and France had been deceived on two points: they believed that the Germans were massing troops for an assault on Switzerland, since the Munich bombing had escalated the war of nerves between Germany and Switzerland; and because of the Venlo provocation Anglo-French forces moved to the north, where they were to be encircled while Hitler delivered his main blow at Sedan. "For such important operations," said Heydebreck, "the Nazis could surely sacrifice a few 'canned goods,' even if they had to take them from their own ranks, as they did in the case of the Munich bombing."

Aside from Heydebreck's observations, examination of the distribution of Allied forces before the offensive leads to the conclusion that the German commander had fully succeeded in deceiving the French General Staff with regard to his real objectives. It was not without reason that Hitler awarded decorations to the men who took part in the Venlo abduction. At Heydrich's request, Schellenberg was given the Iron Cross by the Fuehrer himself.

Those who deny that the Munich bombing was a Nazi provocation use the argument that Himmler and Heydrich would never have ordered an explosion that resulted in casualties among the Nazis themselves: seven dead, sixteen seriously injured, and ten lightly injured. "Thirty other comrades were able to return home after rapid treatment in the hospital for insignificant injuries," said the *Voelkischer Beobachter* on November 10, 1939.

Skeptics reply that there had to be bloodshed in order to prove the brutality of the British; an assassination attempt with no victims would have been much less convincing. Moreover, the SD files contained the names of "warped" Germans who could be eliminated if circumstances called for it, and even SS men were sometimes placed on that blacklist, for faulty discipline or some other reason.

Hitler often said that it did not matter if a few Germans lost their lives in the struggle for an important goal. He had provoked bloody street fighting so that he could have his "martyrs" and demand reprisals. The Nazi party thus always had "canned goods" that the Fuehrer could use if the occasion warranted.

After the occupation of Holland, Theo Hespers, who had been lured into "conspiring" with the false Captain Schaemmel, fled to France. The Dunkirk debacle prevented him from reaching Britain. He was later arrested by the Gestapo and sentenced to death. In a common cell, he told his fellow prisoners that Schaemmel had guaranteed him, as well as Stevens and Best, that "Hitler and his clique" would be eliminated to the last man. Hespers also said that an Abwehr officer who came from Prague by order of Heydrich and Canaris had given Stevens and Best false information on the Czech refugees, and that Schaemmel had succeeded in deceiving everyone by claiming that the Abwehr officer belonged to a Czech secret service.

That officer was Paul Thummel. Heydrich later came to see him as a disloyal collaborator and a dangerous competitor, and had him arrested in Prague in January 1942. It has often been said that Thummel probably acted as a double agent by order of Heydrich and Canaris and that he was finally liquidated because he knew too much about the Munich bombing and the Venlo abduction.

Hespers was executed in the fall of 1943, but Heydrich ordered that Stevens and Best be well treated. He found a pretext for questioning them himself and giving them to understand that they had him to thank for not having been tried before a court that would have sentenced them to be shot. After Heydrich's death, Schellenberg saw to it that Stevens and Best continued to be well treated. Would not Elser also have been allowed to survive, as a living alibi, if he had really carried out the Munich bombing entirely on his own, as former Gestapo members claimed after the war?

Defenders of the Nazis try to make their claims more plausible by presenting those who were instruments of provocations as Resistance fighters: Van der Lubbe had the courage to take action against Hitler when the opposition parties had been reduced to cowardly silence; Grynszpan committed an assassination to draw the world's attention to the plight of the Jews; Elser tried to kill Hitler when the war was barely under way, whereas the German officers who tried to kill him in 1944 waited until the war was nearly over. But if that were true, Elser would have told his fellow prisoners about it. Instead, he constantly complained that he had been imprisoned on false charges.

Combat Duty or Secret Mission?

On May 5, 1940, Heydrich, who had the rank of Captain in the Luftwaffe as well as being the head of the recently created RSHA, sent a postcard from Norway to Himmler in Berlin saying that he had gone on active service with his unit and that while he would need a period of additional flight training, he hoped that within a week he would be able to perform his duties satisfactorily.

Thus five days before the beginning of the offensive in the West, Heydrich was in a combat zone in Norway. In Himmler's reply, dated May 15, he said that he was on his way to the western front in a special train. He reminded Heydrich that they had been together in another special train during the Polish campaign, and told him to send him daily reports on what was happening.

But why was Heydrich at a Luftwaffe base in Norway? Why had he not been sent to make preparations for the offensive in Holland, Belgium, and France? Was he in Norway so that he could win an Iron Cross for himself by flying combat missions? He could have done the same in the western offensive. His presence in Norway meant that he had something important to do in that particular sector.

According to Hans Bernd Gisevius, who got his information from Arthur Nebe, Heydrich was under orders not to go into combat: Hitler and Himmler did not want to lose their superpoliceman. And, still according to Gisevius, when Heydrich left for Norway, no one was able to find out why he had been sent there.

In early October 1939, after the defeat of Poland, Heydrich had been told to gather as much economic and military information as possible on Denmark and Norway, and to work closely with Canaris and Admiral Erich Raeder, Commander in Chief of the navy. Denmark and Norway had to be "protected against British aggression." Thus, the two countries would be occupied—for the following reasons:

1. To prevent the opening of a new theater of operations until the western offensive was over.

2. To install pro-Nazi governments in Copenhagen and Oslo. These governments would place their naval and merchant fleets at the disposal of the Third Reich in its struggle against Britain.

3. To keep open the sea route by which Swedish iron ore was shipped to Germany from the Norwegian port of Narvik. Without an assured supply of that ore, it would be impossible for Germany to win the war.

4. To incorporate Denmark and Norway into a friendly alliance

with Germany. This would have important psychological consequences. Economically and militarily, Sweden and Finland
would put their weight in the balance first against Britain, then
against the Soviet Union.

On October 10, 1939, Admiral Raeder opened discussions on
"the Norwegian question" from the standpoint of strategy.

Heydrich had received reports from Finland indicating that the
Soviet Union was about to take some sort of action. Hitler ordered that operations be postponed until Finno-Soviet relations
had become clarified. The western offensive would begin only
after the supply of Swedish iron ore had been guaranteed by a
lightning amphibious assault. Because of weather conditions in
northern Europe, it would be inadvisable to launch such an assault in winter.

On November 30, 1939, the Soviet Union attacked Finland.
The supply of iron ore immediately became the prime concern of
the Reich. Berlin was afraid that, on the pretext of helping
Finland, Britain might send an expeditionary force into Norway.

Hitler was also concerned with another problem. By invading
Norway and Denmark, both of which were monarchies, he would
greatly alarm the Swedish monarchy. But the Munich bombing
would have a favorable influence on the situation. According to
Nazi propaganda, it demonstrated that the British were willing to
use any means, however vicious and underhanded, to achieve
their ends, and Berlin could now announce that other vile British
plots were to be expected, this time aimed at cutting off Germany's supply of Swedish iron ore. The Munich bombing was
presented as an example of British brutality and a justification of
Hitler's foresight in signing the nonaggression pact with the Soviet Union, which protected the eastern frontier of the Reich.
More than ever, Nazi propaganda hammered away at "Jewish plutocrats and warmongers."

That propaganda found a scapegoat in Oslo: Carl Hambro,
President of the Storting, the Norwegian parliament. The Nazis
attacked him as a "flunky of the Jews" and gave their support to
Vidkun Quisling, a former Minister of Defense who was now the
leader of a Fascist party called the Nasjonal Samling. When
Hambro and his partisans began a campaign against the fifth column in Norway, Goebbels's propaganda called him a warmonger
and a public enemy.

A note found among Otto von Heydebreck's papers after his death sheds light on what later took place.

As the result of activities by the SD and the Foreign Policy Office [a Nazi party organization headed by Rosenberg], Quisling and his assistant [Viljam] Hagelin came to Berlin at the beginning of December 1939 for a secret visit. They had detailed conversations with Hitler, Hess, Goebbels, Rosenberg, Raeder, Himmler, Canaris, and Heydrich. According to the directives and plans adopted, before the western offensive, under diplomatic and military pressure, a government friendly to Germany would be installed in Oslo, with Quisling as its leader.

In 1958, Heydebreck told me that Colonel Oster, an anti-Nazi who was one of Canaris's confidential collaborators, had informed him that Quisling had promised to place the Norwegian fleet at the disposal of the Nazis if they made him the head of his country's government. There were already close relations between Quisling and Rosenberg through the channel of the Foreign Policy Office—that is, so to speak, between the German Nazi party and the Norwegian Nazi party. But in the background, Canaris and Heydrich were maneuvering with their agents and strengthening their influence on Admiral Raeder.

On December 11, 1939, Rosenberg wrote in his diary, "Just informed the Fuehrer of X's visit from Scandinavia." To a historian, there is no mystery: X, the visitor from Scandinavia, was none other than Quisling. On December 14, Rosenberg wrote, "On the twelfth, the Fuehrer again summoned me to the Reich Chancellery to tell me bout Quisling's proposition." And on December 19, "The first phase of the planned action in Norway is completed. On the fifteenth, Quisling, accompanied by Hagelin and [Hans-Wilhelm] Scheidt, my department head, was received by the Fuehrer."

Rosenberg's diary entries concerning Quisling's visit to Berlin show that the Norwegian also met with Goebbels and Hess; that they spoke of "the Jew Hambro," an agitator who was an enemy of Germany; and that they discussed Britain's plan to establish bases in Scandinavia for her fleet.

On April 19, 1940, Rosenberg wrote the following:

The Fuehrer first spoke for twenty minutes: he would naturally prefer to have Scandinavia be neutral, but he cannot allow En-

gland to install a base at Narvik. Then he read Quisling's memorandum: need for a great Germanic alliance. Quisling described
the situation, illegal since January 1, 1940, of the Norwegian
state, which is now in the hands of the Marxists and the Jewish
democrats. The salvation of Norway is crucial to Germany in her
decisive struggle against England.

Hitler received Quisling and Hagelin for the second time on
December 17, 1939. In the course of the one-hour conversation,
it was decided that after the German invasion of Norway Quisling
would be made Prime Minister and the entire Norwegian fleet
would be turned over to the Third Reich. First, however, Quisling's partisans would go to Germany for rapid training. The installation of a Quisling government in Oslo would open new
prospects to the German Navy with regard to Danish possessions
in the Atlantic: the Faroe Islands, Iceland, and even Greenland.

A little more than a month later, on January 27, 1940, Admiral Raeder created a special General Staff for the planned
operations in Denmark and Norway, whose code name was
Weseruebung ("Weser Exercise").

Meanwhile, the British had not remained idle. Suspecting that
Germany was about to strike in Scandinavia, they had intensified
their surveillance of the Scandinavian coasts. On February 16,
the British destroyer *Cossack* attacked the German supply ship
Altmark in Norwegian waters and freed British prisoners of war
who were being taken to Germany.

Ribbentrop immediately called a press conference at which
Professor Bruns, a specialist in international law, accused the
British of having violated Norwegian neutrality. The spokesman
for the German government denounced Hambro for having be-
trayed his country by becoming an accomplice of the British.

The *Altmark* incident obviously served Hitler's interests. He
could now set the Weser Exercise in motion and put pressure on
the King of Norway to make Quisling Prime Minister.

Although General Nikolaus von Falkenhorst had overall command of the operation, Heydrich was responsible for camouflaging it and creating special commando units that would occupy the
main government building in Oslo and key points in the port.
Because of Quisling's valuable aid, Heydrich had no particularly

difficult problems to solve. From his long service in the War
Ministry, Quisling knew the exact location of each fortress and
aircraft hangar and the anchoring berth of every warship.

Hitler was determined to achieve maximum success with minimum engagement of forces. The invasion had to be so rapid that
the King of Norway could be taken into custody; this was a necessary condition for the "legal" installation of a pro-Nazi government. Armed conflict was to be avoided as much as possible.

When the airfields had been occupied, an invasion fleet of
about two hundred ships, carrying troops, munitions, and sup-
plies, would enter the fjords. Quisling's agents would tell the
people that the British were on the way to Norway to violate her
neutrality. Aboard the German ships, English-speaking radio operators would deceive the coastal defenses.

The invasion was scheduled to begin on April 9, 1940. Narvik, the crucial point on the iron-ore route, would be occupied by
two thousand soldiers under the command of General Eduard
Dietl. Seven ports would be occupied in that lightning operation,
including the port of Oslo.

The invasion began on April 9 as planned. In Trondheim Fjord
the cruiser *Hipper* and four destroyers, carrying seventeen hundred troops, were able to reach the harbor without being fired
upon because the *Hipper* signaled to coastal batteries in English,
"I come on government instructions." But at Narvik, after the
landing had taken place, the British battleship *Warspite* and a
flotilla of destroyers inflicted heavy losses on the German warships.

Although General von Falkenhorst announced that the operation had succeeded on the day of the landing, General Jodl wrote
in his diary on April 14 that Hitler was far from being satisfied.
His disappointment came not only from German losses but also
from the fact that the King had refused to place Quisling in
power, which meant that there could not be a peaceful occupation and that Germany could not count on the help of the Norwegian fleet in fighting Britain. Still worse: a British landing,
encouraged by the Norwegians, was imminent.

A scapegoat was needed. Curt Bräuer, special envoy of the
Foreign Policy Office who had not succeeded in making King
Haakon surrender, was suspended from his functions. Heydrich

strongly condemned Bräuer's failure and the "slovenliness of the
military operation" because the complications that occurred directly affected the German secret service. The flagship *Bluecher*,
accompanied by the. pocket battleship *Luetzow* and two other
units, was supposed to take Oslo and its port "peacefully." Instead it was sunk, with Heydrich's entire team aboard, by Norwegian shore batteries. The survivors of the team had to swim
ashore, as did Rear Admiral Oskar Kummetz, commander of the
squadron, and General Erwin Engelbrecht, commander of the infantry troops. The Germans did not capture Oslo until after they
had called in paratroops and airborne infantry.

Thanks to Norwegian resistance, King Haakon and the members of Parliament were able to escape from Oslo. Quisling proclaimed himself Prime Minister, but had to give up his claim to
that position by order of Hitler, who wanted to save face. It was
during these critical days that Hitler was advised to hold at least
twenty prominent Norwegians as hostages and threaten to shoot
them if the King refused to order a cessation of resistance.

On April 13, General von Falkenhorst had twenty hostages
taken, including Bishop Eivind Berggrav and Paal Berg, a famous jurist. As Didrik Arup Seip, Vice-Chancellor of Oslo University, later told his fellow prisoners in the Sachsenhausen
concentration camp, the taking of hostages was an SD operation.

But the Norwegians did not bow to the ultimatum. The King
and his army continued their resistance in the northern part of
the country. On April 20, a British brigade and three French
battalions landed at Namsos, and a second British brigade landed
at Andalsnes. The fighting became so violent that Hitler began to
fear that the iron-ore route might be cut off. By May 5,
when Heydrich sent his postcard to Himmler, there were about
twenty-five thousand Allied soldiers in Norway, and the Norwegians themselves were still fighting tenaciously. On May 28,
British, French, and Polish units drove General Dietl's troops out
of Narvik.

Norwegian resistance ultimately proved to be futile, however,
because after May 10, when the western offensive began, the
British and French had to begin withdrawing forces from Norway
and sending them to defend France. On June 7, King Haakon
boarded the British cruiser *Devonshire* at Tromsø and left for ex-

ile in England. The Allies pulled out of Norway, and the Norwegians surrendered on June 8. But the invasion was a
disappointment for the Germans: they had to give up their hope
of being able to use the Norwegian fleet.

Josef Terboven, a Gauleiter who had Goebbels's confidence,
was appointed Reich Commissar for Norway. He made Quisling
Prime Minister, but not until 1942, after two years of impatience
on Quisling's part.

On April 9, the day when the invasion of Norway began, Rosenberg wrote in his diary:

> Today is a great day in the history of Germany. Denmark and
> Norway are occupied. I congratulate the Fuehrer on that action,
> which I also helped to prepare. He is beaming with joy. Quisling
> can now set up his government . . . The Fuehrer said, "Just as
> Bismarck's Reich began in 1866, the Great Germanic Reich has
> begun today."

But the Norwegian operation did not turn out as Hitler had
expected. According to Himmler, the only truly successful part of
it was the work of Heydrich, who created a new Norwegian regime capable of functioning effectively and temporarily eliminated the unpopular Quisling.

On April 20, Hitler, Himmler, Goering, and Bormann met to
discuss the chaotic situation in Norway. Goering took part in the
meeting as a representative of the Wehrmacht. Josef Terboven,
the Nazi leader chosen to be the Reich Commissar for Norway,
was also there.

It had been Himmler and Heydrich who proposed sending a
high party official to Norway. They also had made another important decision: Heydrich would install in Norway a special SS
group that would not be under Terboven's direct command.

A week after that meeting, Heydrich was in Norway to carry
out his task, camouflaged as a Luftwaffe Captain. In Oslo there
was turbulent infighting among Ribbentrop's men, Quisling's supporters, local politicians, and members of the Wehrmacht and
the SS, and Berlin was unable to bring it under control.
Heydrich's real mission was to put order into that seething mass
of rivalries.

King Haakon's flight from Norway was another disappointment to Hitler. Before the invasion, Heydrich's SD had made plans to take the King and the most important political leaders into custody in order to prevent them from leaving the country. This was to be done in such a way as to make the world believe that they had voluntarily placed themselves under the Germans' protection. Their arrest and the invasion were to take place simultaneously. But, as we have seen, the cruiser *Bluecher*, carrying Heydrich's team of experts, was sunk before it could reach Oslo. That put an end to the plan by which Curt Bräuer, the German special envoy, was to present a memorandum to the Norwegian Minister of Foreign Affairs while the city was encircled. Instead, the King, his ministers, and the members of Parliament were able to leave Oslo and go to Hamar, about sixty miles to the north.

Heydrich had one of his men, Franz Stahlecker, assigned to work with Terboven as an expert on police and security matters. Stahlecker was given the meaningless title of Government Director. Before taking that position, he had been the SD chief in Bohemia and Moravia, where he had earned the reputation of being an incredibly brutal man to whom human life meant nothing. (Early in the war against the Soviet Union, Heydrich placed Stahlecker in command of a murder squad that killed 221,000 people in the Baltic region. In March 1942, Stahlecker was killed by Soviet partisans.)

Heydrich decided that efforts toward solving the "racial problem" in Norway had to begin immediately with a census of Jews. At the same time, all leftists and members of the workers' movement were to be arrested. The man placed in charge of these operations was Dr. Schiedermair, an SS Sturmbannfuehrer who held an important post in the SD.

After the war, apologists for the Third Reich tried to prove that the occupation of Norway had been the outcome of a race between Britian and Germany. They fail to mention, of course, that the operation took place in accordance with a plan to which Hitler and Quisling had agreed in December 1939.

The Norwegian officers and patriots who were sent to German concentration camps knew very well that the main outlines of the invasion and occupation had been settled long in advance by the SD, the Abwehr, and Quisling's men. "They knew exactly which

ships would come into the fjords," the Norwegian poet Arnulf
Överland told me, "and the number of infantrymen and paratroopers. They had also worked out the stratagems that would be
used to overcome Norwegian resistance. Traitors waiting for them
in the harbors signaled to them to show them the way in the
darkness."

Many historians make no mention of Heydrich's mission in
Norway, or else describe it as an ordinary tour of duty by a Luftwaffe officer. Not a word about the thousands and thousands of
people arrested by his henchmen in Norway till 1942, the year of
his death, or the seven thousand sent to German concentration
camps. Among them were Didrik Arup Seip; many doctors, teachers, and students; Arnulf Överland; and Odd Nansen, son of the
explorer and pacifist Fridtjof Nansen. In the concentration camp
where we were together, Överland told me that Heydrich had
personally organized the deportation of members of the Norwegian
Resistance and founded the Grini concentration camp. He said:

> While Heydrich was in Norway, he tried to use airborne troops to
> prevent King Haakon from escaping to England. And he person-
> ally interrogated several political leaders. As for the massive ex-
> ecutions we believed he was capable of ordering, they never took
> place, because they would have caused serious trouble in Sweden
> and Finland.

Överland considered that Himmler and Heydrich had suffered a
defeat in Norway because they had thought they could easily
make the King a collaborator.

Denmark, which had no defenses comparable to those of Norway, had had to surrender immediately to overwhelmingly superior forces. Heydrich's policemen then quickly began hunting
down Danes regarded as "hostile to Germany."

The occupation of Norway cost the Third Reich 1,317 dead,
2,375 missing, and 1,604 wounded, a total loss of 5,296 soldiers. British, French, and Polish units lost about five thousand.

German ideologues of racism, such as Rosenberg, Himmler,
Heydrich, and Canaris, hurried to Denmark and Norway. The
incorporation of those two Viking countries would prove to Germany's allies that the Great Germanic Reich had become a real-

ity. The Nazis immediately set to work, but for the moment they avoided taking their most drastic measures, so as not to alarm Sweden. They explained the repression of Jews and political refugees by saying that Germany had not waged war against the Danes or the Norwegians and that the only goal of the occupation forces was to rid the two countries of their subversive and alien elements and protect them against British aggression.

Heydrich's plan called for all Jews living in Denmark and Norway to be registered, "in preparation for increased emigration." In 1942, he listed their numbers as 5,600 in Denmark and 1,300 in Norway. At the time of his death, their deportation to Auschwitz had been planned in great detail.

Heydrich was eager to "cleanse" Denmark and Norway of their Jews, but he had to take into account reactions among the local populations and in Sweden. His successors waited four months after his death before setting up a camp in Norway. More months went by, then in November 1942, in an operation conducted by the SD, 725 Jews were arrested and 691 refugees classified as "stateless" were deported to Auschwitz. They were followed in March 1943 by a second group of 158 men, women, and children. Of all the Jews sent to Auschwitz from Denmark and Norway, only thirteen were still alive at the end of the war. About eight hundred Jews succeeded in crossing the border and taking refuge in Sweden.

Heydrich was deeply disappointed by the intransigence of the Swedish government. The Nazis' military victories did not deter the Swedes from taking in refugees from Germany and other countries. The Danes also made their contribution: many of the Jews in Denmark were able to escape to Sweden in fishing boats.

Norway remained a source of concern for Heydrich until his death, primarily because the Germans intended to capture the important port of Murmansk by launching an assault against it from Norway after the invasion of the Soviet Union had begun. They never captured Murmansk; they used their best SS units in the attempt, without success.

The SD in France

Since the invasion of Norway had almost ended in failure, Heydrich could scarcely boast of the work his collaborators had done there. But Himmler, whose attention was focused on the development of the military and political situation in France, was fully satisfied. The offensive in the west had moved forward with the speed and power of an avalanche. As Colonel Charles de Gaulle had predicted three years earlier, Hitler's "mechanical force" had plunged through Holland, Belgium, and Luxembourg and then into France.

Even before the invasion, Heydrich had chosen his best SD agents with the intention of sending them into France. He assumed command of the psychological front during the "phony war." His spies reported on Frenchmen in important positions and divided them into three categories: friends, enemies, and neutral. His fifth column included intellectuals, journalists, government officials, and renegades from various parties.

German military espionage in France zealously tried to make sure that the Norwegian "betrayal" of the New Europe would not be repeated. The legal French government had to be prevented from fleeing to Africa or Britain. Meanwhile, Himmler, Heydrich, and Ribbentrop had realized that certain French generals and police chiefs were not inclined to follow the example of the Poles and Norwegians. Prime Minister Paul Reynaud was regarded as a particularly dangerous adversary: he was known for maintaining close relations with Britain and exercising a strong influence on all officers with "anti-Marxist" ideas.

On June 6, 1940, while the offensive was still under way, Charles de Gaulle was promoted to Brigadier General and made Undersecretary of War in Reynaud's cabinet. This worried Hitler and his strategists, despite their continuing victories, because they took it to mean that they were now less likely to succeed in their plan to have the French government headed by a military man who would recommend surrender and participate in building the New Europe.

Himmler and Heydrich were also determined to have France incorporated into the New Europe, a move that would deal a damaging blow to the "warmongers" in London. For Winston Churchill, the loss of positions on the Continent was only a temporary setback and not an indication of total defeat. If Reynaud adopted that viewpoint, the final victory of the Third Reich would be placed in question. A continuation of hostilities in North Africa would strengthen Churchill's position and encourage increased arms production in the United States. In the Mediterranean, Italy, Germany's ally, could not withstand a British and French onslaught.

Even after German troops entered Paris, unopposed, on June 14, Hitler was still wondering if the Reynaud government would go on fighting from Britain or North Africa. "A repetition of the example given by King Haakon of Norway would have been disastrous," Heydrich said in Paris, after the armistice, to Major d'Hôpital, former aide-de-camp of Marshal Foch. D'Hôpital, who was later arrested by the Nazis and sent to the Sachsenhausen concentration camp, said that the leaders of the fifth column in France had been impatient to learn whether or not the Reynaud government and the top military commanders would decide to leave France. Heydrich was sure that Georges Mandel, Minister of the Interior, favored taking the government into exile. Major d'Hôpital became acquainted with discussions on these matters within the SD through Brigadefuehrer Alfred Thomas, who was known for talking a little too much when he was drunk. In Paris, everyone knew that Thomas's daughter was on intimate terms with Heydrich.

The Germans were reassured on June 16, when Marshal Pétain, a great hero of World War I, delivered an ultimatum to Reynaud, threatening to resign if hostilities were not ended immediately. He felt confident in taking that stand because he knew that most of Reynaud's ministers recommended signing an armistice with the Germans.

"When Pétain threatened to resign," General de Gaulle said to me in 1956, "he already had in his briefcase a list of the men who would compose the new government he expected to head. And when Lebrun gave him the presidency, the fate of France was sealed." (Albert Lebrun, President of France, resigned in July 1940.)

In June 1940, de Gaulle fled to London and, on BBC radio, broadcast his famous appeal to the French people: "We have lost a battle, we have not lost the war."

On June 22, when a delegation sent by Pétain signed an armistice that was essentially a surrender, Hitler was triumphant in front of his Generals, not so much because of his spectacular military victory as because the French government had remained in France and agreed not to let the French Navy and Merchant Marine fall into the hands of the British.

The Germans now controlled the Atlantic coast from Belgium to the Spanish border. They occupied "only" three-fifths of France's territory, which was under their direct rule. France had undertaken to pay Germany four hundred million francs a year for the maintenance of two million German soldiers. An equal number of French soldiers remained prisoners of war. French industry would work for Hitler's war machine.

The German victory over France owed a great deal to Heydrich. Using anti-Marxist and anti-Semitic slogans, his agents had succeeded in launching the fifth column into subversive action. Two clandestine radio transmitters, installed and operated by Heydrich's men, had hastened the collapse of France by broadcasting false information and undermining the morale of the French; "Radio Humanity" and "The Voice of Peace" had accomplished their mission.

Hitler needed a peaceful and collaborating France for his plan of world conquest. Paris would remain intact, even though seventy years earlier Richard Wagner had said that it ought to be destroyed. For the moment, Hitler wanted to make the French capital illustrate a collaboration that functioned perfectly. On Himmler's advice, he decided not to disarm the Paris police.

Heydrich realized that the police could be turned into a force that would support the occupation authorities and help to incorporate France into the new order. He was well aware that, at first, direct domination by the Gestapo had to be avoided, in order not to alarm those willing to collaborate. The conquered French had to be treated on equal terms to encourage them to take part in the restructuring of Europe. At the beginning of the occupation, therefore, the SD limited itself to arresting and deporting German refugees, while order was maintained by the Geheime Feldpolizei (secret army police) and the Feldgendarmerie (military police) under the sole authority of the Wehrmacht. The Geheime Feldpolizei began with a force of twenty-six hundred men and quickly increased it to six thousand. Each man was given special training by the SD.

In Paris the SD, which worked closely with the Geheime Feldpolizei, had a team of twenty secret agents headed by Helmuth Knochen, an energetic SS man who was an expert on life in France and, of course, spoke French well. Heydrich had taken him into the SD in 1937, with the rank of Obersturmfuehrer. On June 14, Knochen came to Paris and, with his team, settled into the Hôtel du Louvre. He later stayed in the Hôtel Scribe, then at 57 Boulevard Lannes, and finally in an elegant building at 72 Avenue Foch.

Heydrich saw to it that the occupied zone was kept under surveillance by men in whom he had complete confidence. Boemelburg, the police attaché of the German embassy, had worked with Heydrich as a secret agent in France before the occupation and was considered to have a thorough knowledge of the French police. SD operations in Paris were ultimately controlled by a close friend of Heydrich, SS Brigadefuehrer Alfred Thomas, who maintained relations with the German embassy and the military High Command in France. Werner Best, Heydrich's assistant, had a post in the military administration. He was concerned mainly with the Geheime Feldpolizei and the Feldgendarmerie. Although those two police forces were officially within the jurisdiction of the military Commander in Chief, they were kept under secret surveillance by Best. His surveillance also extended to the French police.

Heydrich's agents in Paris tracked down German and Austrian refugees, Jews, Freemasons, and Communists; they gathered art treasures and "put them in safekeeping"; they had ethnic and racial studies made; they coordinated groups of collaborators, so successfully that they soon had friends in some of the highest circles of French society.

At first the SD establishment in Paris left little to be desired, but Heydrich later became dissatisfied with it and decided that it had to be reorganized. Despite the tireless and merciless efforts of his friends Thomas and Dannecker, he was never able to bring about a "spontaneous" pogrom of the kind that had occurred in Germany in 1938. On the contrary, the persecution of Jews and the operations of Heydrich's men in Paris aroused great hostility. Thousands of men, women, and children disappeared; they were first taken to temporary camps, then sent by train to death camps in Germany. General de Gaulle's appeal had not been in vain. Little by little, French resistance was stiffening.

The history of the German secret service in France is insepara-
ble from the activities of Reinhard Heydrich. He was directly or
indirectly involved in all operations intended to insure the do-
cility of France. Twenty days before his death, he returned to
Paris to give his agents new instructions for increasing the efficiency of their efforts toward "racial purification."

Paris, the city that was loved by so many German invaders,
did not find favor in Heydrich's eyes. As a Wagnerian, he was
repelled by its universality and its revolutionary tradition. For
him, collaboration was only a temporary tactic; the French people, a mixture of "non-Germanic elements," would eventually
have to be thoroughly purged.

Heydrich's Contribution to Hitler's Reputation as a Great Strategist

Heydrich attributed much less importance to his security measures than to SD operations that helped the Fuehrer to achieve
his political and military objectives. According to Major
d'Hôpital, SS Brigadefuehrer Alfred Thomas once said that the
Western powers had been deluded about Hitler's war plans after
the Munich bombing and the Venlo abduction, and that Heydrich
deserved all the credit for misleading them. A brief look at the
situation just before the beginning of the offensive in the West
will show that Thomas had good reasons for making that statement.

Swiss historians have reported that in October 1939 the German secret service was able to convince the Swiss military leaders that the Third Reich was about to invade their country. The
German military historian Wilhelm Ritter von Schramm is also of
the opinion that German accusations against Switzerland after the
Munich bombing strengthened the Allies' belief that the opening
phase of Hitler's offensive would be an invasion of Switzerland.
Thanks to Heydrich's SD, the Germans were able to make the
French High Command go on believing it until the offensive actually began on May 10, 1940.

In the Ardennes breakthrough, General von Rundstedt's Army
Group A had forty-five divisions, including seven armored and
three motorized divisions. The Allied forces confronting them
were in a state of chaos created by the deceptive machinations

and propaganda of the German secret service. According to
Wilhelm von Schramm, "To German officers, Hitler seemed to be
the greatest strategist of all time. When he returned to Berlin
after the surrender of France, he was almost worshiped as a god."

Himmler and Heydrich were given no official recognition in
that victory celebration. Since 1934—that is, since the Night of
the Long Knives—Heydrich had not been promoted in rank. Was
that simply the result of ingratitude, or was it part of a deliberate
effort to keep him in the background? In any case, after the
victory in the West he continued working in the shadows, as
always.

The SD in the Campaign for Peace with Britain

Heydrich was prepared for the occupation of Britain. He had lists
of prominent people to be arrested and sent to concentration
camps, and he had worked out the details of how the population
would be treated. But Hitler did not really expect to invade Britain. He believed the British would be willing to make peace after
the fall of France, and that was the solution he preferred. Contrary to Ribbentrop's assurances, however, German peace offers
continued to be rejected. Heydrich began taking a new approach
to the problem, using the resources of his SD.

Meanwhile, the invasion of the Soviet Union was still scheduled for the summer of 1941. Hitler had not lost hope that Britain, in view of the surrender of Scandinavia and the German
victory in France, would accept peace rather than face possible
annihilation. He could use two means to bring that about: the
threat of an imminent invasion and propaganda efforts directed
toward British conservatives, who were regarded in Berlin as
being opposed to the war.

A secret report from London stated that, as a precondition for a
peace settlement with Britain, the Munich bombing must no
longer be attributed to the British Intelligence Service, and that
great emphasis must be placed on Germany's good relations with
the Soviet Union, so that Britain could have no hope of an alliance with the Soviet Union against Germany.

In Colonel Vladimir Vauhnik, the Yugoslavian military attaché in Berlin, Heydrich found an ideal instrument for transmitting propaganda and misinformation. A former officer in the Austro-Hungarian Army and a hardened anti-Communist, Vauhnik was a close friend of Prince Paul of Yugoslavia, who was married to Princess Olga of Greece, sister of the Duchess of Kent. Heydrich and Schellenberg immediately realized how valuable Vauhnik could be to them; they would have only to maneuver him skillfully, without letting him realize that he was being used.

And so one day, Vauhnik met a young woman who worked as a cashier in a Berlin restaurant that was frequented mainly by military men. She quickly became his mistress and began regularly giving him information that she happened to pick up from Wehrmacht officers who came to the restaurant. She also told him that she sometimes got information from a relative who, though opposed to Hitler, was a member of the General Staff. It goes without saying that the SD was the real source of her "revelations" to Vauhnik. He repeated many of them to Ivo Andrić, the Yugoslavian ambassador (who in 1961 was awarded a Nobel Prize in literature).

Heydrich used this channel to Yugoslavia to transmit certain parts of the plan for invading Britain, without revealing that it had been abandoned. The reports reached Britain, as expected, and caused great concern by fostering the belief that the invasion was going to be launched from Western Europe and Norway at the same time. Vauhnik specified that Goering had assembled a fleet of eighteen thousand planes and an airborne army of a million men for the assault.

Heydrich gathered information on all the most influential families of Britain. On the basis of dubious reports, he believed that part of the upper classes did not wholeheartedly accept Churchill's policy of war to the bitter end, and that before the defeat of France it had been assumed that if French resistance collapsed Churchill would be forced either to alter his policy or abandon it altogether. It was therefore not by chance that when France had been conquered, Hitler made a peace offer to the British.

Soon afterward, Rudolf Hess had a discussion with Professor Karl Haushofer and his son Albrecht, specialists in geopolitics, on the possibility of contacting influential circles in Britain. The Haushofers were known for having excellent relations with British scholars, who regarded them as experts on the Commonwealth.

Those two men, thought the Nazis, could effectively vouch for the sincerity of Hitler's peace initiative and get in touch, via Lisbon, with certain prominent Britons, including Lord Hamilton, who were considered to be opposed to the war. But first Heydrich's intervention was needed. A series of false reports had to reach the British leaders and convince them that an overwhelmingly powerful invasion force was about to attack their country.

Many of the historians who have tried to describe the real Heydrich believe that flying was only a pastime for him. That is not true. To Heydrich, being a pilot meant that in some cases he could do his work more efficiently. It was his widow who, after the war, transformed his enthusiasm for flying into the innocent hobby of an adventurous hero. According to her, he was severely reprimanded for having flown in Norway without permission. "That was the end of his career as a pilot."[10]

But in view of the fact that for his services in Norway he was awarded the Iron Cross, Second Class, as well as the bronze bar of a combat pilot, it is safe to assume that he was not reprimanded. And Lina Heydrich makes a second mistake when she claims that her husband's career as a pilot ended with that Norwegian episode: a year later, in May 1941, he was flying again, this time over the English Channel.

It was a period of calm on the western front because the Wehrmacht was engaged in "the greatest camouflage maneuver," as it was described by Keitel, Hitler's Chief of Staff, a maneuver that was to precede the invasion of the Soviet Union. The Nazis wanted to make the world believe that they intended to invade only Britain. Heydrich was told to draw up a detailed report by June 10, 1941, "proving" that the Soviet Union was planning to attack Germany that summer. But early in May, he unexpectedly left to make a flight over the Channel, and Schellenberg was ordered to finish the report.

Some years later, Gisevius said, "Nebe's attention was always alerted when Heydrich, his chief, was sent on a mission as a pilot; he sensed that something secret was under way."[11] Nebe later said that Heydrich sometimes boasted of those flights and showed aerial photographs of England and Scotland taken by him and his squadron.

May 10, 1941, the day when Heydrich made his reconnaissance flight over the Channel, was also the day when Rudolf Hess made his historic flight to Scotland. After the war, Lina Heydrich claimed that the two flights had taken place on the same day only by coincidence. But it must be pointed out that the superpoliceman of the Third Reich surely did not confide all important state secrets to his wife.

Soon after Hess had safely reached Scotland, Heydrich was called back to Berlin, and he then flew to Obersalzberg, where Hitler was staying. After the war, all the surviving Nazi dignitaries maintained that Hitler was enraged by Hess's flight and the fact that he had been able to make his preparations for it in secret. That is a fabrication. Professor Haushofer, the expert on geopolitics, was aware of the increasingly frequent contacts between Hess and certain British circles. He was not accused of treason, and neither was Hess himself.

An official communiqué stated that British agents had drawn Hess into a trap, using his hope of peace as bait. This was a ruse by the Nazis, designed to convince the Russians that Hess was one of those who rejected the idea of an invasion of Britain. To make the ruse more plausible, Heydrich had members of Hess's staff arrested.

After landing by parachute in Scotland, Hess tried to persuade the British to accept Hitler's peace offer and described the terrible fate that lay in store for them if they refused. But when he was forced to recognize that his dramatic effort had failed, he suddenly claimed to have amnesia and made such a realistic pretense of insanity that psychiatrists were taken in by it. In a letter to his wife after the war, he boasted of his clever performance. His insistence that he remembered nothing of his time in the Third Reich had only one purpose: to keep secret the plans of the conspirators responsible for World War II. In a speech that he made before his flight, at his trial in Nuremburg after the war, and during his subsequent imprisonment at Spandau, he persistently maintained that Germany had always struggled for peace.

It can be argued that the Nazi leaders must have been demented to believe that they could change the face of the world and separate peoples from their governments by using skillfully staged provocations. Their attempts at deception succeeded only in their own country, not because the German people had a special mentality that made them vulnerable to such machinations, but because the Nazi reign of terror left them no choice

7

The Generalissimo of the Racial War

Heydrich knew that the invasion of the Soviet Union would provide an opportunity to begin work on the "Final Solution of the Jewish problem." Before the offensive in the West, that solution had never been among the Nazis' most immediate concerns; they had alluded to it only in passing. Hitler had felt it was best not to arouse too much indignation and alarm among the Jews in Western countries. After the defeat of France, it became possible to deal with the problem more effectively, presenting it as an internal matter: each occupied country would promulgate its own anti-Jewish laws and act accordingly. But the main operation would not begin until the invasion of the Soviet Union was under way. The turmoil created by that vast assault would serve to camouflage the Final Solution.

For Hitler, the Soviet Union was only an extension of international Jewry. He believed that the British had rejected his peace offer because they thought they could count on the Russians. In conquering the Soviet Union, he would be striking a decisive blow at the worldwide conspiracy of Judeo-bolshevism.

The Nazis' anti-Semitic views were expressed in three films released in the second half of 1940: *The Rothschilds* (first shown on July 11, shortly after the fall of France), *The Jew Suess* (first shown in Venice on September 6), and *The Eternal Jew* (first shown on November 29). The last film was a "documentary" on world Jewry with a scenario by Eberhard Taubert, one of Goebbels's collaborators and a specialist on the struggle against Judeo-bolshevism. Taubert worked closely not only with Goebbels

235

but also with Rosenberg, Himmler, and Heydrich. It was Heydrich and Adolf Eichmann who had provided him with material for *The Eternal Jew.*

The Madagascar Plan

After the victory over France, Heydrich turned his attention to the Madagascar Plan, which called for deporting European Jews to that large island off the southeast coast of Africa. But he regarded this plan only as a partial measure and did not give up the idea of a total solution.

At his trial in Israel in 1961, Adolf Eichmann, who had been Heydrich's assistant, naturally did his best to present his activities in a favorable light. He maintained that the purpose of the Madagascar Plan was to "put firm ground under the feet of the Jews" by providing them with their own state, and that their future would have developed to their satisfaction, as well as that of the Nazis, if political circumstances had not caused the plan to be abandoned.

Eichmann's judges were not taken in by his attempt to deceive them. The details of the Madagascar Plan that have been preserved in writing show that the four million Jews chosen as victims would have had no chance of surviving on the island. The "independent state" would have quickly degenerated into a police state ruled by the RSHA.

The Madagascar Plan was a camouflage maneuver by which the Nazis tried to conceal their real intentions from the world and prevent Jewish opposition to their Final Solution, that is, the extermination of the Jews in Europe. They hoped to blind their victims to the point where they would cooperate in their own destruction—and to a large extent they succeeded. Heydrich was able to build up files on Jewish communities with the help of their leaders, who believed they were working to prepare for an emigration that would save Jewish lives. Jews who had been registered in this way were often told to fill out forms in which they listed all their property and consented to being evacuated.

The Nazis claimed that carrying out the Madagascar Plan would take four years—exactly the length of time in which Hitler expected to subjugate all of Europe. Meanwhile, the SD quietly continued its efforts toward achieving the Final Solution.

That tissue of lies and blackmail that constituted the Madagascar Plan eventually appeared as what it actually was: an anti-Jewish operation disguised as the realization of the Zionist ideal. It was officially presented for the first time in speeches made by Rosenberg in 1939. During the war, it was manifested in various forms, but took on a particularly ignoble aspect with the "evacuation" of the Hungarian Jews in 1944, when Himmler's emissaries began negotiating with representatives of Jewish organizations in Stockholm for the release of Jews in concentration camps. Himmler sent Schellenberg and Felix Kersten, his masseur, to establish the first contacts in Sweden. Their instructions were to advocate the Madagascar Plan once again, but this time for a different purpose: to obtain better treatment for the SS after Germany's defeat.

Defenders of the Third Reich claim that the extermination of the Jews did not begin until after the invasion of the Soviet Union and that, before then, the Nazis had tried to transplant the Jewish population, as was exemplified by the Madagascar Plan. The Final Solution was thus a historical accident brought about by the war and one of the many crimes of that war: the chance of Jewish salvation represented by the evacuation program was lost because of the Allies' intransigence.

It is understandable that after the war Kersten and Schellenberg falsely described the mission they had been given by Himmler. They could not have been expected to admit that the goal of their trip to Stockholm was to provide an alibi for the SS. Hjalmar Schacht, former Finance Minister of the Third Reich, and the man who made possible the financing of the war and let Himmler use his services for the Madagascar Plan, also gave a distorted version of the whole affair. He said that no German Jews would have lost their lives if his plans for massive emigration had been accepted internationally.

To understand the context of Schacht's statement, we must go back to 1938, when Heydrich was able to convince several countries that Germany was trying to solve the Jewish problem in the best possible way. Hitler also used Schacht in that diversionary maneuver, since Schacht had excellent relations with influential people in Britain and the United States. At that time, when the

Third Reich was just beginning to expand, Hitler did not want to arouse international opposition by overt persecution of Jews. The Nazis therefore let it be known that the German authorities were willing to allow a massive Jewish evacuation, but that the operation would take more money than Germany could supply alone.

Schacht contacted the Americans, the British, and Jews all over the world to propose that they gather funds for an international loan that would make it possible to transport Jews to Madagascar, where they could create a Jewish state. It goes without saying that he would not have made such contacts without the consent of Himmler and Heydrich, not to mention Hitler himself. In the course of the negotiations, Schacht stated that the Third Reich would repay the loan in twenty years by means of compensation for confiscated Jewish property.

According to Schacht, the Madagascar Plan failed because world banks influenced by Jews refused to give Germany a loan and Britain refused to grant free passage to ships carrying Jewish emigrants. He stated further that only as a result of that failure was the Wannsee Conference held in 1942 to deal for the first time with the "Final Solution of the Jewish problem." In this view, the British and the Jews themselves were responsible for the horrible fate of European Jews.

In the 1950's, I was told by one of Schacht's former collaborators, and by a Munich journalist, that Schacht had become involved in the Madagascar Plan for purely humanitarian reasons and that he had seriously considered it to be workable. I then had a telephone conversation with Schacht himself.

After he had told me that Hitler really intended to create "at least one Jewish state," I asked him, "Just after the occupation of France, why did the evacuation of several million Jews and the creation of a Jewish state become so urgent that you and several humanitarian organizations were called upon to help bring it about?" He replied that he did not know. I asked him if he thought it was possible that Hitler had deceived him, intending to use the fate of the Jews as a means of inducing Britain to make peace. "I don't know what was in Hitler's mind," he said, "but I can assure you that I never suspected the existence of an extermination plan. I acted in the firm conviction that Himmler and Heydrich intended to get rid of the Jews by expelling them."

It is regrettable that Schacht, who knew about Hitler's war plans and therefore must have guessed what was behind the Madagascar Plan, defended it after the war, as Eichmann did at his trial in Israel. To this day there are still people who try to exonerate the Nazis by asking why the Allies did not support that plan.

Extermination

In 1940, after the fall of France, Heydrich knew that the following year Hitler would take his next step toward world mastery: conquest of the Soviet Union, that "satanic creation of international Jewry." Besides gaining the "living space" it needed, the Third Reich would have access to the grain of the Ukraine, the petroleum of the Caucasus, and a labor force composed of a hundred million slaves. Then all the resources of the European continent could be used for subduing Britain and the United States. Heydrich had carefully studied each phase of this project because he would have to develop the structure of an enormous system of domination and supervise its functioning.

To him, the struggle against Britain was primarily a matter of psychological warfare. He believed that the British would hold out as long as they had any hope of help from the armed forces of other European countries. France had already been disarmed, and the Soviet Union would soon meet the same fate.

The German plan for an invasion of Britain (code name Sea Lion) was now well known in the world of international espionage. Military attachés in Germany and other countries regularly received supposedly secret information intended to fill them with respect for the enormous war machine that Hitler was going to use in the invasion. According to Nazi propaganda, German submarines in the Atlantic would increase their activity to a devastating level, then the Luftwaffe would launch massive bombing attacks that would wipe British cities off the face of the earth.

These dire prospects were supposed to make the British negotiate a peace settlement. As early as November 1940, Heydrich had said that peace with Britain was certain. After the defeat of the Soviet Union, at the very latest, the British would accept the inevitable, especially since some political circles and part of the aristocracy already disapproved of Churchill's war policy.

While final preparations for the invasion of the Soviet Union were being made, Hitler ordered Himmler, and therefore Heydrich, to begin preparing for the total elimination of the Jews.

All those in the zone controlled by the Reich would be deported. The operation would begin suddenly but would last for three or four years, until the death of the last Jew. At the same time, the vanquished Soviet Union would be completely pacified. For the Generalissimo of that racial war, the extermination of eleven million human beings posed only a technical problem.

To carry it out, Heydrich enlisted the services of doctors, chemists, transportation experts, truck drivers, commanders of concentration camps, administrators, accountants, crematory designers, engineers, carpenters, guards, and others. Murder squads, known as Einsatzgruppen, were created to follow combat troops into occupied territories. They, in turn, were followed by trucks carrying collapsible barracks, gasoline, drinking water, and tools, such as shovels, picks, and rakes. Whenever they stopped to set up a camp, they used forced labor from the local population. The four thousand murder experts of the Einsatzgruppen, their technical personnel, and their slaves constituted an army of more than a hundred thousand men.

We have no official documents giving an exact description of those death camps where the Einsatzgruppen operated; we have only accounts by survivors. I will not repeat those that are already well known, but I think the reader will be interested by the story of a thirteen-year-old boy named Mendel, who lived in Poland:

> The police surrounded the streets and houses. My father hid my mother, my two sisters, and me, making us lie on the ground, then he went off by himself to see what was happening. . . . We never saw him again. . . . The first people were taken into the forest in cars. . . A very big grave was dug, and people were thrown into it after being shot. Children were thrown into it alive. This was on a Thursday; the grave was not filled in till Friday morning. Ten children and several women who had been only wounded were able to crawl out of the grave during the night, after lying under dead bodies.

A few Nazi murderers later confirmed these facts by their own statements, and others took photographs that have been preserved.

We know that Heydrich began developing his methods of annihilation as soon as German troops marched into Czechoslovakia, that he developed them further in Poland, and that in preparation for the invasion of the Soviet Union he organized the largest and most efficient mass-murder system of all time. He acted in accordance with specific principles that followed from his nationalistic (voelkisch) attitudes: "We do not want to conquer the souls of the Jews, Catholics, and Marxists; we want to conquer living space. We want to settle Germanic peasants on that land."[1]

Besides the victims who were killed directly, others died "naturally," from epidemics, starvation, and cold. Inhuman conditions in ghettos and concentration camps did part of the work; gas chambers and bullets did the rest.

After the war, apologists for the Nazis tried to disguise the real nature of their murderous system. They often spoke of individual crimes committed by subordinates who, exasperated by the situation in the occupied territories, were driven to acts that went beyond their duty. According to those apologists, the killings occurred only because of the chaos that resulted from the state of war. But the fact is that, long before the invasion of the Soviet Union, the Nazi leaders already knew how their civilian "enemies" were going to be slaughtered.

The four Einsatzgruppen—designated A, B, C, and D—with their four thousand specialists and some hundred thousand assistants, had complete autonomy of action but were officially under the supervision of the Wehrmacht. On March 26, 1941, Field Marshal Walther von Brauchitsch, the Wehrmacht Commander in Chief, issued directives to his subordinates concerning the operations of the Einsatzgruppen. They were first to exterminate "inferior Asians," Gypsies, and Jews. An order from Heydrich designated some of the victims more specifically: Red Army People's Commissars; Jews holding positions in the Communist party and the state; warmongers, guerrillas, and propagandists.

Heydrich repeatedly explained to SS leaders and Einsatzgruppen commanders how the extermination operations were to proceed. The "great suppression of the Jews" was to begin within hours after a piece of territory had been occupied. The Einsatzgruppen would try to stir up the local population to the point where they would take part in killing the Jews. The whole territory had to be carefully searched to make sure that not one Jew was left alive, and an especially close watch had to be kept on young people, because they had a tendency to run away and join Resistance groups.

Here are the operational results of those elite SS units: Einsatzgruppe A (commanded by Stahlecker) reported killing 229,052 Jews by the end of August 1941; Einsatzgruppe B (Nebe): 45,467 by mid-November; Einsatzgruppe C (Rasch): 95,000, also by mid-November; Einsatzgruppe D (Ohlendorf): 92,000 by the beginning of April 1942.

On December 20, 1941, Heydrich informed the Fuehrer that 363,211 other Jews had been killed.

Most victims of that extermination campaign led by Himmler and Heydrich were killed in death camps, usually by means of gas chambers, and in mass executions by the Einsatzgruppen, but there were also many who died while they were being transported under bestially cruel conditions.

It is not true that Hitler persecuted only Jews, as his propagandists tried to make the Eastern peoples believe. Slavs and "inferior Asians" were also slaughtered. The invasion of the Soviet Union provided an opportunity to wipe out several million people and clear the way for German colonization. This plan had been adopted even before the invasion began.

Hitler stated on April 30, 1941, that the Red Army would be annihilated within four weeks. He expected half of its ten million men to be taken prisoner, yet no plans were made for feeding or sheltering that great mass of human beings.

The historian Christian Streit has calculated that of the 5,734,528 Soviet prisoners of war, about 3,300,000, more than 57 percent, were either executed or died of starvation, disease, or cold.[2] That is, the death rate was twenty times higher than among prisoners in World War I. In World War II, the Soviet Union lost more than twenty million people.

Heydrich's Mission in Prague

After the first months of the war in the East, Hitler had to recognize that he had failed to achieve his goal of destroying the Red Army within a few weeks. He now had to draw on all his economic resources to equip new divisions. The Protectorate of Bohemia and Moravia, in what had once been the independent state of Czechoslovakia, offered him both manpower and a safe location: there, far away from British bombers, war production could be carried on without interruption.

The Protectorate gave Himmler his first chance to place an occupied territory under the total control of his SS. An intrigue was quickly organized to oust Konstantin von Neurath, the first Protector appointed by Hitler. On September 21, 1941, after careful preparation of all details by Martin Bormann, Hitler's closest collaborator, Heydrich went to the Fuehrer's headquarters at Rastenburg. Just before this visit, General Alois Elias, President of the government of the Protectorate, had been accused of having contacts with "the Beneš clique" in exile in London. The difficulties being encountered in the Protectorate were presented as being the result of Neurath's administration. A man with an iron fist was needed in Prague!

Hitler conferred with Heydrich and Bormann for two days. SS Gruppenfuehrer Karl Hermann Frank, the number-two man in the Protectorate, with the official title of State Secretary, also attended the meetings. Finally, a decision was made: Neurath would go on sick leave and Heydrich would become Acting Reich Protector of Bohemia and Moravia; for reasons of prestige, Neurath would officially remain the Protector

A week later, Heydrich, now aged thirty-seven, assumed his new post in Prague. He was still head of the RSHA, and from Prague he would continue to oversee the progress of the Final Solution.

On October 2, he made his first official appearance, at a gathering of army and party dignitaries in Hradcany Castle, which housed the office of the Reich Protector and was also Karl Hermann Frank's residence. Frank greeted his guests at the door of the meeting hall. They had been ordered to be in their seats ten minutes before Heydrich's arrival. While they waited, they were addressed by SA Brigadefuehrer von Burgsdorff:

Party comrades, before the Protector speaks to you, I am authorized to tell you emphatically that all statements by SS Obergruppenfuehrer Reinhard Heydrich concerning the secret affairs of the
Reich are of the greatest political importance. They must be regarded as state secrets, in accordance with Paragraph Eighty of
the Reich penal code. Divulging any part of what will be commu-
nicated to us at this meeting will constitute treason and be punished by death or imprisonment. I warn you in the name of the
Protector that not one word spoken here must ever be repeated.
At the end of the meeting, everyone present will confirm the responsibility he has assumed by signing the minutes of the meeting
before he leaves the room. Needless to say, no notes of any kind
may be taken during the proceedings.

This was an unusual prelude to a meeting of such high-ranking
officials, and it had obviously been ordered by Heydrich himself.
He wanted to make it clear to his subordinates that a new era was
beginning in that part of the Great German Reich. In the future,
there would be less discussion; the Fuehrer's orders had to be
obeyed without comment. And as an expert on the dramatic staging of events, Heydrich felt that this new procedure would firmly
fix his words in the minds of his listeners.

At two minutes to nine, Frank greeted Heydrich at the top of
the stairs with his arm upraised in the Nazi salute. Heydrich
walked into the meeting hall. The elite of the occupation forces
stood up and saluted. In his SS uniform adorned with medals
from the party, the state, and the army, Heydrich made his way
to the speaker's platform.

Although members of the audience were forbidden to take
notes during the meeting, Heydrich had his secretary, out of
sight from everyone, record his speech in shorthand. We therefore know what he said that day, despite the oath of secrecy that
his listeners were required to take.

Knowing that his audience was curious as to why he had been
sent to Prague to replace Neurath, he began by addressing that
subject:

Party comrades, gentlemen, three days ago, by order of the
Fuehrer, I assumed control of affairs incumbent upon the Protector, in place of Reich Minister and Reich Protector von Neurath,
who is ill.

But he gave his listeners no further explanation. They were not to know that Neurath's illness was a pretext for sending the ruthless head of the RSHA to put an end to rebelliousness in the Protectorate. The situation had deteriorated alarmingly, and an experienced surgeon was needed to perform the necessary operations.

He told that gathering of high officials that "in accordance with the Fuehrer's instructions" he intended to act "with all possible severity" because the Protectorate of Bohemia and Moravia was "part of the Reich." The SS, along with the SD and the security police that belonged to it, were

> the shock troops of the party in everything that concerns the safeguard of our space from the standpoint of internal policy, as well as the safeguard of the National Socialist idea. As shock troops, we are always in the forefront of the army, we are particularly well armed, we are ready for action, and we know how to fight. . . . Thus we act as an organ of execution, conscious of the mission of the Fuehrer and the Reich, that mission which will take us from the Great German Reich to the Great Germanic Reich. And since the Fuehrer has said to me, "Bear in mind that, wherever I see the unity of the Reich endangered, I choose an SS leader and send him there to preserve that unity," from those words of the Fuehrer you can infer the overall task of the SS, and my special task here.

When he had finished that "special task," he said, he would resume his main activities, that is, his duties as head of the RSHA.

Those who listened carefully to his speech were able to understand why Hitler had sent him to the "citadel of Europe," as Bismarck called the Bohemian plateau: it was to become a "bastion of Germanism." Norway, Holland, Flanders, Denmark, and Sweden would also be included in the "great space" of the Reich within the near future.

> These are lands which are inhabited by Germanic peoples and which—we must be clear on this—will belong to us in one way or another, whether as a federate state or an administrative district, or in some other form.

Those Germanic peoples, "warped by bad political leadership and the influence of Jewry," were to be colonized and assimilated.

Heydrich then turned to the Eastern European territories, going on the assumption that a German victory over the Soviet Union was a foregone conclusion:

> The second is the East and its regions partially inhabited by Slavs. These are regions where, we must understand, kindness is seen as weakness. They are regions where the Slav himself does not want to be treated as an equal, where he is used to having a master different from himself. They are therefore regions where we must rule, and which we will keep. They are regions which, after a military advance into the depths of Russia, to the Urals, will be firmly governed by a German upper class and turned into a source of raw materials for us, and also of workers for great agricultural enterprises—serfs, to put it bluntly.

After a few brief allusions to the history of the Czechs, Heydrich spoke of recent attempts to create "illegal Resistance movements" which tried to "stab the Reich in the back" during its "crucial fight against bolshevism." In the last few weeks, "sabotage, action by terrorist groups, destruction of crops, and slowdowns by workers, all obviously organized by a resistance movement," had led to a situation in which the unity of the Reich was "clearly endangered."

Not only was it necessary to take preventive measures against those "stabs in the back," but the Protectorate itself must become a dagger that would inflict mortal wounds on the adversaries of the Reich.

In a report dated October 11, 1941, which he sent to Hitler by way of Bormann, Heydrich described how critical the situation in the Protectorate had been when he arrived there: if he had not taken action, within two weeks there would have been uprisings intended to foment resistance among the entire population.

Meanwhile, to his audience in Hradcany Castle, he declared that it was time to show the Czechs who their master was. For those who rebelled against German rule, there could be no pardon. The Czechs could not be treated any more leniently than the Jews in the Reich. Unlike the Jews, however, the Czechs were basically decent people and would therefore be treated decently when they deserved it. The police would see to it that Germans behaved "properly" in the Protectorate. It was important to convince the Czechs that disturbances and acts of sabotage would have only harmful consequences for them.

Propaganda alone would not be enough; concrete measures would be taken. It did not matter what the individual thought, as long as he worked and produced as much as possible. "I need calm in this region so that the worker, the Czech worker, will work to the best of his ability for the German war machine," Heydrich said.

At the end of his speech, he expressed "a few thoughts on the Final Solution." His audience realized that he had no intention of Germanizing "that Czech rabble." He wanted to "probe the population from a national [voelkisch] and racial viewpoint"; everyone in the room knew what that meant. During the brief time he expected to spend in Bohemia and Moravia, he believed he could "pave the way toward the Final Solution in this region." He was able to speak frankly because his listeners had all been chosen in accordance with his directives. He knew that their experience and specialized knowledge would allow them to make valuable contributions to his plans.

He concluded by saying that he was willing to answer any questions that his listeners might want to ask; but after the thunderous applause that he was given, no one dared to say a word.

Heydrich put the transcription of his speech into his safe and treated it as a secret document. Twenty years later, however, it was published by the Czech Ministry of Foreign Affairs.

A short time after the meeting on October 2, 1941, Heydrich told his collaborators that the Czechs could be divided into two sharply distinct categories: "Some are of good race and well disposed toward us; with them, it is simple: we can Germanize them. Then we have the others, at the opposite pole: those who are of bad race and hostile to us. I must get rid of them. There is plenty of room for them in the East."

Heydrich's first concern was to restore order in the Protectorate. Then the process of Germanization could begin. Those who were racially unfit for it would be sterilized and made to work until they died. "Hostile elements" would be killed. With regard to the time when this extermination would take place, Heydrich said, "That is a matter which the Fuehrer will decide. But we can already begin making plans and assembling the necessary matériel."

We can now see why Heydrich wanted that temporary assignment as the ruler of Bohemia and Moravia. He was eager to prove his ability as a political and economic organizer because, having passed that test, he would be ready to take command of a larger territory. He wanted to turn the Protectorate into a command post of the Final Solution.

During his stay in Prague, he continued to keep close watch on what was happening in the other occupied countries. As a preparation for the Final Solution, he ordered an increase in propaganda against "Jewish warmongers" in France. On October 3, he received several telegrams from Paris; the night before, there had been bomb explosions in the French capital which damaged synagogues on the Rue des Tourelles, the Rue Notre-Dame de Nazareth, the Rue de la Victoire, the Rue Saint-Isaure, and the Rue Copernic. The Nazis presented these incidents as proof of growing anti-Jewish feeling among the population. But General von Stuelpnagel, the military governor of occupied France, saw the bombings as the work of the SD and the SS and even named those he considered responsible for them: Helmuth Knochen, Alfred Thomas, and SS Obersturmfuehrer Sommer. On October 21, the military administration addressed an official complaint to Heydrich, since it was obvious that such an operation could not have taken place without an order from him, or at least his authorization. In both the military administration and the police it was openly said that Thomas had placed the French collaborator Eugène Deloncle in charge of the operation. Heydrich was furious when he learned that his men had not been able to maintain secrecy. Thomas was transferred to Kiev, but Knochen remained in his post.

The reproaches of the military administration finally came to Hitler's attention. Heydrich then convinced the Fuehrer that the army's secret police had to be totally reorganized and that only the SD could control the security forces in France effectively enough to prevent German soldiers from being threatened by Judeo-Bolshevik agitation. For the next six months, from Prague, Heydrich supervised the reorganization of terror in France.

His duties in Prague also left him enough time to go on directing the RSHA. His appointment as Acting Reich Protector of Bohemia and Moravia had marked a strengthening of the SS empire and therefore of his personal position within the Third Reich. As we have seen, Neurath's illness was only a pretext for sending Heydrich to Prague. Hitler wanted a Reich Protector who would take firm control of the munitions industry in Bohemia and Moravia and turn that region into a second Ruhr by increasing production in existing factories and creating new ones.

A reign of terror began as soon as Heydrich arrived in Prague. He formed courts-martial, each composed of three Gestapo officials, and in less than two months they delivered four hundred death sentences followed by immediate execution. Four thousand patriots and intellectuals were put into prisons and concentration camps. The Czechs had to be shown by forceful means that any resistance, however slight, would have disastrous consequences for them.

A week before his death, Heydrich gave this explanation of his behavior: "It is much easier to be just and humane after inflicting harsh treatment, when it has become necessary, than during a constant series of compromises that are always interpreted as weakness and therefore lead to insubordination."[3]

In deciding on measures to be taken against workers' leaders and left-wing intellectuals, he sought advice from professional anti-Marxists and former Communists, Social Democrats, and Trotskyites who claimed to be experts on the Comintern. One of those advisers was Melitta Wiedemann, editor of *Die Aktion*, a periodical supported by Goebbels and Heydrich. A year after Heydrich's death, she wrote a nine-page letter to Himmler containing this characteristic sentence: "The starting point of my reflections is the irreplaceable loss of precious German blood on all fronts." She recommended the formation of "Germanic units" composed of non-German soldiers as a means of saving pure German blood. Frenchmen and East Europeans could be used as auxiliary troops to repel the "plutocratic invasion." With regard to the conquered territories, she wrote, "It is obvious that unpleasant phenomena will occur among those vast, racially mixed populations, especially those under Bolshevik influence. This certainty, based on our racial knowledge, indicates our great task for the future, and will be the source of our greatest successes."

And she advocated a special role for the SS: "In all Eastern European populations organized nationally under German administration, the SS must make a thorough selection which, in the course of decades and centuries, will create an increasingly strong Nordic-German ruling class."

Heydrich had often exchanged ideas with Melitta Wiedemann. She maintained that putting into practice the principle of domination based on race was the only way to insure the duration of the European Reich under German rule. In the brief period of the Reich's existence, eleven million people died in organized genocides, including six million in Poland alone, and two million in Yugoslavia. However, it is not my intention here to give a detailed account of those massacres in each of the countries where they took place. Their extent is revealed by the official statistics reported in the Netherlands, Belgium, Luxembourg, France, Czechoslovakia, Italy, Albania, Greece, Denmark, Norway, and the Soviet Union.

During his stay in Prague, Heydrich gave some examples of his talent as a demagogue. On October 24, 1941, he invited a hundred delegates from factories in the Protectorate to visit him. He shook hands with them, assured them that they could express themselves freely, and encouraged them to tell him their grievances. But this show of friendship was nothing but an empty pretense: the Nazi regime continued its policy of harshness against "the Czech rabble."

On April 1, 1942, Heydrich ordered that pensions be increased by 20 percent. But he lost nothing because, at the same time, severe measures of forced saving brought back the money paid out in pension increases. This maneuver was suggested to him by Ohlendorf, his economic adviser.

The Protectorate was covered by a network of Gestapo posts with agents and informers who kept watch on the whole population. Heydrich also had the Czech police at his disposal. In Bohemia and Moravia he was able to apply his principles in all their cruelty.

To him, the struggle taking place in the Protectorate represented the centuries-old conflict between the East and the West. He viewed that supposed conflict in romantic and metaphysical terms. Like his father, he remained a fervent Wagnerian till his

death, and he showed his talent for Wagnerian drama in Hradcany Castle on November 19, 1941, when he staged a pompous
ceremony in which President Hácha presented him with the
seven keys to the room in which the crown of Duke Wenceslaus
was kept. Heydrich considered that Wenceslaus, who had been
assassinated in the tenth century as the result of a conspiracy led
by his brother Boleslav, had been a friend of Germany killed by
infamous partisans of the East. That ancient wrong had now been
righted by Hitler's creation of the German Protectorate and President Hácha's symbolic act of giving the seven keys to Heydrich,
Hitler's "Viceroy." In a grand gesture, Heydrich gave three of
the keys back to Hácha and said, "See this as a token of our
trust, and also of your obligation." The whole melodramatic performance, complete with flowers, candlelight, and music, was
intended to show the Czechs that the German Reich would preserve their traditions.

A Visit to Paris

Hitler expressed his satisfaction with the measures that Heydrich
had taken in Czechoslovakia. He also fully approved of
Heydrich's directives to the Einsatzgruppen that were murdering
civilians and prisoners of war behind the eastern front.

When concentration camps were first established, Heydrich
himself had decided all details of the treatment to be given to
prisoners—from torture to "liquidation"; and now, during the war
against the Soviet Union, he gave specific instructions on how
Red Army prisoners were to be selected for execution, and how
they were to be killed. In an order dated July 17, 1941, he
stated, "The executions must not take place in the camp or near
it; they are not official and must be kept secret as much as possible."

He tirelessly issued directives to the leaders of his Einsatzgruppen and demanded that they send him regular reports on
the number of their victims and how they had been killed. Hitler
felt that a "cleansing" was also needed in the West. Knowing that
the difficulties being encountered by the German Army in the
Soviet Union had enabled the French Resistance movement to
increase its strength, he decided, in agreement with Heydrich,

that a kind of protectorate should also be established in France to facilitate eliminating enemies of the Reich. A high SS official would be given broad powers and sent to work with the military governor of occupied France.

There were already such officials in other occupied territories; they bore the title of High SS and Police Leader. On March 9, 1942, Hitler decreed that France would also have one. The official order stated that the new Leader would be "personally and directly" under the command of the military governor, but that was intended only to deceive the many French political collaborators who preferred to deal with the army rather than with the SS. In reality, the High SS and Police Leader would dominate both the military governor and the French police.

On May 7, Heydrich flew to Paris for the official installation of the man who had been given that post: SS Gruppenfuehrer Karl Oberg.

Born in 1897, the son of a Hamburg professor, Oberg had been a volunteer in World War I and then, like Heydrich, he had fought in the Free Corps. He was well qualified for the duties assigned to him; he could be counted on to make deportations continue without difficulty and increase the number of executions.

Heydrich took advantage of his stay in Paris to confer with the Secretary General of the French police, René Bousquet, on cooperation between the French and German police organizations.

He established his headquarters at the Ritz. Surrounded by his subordinates, he discoursed on the need to crush all resistance in France now that the "fateful struggle" was taking place in the East. Victory over the Soviet Union was essential to the Final Solution and pursuit of the war against the "Judeo-Bolshevik enemy."

He also negotiated with representatives of the Vichy regime, advised them on ways to solve problems of collaboration, and inquired about arrests of Jews to be deported.

He was confident that Karl Oberg would be able to keep France firmly in hand. One of the first things Oberg did was to mobilize the army's secret police and add it to the SD and Gestapo contingents in France.

Convinced that the French problem could be solved by the

same methods used in the Protectorate, Heydrich went back to Prague. His intervention in France was to result in thirty thousand deaths and a hundred and fifty thousand deportations. Of those deported, only thirty-five thousand returned.

Back at his desk in Prague, Heydrich studied reports on the progress that had been made in eliminating non-Aryans. Meanwhile, his subordinates, at his request, organized a concert in honor of his father, Bruno Heydrich, the composer.

The concert took place on May 26, 1942, the day before Reinhard Heydrich was assassinated. He had personally chosen the musicians who would perform his father's works. Sitting in the first row of the attentively listening audience, he had no suspicion that Czech patriots were preparing to kill him.

The Death Sentence

Immediately after the attack in which Heydrich received the wounds that proved fatal a week later, 13,119 people were arrested, 232 were executed for having expressed approval of the attack, and 462 were executed either for illegal possession of weapons or for having disobeyed an order to report to the police. And after Heydrich's death, the village of Lidice was destroyed as a reprisal: the SS killed the men, sent the women to concentration camps, and deported the children to Germany.

We now know about the assassination in great detail. The decision to kill Heydrich was made by the Czech government in exile in London, headed by Eduard Beneš, and the operation was organized by Frantisek Moravek, chief of the Czech secret service, who had fled to London, taking several boxes of secret documents with him, before the Germans arrived in Prague. After the murder of Rudolf Formis, he had devoted special attention to the activities of German agents in Czechoslovakia. It was to him that Otto Strasser had said, "Each of us does what he can for his country," when Moravek asked him why he was risking his life in working against the Third Reich.

According to Czech sources, Moravek repeated Strasser's words to two Czech paratroopers, Jan Kubis and Josef Gabcik, when he met with them in London to give them the mission of killing the cruelest enemy of their people.[4] Kubis and Gabcik were given special training in England. On the night of December 28, 1941, they parachuted into the Protectorate with two other groups from a British Halifax bomber. Until May 27, 1942, they lived in hiding, making preparations to insure the success of their mission.

On the morning of May 27, when Gabcik stepped in front of Heydrich's car and tried to shoot him, his Sten gun failed to fire. But then Kubis threw his Mills bomb. It exploded under the right rear wheel of the Mercedes, wounding Heydrich. Klein, the chauffeur, ran after Kubis. In vain. The two Czechs escaped.

A traitor named Karel Curda told the Gestapo what he knew about the agents who had come from England. The manhunt became more precise. Kubis and Gabcik took refuge in the Karel Boromaeus Greek Orthodox Church, where priests hid them in the underground crypt. On June 18, the church was surrounded by no fewer than 750 SS men. When Kubis and Gabcik refused to surrender, they were killed. All the priests involved in hiding them were sentenced to death and executed.

Because of the German reprisals that shook the whole Protectorate, many Czechs condemned the assassination, feeling that it could have no effect on the course of the war and that it had only given the Nazis a pretext for intensifying their brutality.

After the war, the reasons for the decision to kill Heydrich became a subject of controversy. So far, neither the British nor the Czech government has given an official explanation. Some leftist historians have maintained that the Czech government in exile ordered the assassination only to strengthen its position, deliberately disregarding the reprisals against its own people that were certain to follow. Others have even accused the exiles in London of having ordered it as a means of provoking the Nazis to take even harsher actions against Marxists in the Protectorate.[5] Still another opinion is that Moravek, head of the Czech secret service in London, wanted Heydrich killed because his best agent, Paul Thummel, had just been arrested in Prague. That opinion is untenable, however, because Kubis and Gabcik went to Czechoslovakia five months before the assassination and were already under orders to kill Heydrich when they left England.

The truth is simply that Heydrich's crimes had accumulated to the point where the British Intelligence Service and the Czech government in exile felt that he had to be killed. And it was also a way of demonstrating that "the world's best secret service," as Heydrich called it, had not been able to protect its chief from the punishment he deserved.

It is now an established fact that Heydrich's death did nothing to change the Nazis' program of mass murder. Shortly before he died, he learned that the Wehrmacht had just suffered its first serious defeat, in its attempt to take Moscow, and six months later there was another defeat, at Stalingrad. But those reverses did not alter Hitler's determination to continue carrying out the Final Solution.

That attempted genocide lasted three and a half years. It was carefully planned and methodically executed, and the gigantic machine went on functioning even after Heydrich's death. He had been only one element, though a crucially important one, in the war of extermination waged by the Nazis.

At his funeral, Heydrich was extolled as a hero of the Nazi movement by the Fuehrer himself. Admiral Wilhelm Canaris, his friend and teacher, wept beside his coffin. Three years later, on April 9, 1945, Canaris was hanged by order of the Fuehrer in the Flossenburg concentration camp. He was made to stand naked on a wooden coffin; the noose was put around his neck, and an SS man kicked the coffin out from under him. According to Otto von Heydebreck, for Himmler and Schellenberg, Canaris had become "too dangerous: he knew too many secrets because he had been an accomplice in some of their machinations and seen through the others." He was executed within the enclosure surrounding the crematorium, in accordance with the procedure that had been developed by his friend Reinhard Heydrich for eliminating enemies of the Reich.

8

Conclusion

The personality of Reinhard Heydrich is too complex to be depicted by general remarks or a description of his outward characteristics. His nature impelled him to take an interest in all fields of knowledge, and his functions led him into the labyrinth of secret state affairs and public life. Without being thoroughly acquainted not only with the relevant historical events but also with the structure of the Nazi state, it is impossible to present an accurate picture of him. Many documents concerning him no longer exist, and we cannot fully understand him simply on the basis of the highly subjective accounts given by his family, friends, and collaborators.

Heydrich was obviously not only the good husband and father presented to us by his widow, or the loyal comrade described by his friends, or the man of extraordinary professional abilities who appears in the memoirs and testimony of his collaborators. His real nature was certainly not what so many people have now come to believe. He could not have reached his final development without the nourishing soil of Nazism and the Third Reich, and anyone who tries to describe that plant without knowing its roots will produce only a deceptive image with little relation to reality.

I do not claim to have discovered all the secrets of the Third Reich and of Heydrich's life. I may have made mistakes that will have to be corrected in the light of new discoveries. But one thing is certain: the cloud of mythology that has been deliberately created around the Third Reich and its leaders must be dispelled if the truth about them is to be known. The forces trying to con-

257

ceal that truth are powerful even today, as is shown by the fact that children in West Germany are not always given an opportunity to learn about the catastrophic ways in which the world was affected by Hitler and his regime.

If young Germans grow up ignorant of the Nazi past, there is a risk that they may repeat it. And the same risk exists in other countries where fascism once prospered in one form or another. I hope that my attempt to paint a realistic portrait of Heydrich will be of some use in preventing such dangerous ignorance. He was an important factor in the Nazis' seizure of power in Germany and their launching of the most destructive war in history. The story of his life therefore has vast ramifications, even though many of its details remain unknown.

There have been efforts to explain Heydrich's monstrous acts by attributing to him a virulent anti-Jewish complex resulting from his awareness that he himself had "impure blood." This simplistic explanation shows an inability to grasp the implications of the situation created when modern technology and the resources of a powerful industrial nation were placed in the service of Nazi ideology. I have been unable either to verify or disprove the assertion that Heydrich had "Jewish blood." It is beyond doubt, however, that his fanaticism and his total devotion to Nazism and his Fuehrer were not caused by any feeling that he was not of pure Aryan descent. He felt himself to be thoroughly German, a worthy member of the Master Race, and as such he enjoyed the unshakable confidence of Hitler and Himmler.

The great diversity of Heydrich's interests and activities makes it hard to analyze his personality. Using his wide range of knowledge and skills, he turned his secret service into the Nazi state's strongest lever of power. He did not devise its methods entirely on his own, however; the germ of them was in Nazism from the beginning.

He was driven by pathological ambition, and his appetite for personal privileges increased with his power. Although he was not promoted to Obergruppenfuehrer until September 1941, his status was out of all proportion to his official rank. While he was still a Gruppenfuehrer, he lived in the grand manner of a feudal lord: he had a villa on the Schlachtensee, a secret apartment in Berlin, a summer house on the island of Fehmarn, and a hunting preserve on the Schorfheide moor; he had servants, gamekeepers, and several chauffeurs; besides his car, his sailboat, and his motorboat, he also had his own private plane. Hitler, Goering, Goebbels, and Ribbentrop were the only other Nazi leaders who lived on such a regal scale. Heydrich enjoyed his privileges to the fullest, but without letting them distract him from the ardent desire for power that was the dominant trait of his character.

Heydrich and his fellow murderers considered that they were acting in accordance with a "superior morality." But there were few Germans willing to live by such a "morality," so the acts it entailed were carried out in secrecy. Because of that secrecy, and because Heydrich destroyed the documents that would have made it possible to reconstruct his crimes in detail, postwar defenders of the Nazis were able to invent justificatory myths and spread them to the point where they have influenced the views of many historians. Examining those myths to expose their falsity is an unpleasant task, but it must continue to be done.

Notes

Introduction

1. Dušan Hamšik and Žiri Pražák, *Eine Bombe für Hitler*. Berlin, 1964.
2. Max Domarus, *Hitler Reden und Proklamationen 1932–1945*, Würzburg, 1962.
3. Hamšik and Pražák, op. cit.
4. Karl-Heinz Janssen, *Die Zeit*, September 14, 1979.

Chapter 1

1. Houston Stewart Chamberlain, *Die Grundlagen des Neunzehnten Jahrhunderts*, Munich, 1903.
2. Otto von Heydebreck, communication to the author.
3. Shlomo Aronson, *Reinhard Heydrich und die Frühgeschichte von Gestapo und S.D.*, Munich, 1971.
4. Ibid.
5. Ibid., and communication to Otto von Heydebreck from Karl von Eberstein.
6. Aronson, op. cit.
7. Günther Gereke, communication to the author.
8. Ibid.
9. Reinhard Heydrich, SS-Personalakte, Document Center, Berlin.

Chapter 2

1. Shlomo Aronson, *Reinhard Heydrich und die Fruhgeschichte von Gestapo und S.D.*, Munich, 1971.
2. Ibid.
3. Ibid.
4. Ibid.

5. Ibid.
6. Heinz Höhne, *Canaris—Patriot im Zwielicht*, Munich, 1976.
7. Lina Heydrich, *Leben mit einem Kriegsverbrecher*, Pfaffenhofen, 1976.
8. Aronson, op. cit.
9. Otto von Heydebreck, communication to the author.
10. Aronson, op. cit.
11. Günther Deschner, *Reinhard Heydrich*, Esslingen, 1977.
12. Aronson, op. cit.
13. A. Neuberg, *Der bewaffnete Aufstand*, Berlin, 1928.
14. Höhne, op. cit.
15. Ibid.
16. Ibid.
17. Aronson, op. cit.
18. Ibid.
19. Deschner, op. cit.

Chapter 3

1. Shlomo Aronson, *Reinhard Heydrich und die Fruhgeschichte von Gestapo und S.D.*, Munich, 1971.
2. Ibid.
3. Ibid.
4. Otto von Heydebreck, communication to the author.
5. Ernst Hanfstaengl, communication to the author.
6. Ibid.
7. Otto Heydebreck, communication to the author.
8. Emmy Breiting, communication to the author.
9. Günther Gereke, communication to the author.
10. Ibid.
11. Günther Deschner, *Reinhard Heydrich*, Esslingen, 1977.
12. Ibid.
13. Werner Best, notes, October 1, 1949, Bundesarchiv, Koblenz.
14. Aronson, op. cit.
15. Otto von Heydebreck, communication to the author.
16. Udo von Mohrenschildt, communication to the author.
17. Otto von Heydebreck, communication to the author, corroborated by Franz Knospe and Alfred Raeschke.
18. *Voelkischer Beobachter*, August 24, 1932.

Chapter 4

1. *Rheinischer Merkur*, November 10, 1978; *Le Monde*, March 4–5, 1979; *Der Tagesspiegel*, December 3, 1978; *Süddeutsche Zeitung*, May 2, 1979; *Haagse Courant*, October 28, 1978; *The Sunday Times* (of London), October 29, 1978.
2. Karl Dietrich Bracher, *Die Deutsche Diktatur*, Cologne/Berlin, 1969.
3. Wilhelm von Schramm, "Das Fanal des brennenden Reichstages," *Rheinischer Merkur*, November 24, 1978.

4. Franz Knospe and Alfred Raeschke, communications to the author.
5. Lina Heydrich, *Leben mit einem Kriegsverbrecher*, Pfaffenhofen, 1976.
6. Ernst Hanfstaengl, communication to the author.
7. Paul Schmidt, *Statist auf diplomatischer Bühne*, Bonn, 1949.
8. Ibid.
9. Ibid.
10. Ibid.
11. Ibid.
12. Ibid.
13. Ibid.
14. Louis de Jong, *Koninkrijk der Nederlanden in de Twee Wereldoorlog*, The Hague, 1969.
15. Rudolf Diels, *Luzifer ante portas*, Stuttgart, 1950.
16. André Malraux, communication to the author.
17. Ernst Hanfstaengl, communication to the author.
18. Otto von Heydebreck, communication to the author.
19. Ibid.
20. Heinrich Bennecke, *Die Reichswehr und der "Röhm-Putsch,"* Munich, 1964.
21. Dr. Helmut Stange, communication to the author.
22. André François-Poncet, communication to the author.
23. Max Domarus, *Hitler Reden und Proklamationen 1932–1945*, Wurzburg, 1962.
24. Otto von Heydebreck, communication to the author.
25. Botho Bauch, of the criminal police, communication to the author.
26. Kurt Gildisch, testimony at the trial; and Dr. Erich Klausener, Jr., communication to the author.
27. Henry Picker, *Hitlers Tischgespräche im Führerhauptquartier*, Stuttgart, 1976.

Chapter 5

1. Ernst Hanfstaengl, communication to the author.
2. Hans Bernd Gisevius, communication to the author.
3. Juraj Demetrović, communication to the author.
4. Alexandre Guibbal, "Dokumentation über das Attentat in Marseille," in Vladeta Milićević, *Der Königsmord von Marseille*, Bad Godesberg, 1969.
5. *Das politische Tagebuch Alfred Rosenbergs*, Munich, 1964.
6. Otto Strasser, communication to the author.
7. Ibid.
8. Günther Deschner, *Reinhard Heydrich*, Esslingen, 1977.
9. Otto Strasser, *Exil*, Munich, 1958.
10. Otto Strasser, communication to the author.
11. Otto von Heydebreck, communication to the author.
12. *Der Spiegel*, January 28, 1980.
13. Paul Schmidt, op. cit.
14. *Der Spiegel*, January 28, 1980.
15. "Der antifaschistische Widerstand," Bilder und Dokumente, Frankfurt, 1975.

16. Georg Kaczmarek, of the criminal police, communication to the author.
17. Hans Buchheim, Martin Broszat, Hans-Adolf Jacobsen, and Helmut Krausnick, *Anatomie des SS-Staates*, Freiburg, 1965.
18. Ibid.

Chapter 6

1. Margarete von Blomberg, communication to the author.
2. Max Domarus, *Hitler Reden und Proklamationen 1932–1945*, Wurzburg, 1962.
3. Lina Heydrich, *Leben mit einem Kriegsverbrecher*, Pfaffenhofen, 1976.
4. Ibid.
5. Heinz Höhne, *Der Orden unter dem Totenkopf*, Frankfurt, 1969.
6. Alfred Spiess and Heiner Lichtenstein, *Operation Tannenberg, Bericht zur Konferenz: Der Nationalsozialismus und der Hitlerkrieg vor der Geschichte*, Paris, 1979.
7. Ibid.
8. Jürgen Runzheimer, "Die Grenzzwischenfälle am Abend vor dem deutschen Angriff auf Polen," in Wolfgang Benz and Hermann Graml, *Die Grossmächte und der europäische Krieg*, Stuttgart, 1979.
9. Fritz Heberlein, communication to the author.
10. Lina Heydrich, op. cit.
11. Hans Bernd Gisevius, communication to the author.

Chapter 7

1. Friedrich Zipfel, communication to the author.
2. Christian Streit, *Die Wehrmacht und die sowjetischen Kriegsgefangenen 1941–1945*, Stuttgart, 1978.
3. *Die Aktion*, May–June, 1942.
4. Dušan Hamšik and Žiri Pražák, *Eine Bombe für Hitler*, Berlin, 1964.
5. R. Kühnrich, *Der Partisanenkrieg*, Berlin, 1968.

Index